Technology Handbook
for School Librarians

Technology Handbook for School Librarians

William O. Scheeren

LIBRARIES UNLIMITED™
An Imprint of ABC-CLIO, LLC
Santa Barbara, California • Denver, Colorado

Copyright © 2015 by William O. Scheeren

All rights reserved. No part of this publication may be reproduced, stored in a retrieval system, or transmitted, in any form or by any means, electronic, mechanical, photocopying, recording, or otherwise, except for the inclusion of brief quotations in a review, without prior permission in writing from the publisher.

Library of Congress Cataloging-in-Publication Data

Scheeren, William O.
  Technology handbook for school librarians / William O. Scheeren.
      pages cm
  Includes bibliographical references and index.
  ISBN 978-1-4408-3396-0 (paperback) — ISBN 978-1-4408-3397-7 (e-book)
1. School libraries—Information technology.   2. Internet in school libraries.
3. Libraries—Special collections—Electronic information resources.   4. School librarian participation in curriculum planning.   5. Educational technology.
I. Title.
  Z675.S3S2593 2015
  025.042—dc23   2015012912

ISBN: 978-1-4408-3396-0
EISBN: 978-1-4408-3397-7

19 18 17 16 15   1 2 3 4 5

This book is also available on the World Wide Web as an eBook.
Visit www.abc-clio.com for details.

Libraries Unlimited
An Imprint of ABC-CLIO, LLC

ABC-CLIO, LLC
130 Cremona Drive, P.O. Box 1911
Santa Barbara, California 93116-1911

This book is printed on acid-free paper ∞
Manufactured in the United States of America

Contents

1

School Libraries: How It Was

WHY TECHNOLOGY IS IMPORTANT

School librarians entering the field in the past twenty-five years have little or no recollection of the school library without technology. Even so, within school libraries there are widely varying levels of technology hardware, software, and expertise. The use of technology in the school library is a given among the practitioners of today, "but the questions of 'what,' 'how,' and 'who' as they relate to school library technology are ones that must be addressed; and if we do not address them in a satisfactory way, the job of the school librarian and even the existence of the school library as we know it is in danger" (Scheeren, 1). This challenge to the existence of school libraries and school librarians is discussed in more detail in chapter 2.

Does this situation alarm school librarians? It should, because our future as a profession is at stake. To realize this is true, one has only to read the newspapers (yes, reading newspapers is still important) and see how the media portray the way people have changed their information-seeking behavior. The media collectively says that today we are a society based on information. If that is so—and there really is no reason to doubt it—shouldn't the library be at the very center of this search for information? One would think so, but too often librarians, especially school librarians, are presented as being unnecessary to the "new" information loop. Recently I heard a member of a local school board say that there really wasn't any need for a budget for school libraries—or, for that matter, any need for school librarians—because everything the students need as far outside textbooks is available on the Internet for free. Unfortunately that school board, with acquiesce of the school librarian, has removed all books from the school library, carrying through with the idea that all the information students could possibly need is freely available on the Internet. For all the power and information the

Internet has given us and our students, saying that using the Internet can be the sole source of information for students is a gross overstatement.

How do we school librarians counter such statements? We counter them by demonstrating our leadership and expertise in using technology to provide accurate, timely, and relevant information in our school libraries. How many librarians have the knowledge about and the level of expertise in technology to be leaders in our schools? Just out of curiosity, how many librarians do you know who still keep and maintain a hard-copy shelf list because they just do not trust the electronic database not to crash and instantly erase all the information about their collections? How many of our colleagues know that it would be good for your students to be able to access library materials remotely but do not know how much is actually available to them through many "hidden" resources to make that case to your technology coordinator or your administration? If you know any, you need to help them take a hard look at their technology skills, the technology available in their library, and their ability to be a leader in the field of educational technology. They are well on the way to irrelevance in their school. When one principal decides to close the library and dismiss the school librarian, sometimes under the guise of a cost-saving necessity, other principals may follow.

So far we have addressed the shortcomings in technology and technology expertise that could be disastrous for the school librarian. Has the role of the school librarian changed to the point at which we are only electronic "information managers" rather than school librarians? Though a case could be made for this point of view, that is not what I am saying. What is said is that if the school librarian does not add technology leadership and technology expertise to the litany of skills (information literacy instruction, development of critical thinking skills, promoting guided inquiry, implementing Common Core Standards, encouraging recreational reading, and building lifelong learners) they have now, then teachers and students will indeed pass them by, and school librarians will seem less and less relevant in the world of information and in their schools.

HOW TECHNOLOGY HAS CHANGED THE SCHOOL LIBRARY

How has technology changed the school library and the school librarian? Go back fifty years to see how the school library typically worked. The first of the baby boomers were completing high school and moving on to college or into jobs. In many cases smaller schools were overwhelmed with more students than they could handle and the first school consolidations were taking place. The launch of *Sputnik* in 1957 caused increased emphasis on mathematics and science in American schools but in some ways schools were much the same in 1968 as they had been 100 years before. Take, for example, the school year. In 1968, as well as today, the school year is based on the farm cycle, with nine months of school and three months off in the summer. The school year was like that in 1868, 1968, and it remains so today in most school districts. Continued discussion of lengthening the school year or the school day continues, but in most school districts, nothing has changed.

In many ways, the school library might look very familiar to us. It would have books, magazines, and perhaps some other types of print media. In the late 1960s, there would probably be a nascent audiovisual collection: films, filmstrips, and records available for teacher use. These audiovisual materials were the extent of technology in the school library except for the librarian's typewriter, which turned out endless catalog cards to be filed in the card catalog, a set of drawers with cards allegedly created to help find books and other materials but perceived by some as having been created to torture unwary students or teachers. The school library was the home of the record players and projectors needed to use the audiovisual collection.

Physically the school library of 1968 would closely resemble many of today's facilities in many schools. The door still leads into an essentially rectangular room with tables and chairs for students. Book stacks line the walls and perhaps extend from the wall perpendicularly and, if the collection is large enough, into rows of shelves. Magazines and newspapers are available. Near the door, or perhaps in the center of the facility, is the charging desk, the domain of the librarian and the student assistants. However, in 1968, somewhere nearby would be the card catalog. Let's jump forward forty-five years to the typical school library of 2014. The room is still a rectangle, the books and book stacks are still there, as are the magazines and newspapers, but the number of shelves has been greatly reduced. Gone is not only the card catalog but the reference section. However, the biggest difference between the school library of 1968 and that of 2014 are the computers and other social media devices that your students and teachers are using both in the library and in their classrooms.

This does not include the movement to the Learning Commons, where the school library has truly become the center of the school. In this scenario, the "room" is totally free from obstructions. Book shelving may be around the room, but any shelving in the center is on bookshelves with wheels. All tables and chairs can be rearranged at a moment's notice, and technologies and experts to help with them are readily available.

Described above are the new levels of technology available in school libraries. The question then arises: How much is enough technology? How much is too much, if that is possible? What is the correct level? If we were

At what point is the joy of books replaced by technology?

to ask our students, they would say that you can never have enough technology. Members of the Millennial Generation, who are in schools today, are truly technology natives. They have been exposed to technology and have used it their entire lives. They spend much of their time texting their friends, sometimes even during class.

Teachers would support technology that did not interfere with instructions. Many teachers prohibit the presence of cell phone technology in their classrooms and confiscate any they see.

Parents would probably agree with teachers up to a point, but parents would support the use of technology that would assist their children's learning. Many parents who are less affluent than others cannot provide technologies for their children at home, and those parents are probably less aware of what could be available.

The school administration and governing body would probably say that any technology that can be paid for is the correct level to offer. To purchase technologies when these technologies are constantly in need of upgrades will put enormous stress on an already overextended budget.

The school librarian should agree that enough technology is what will make an equal opportunity for all students in the school. If students do not have access to the Internet at home and do not have the needed electronic devices to do so, they should have access to those devices through their school library.

It is interesting to note that several of the individual state studies conducted by Keith Curry Lance and others have reached similar conclusions regarding the needs for technology in all studies, regardless of the state. That is, technology extends the reach of an effective library program, with the evidence showing that schools that have good technology programs are more effective. Lance further stated that the best school libraries were integrated into computer networks and provided remote access to library resources to their students.

LEVELS OF TECHNOLOGY ACCEPTANCE

Acceptance of the use of technology in the library obviously begins with the librarian. Kochtanik and Matthews, in their work dealing with technology in all types of libraries, identify four different levels of acceptance of technology among librarians. Though their conclusions relate to all types, school librarians can identify among those at the different levels of acceptance.

Bleeding-Edge Technologists

The first level of acceptance Kochtanik and Matthews identify as the "Bleeding Edge." Librarians in this category are far out ahead of the pack and are eager to implement any new type of library technology application as soon as it is released. Along with the desire to lead, they want state-of-the-art hardware on release. School librarians at this bleeding edge of technology are the envy of many, because they always seem to have the resources at their disposal to move forward with library technology.

Many school librarians do not envy those at the bleeding edge. These are the school librarians who are generally satisfied with the level of technology in their libraries and have a great deal of trepidation about moving forward. Worse, their students, their parents, and their administration may be comparing them to those at the bleeding edge, to their chagrin.

Being at the bleeding edge of technology is not always an unalloyed positive. The possibility of buying technology that is inefficient or rapidly out of date is a real possibility. Furthermore, there is always technology that promises much and delivers little. As a cautionary tale, school librarians should keep in mind the teaching machines of the 1960s and 1970s. School districts may still have storage areas full of teaching machines, a technology that promised much and delivered little. Many districts were a bit skeptical of the proliferation of computers, asking whether they were the second coming of the teaching machines.

Leading-Edge Technologists

The second level of technology acceptance in the school library, according to Kochtanik and Matthews is the "leading edge." School librarians in this category are still considered to be leaders in the use of technology, but not to the extent of those at the bleeding edge. Typically school librarians in this category are eager to move forward with technological innovation but are willing to sit back and see how successful these innovations will be. These are the school librarians who are not using beta versions of software or the latest operating systems as soon as they are released; nor are their libraries demonstration sites for the most advanced library technology applications.

Instead, people on the leading edge carefully evaluate new technology. After it has been proven in the field, they are ready to move. Librarians at the leading edge seldom have a storage area filled with outdated technology that never quite served its purpose or never quite worked right. School librarians at the leading edge are largely supported in their technology initiatives by their administration, because they seldom make foolish purchases, seldom waste funds, and generally keep their school libraries leaders in technology. School librarians on the leading edge give their students the latest and greatest only after it has been proven to be so.

The Wedge Technologists

The third level of technology acceptance is where some librarians and some school librarians fall, for better or worse. This is the level known as being in the wedge. They are not risk-takers and are satisfied to be in this wedge area. These school librarians accept this situation and, if asked, may report to their administrators that the level of technology in their libraries is the same as in most schools in their area. This response and this approach could also be called the "safe" approach: If you never take a risk, you will never make a mistake. A visitor to a school library in the wedge would certainly see an online catalog and online databases, but also a limited number of computers for students. The school librarian is not one of the leaders in technology in the school, and his or her technology skills are often not respected by those who are trying to move forward with technology. They are often left out of the decision making process and are just as happy to be so.

Trailing-Edge Technologists

The fourth and final level of technology acceptance is known as the trailing edge. In World War II flying parlance, they would have been known as "tail-end Charlies." Librarians in this category have to be dragged kicking and screaming to accept any kind of technology in their libraries. For school librarians, it is not a matter of money but more the inertia or unwillingness to move forward. These are the school librarians who still have their shelf list cards because they think the system may crash and they will lose all of their data.

Librarians on the trailing edge always have an excuse for why they haven't moved forward with library technology. "I only have ___ (you fill it in) years until retirement." "I am too old to learn all of this technology stuff." "My administration won't let me spend any money." "I still like to hold that book in my hands." We have all heard these excuses; if each one were overcome, there would be others. Librarians at the trailing edge rarely change: They will not move forward with technology no matter what, and they are becoming increasingly irrelevant in their schools.

So who would be in danger if they do not move forward with technology? It goes without saying that those school librarians in the trailing edge are at risk if they have not already been removed. Many will be glad that they don't have to learn something new and will appreciate the opting-out solution. It is those school librarians in the wedge who are at risk but don't understand why. As we move further into the second decade of the 21st century, it is not enough to be in the wedge crowd as a school librarian.

As a profession, we must be leaders in technology. We must provide our students with the best-quality library services available, and that means being a leader in technology. The technology train for school librarians is leaving the station: If you are not on it, you will be left alone on the platform!

THE EVOLUTION OF TECHNOLOGY IN THE SCHOOL LIBRARY

In this section, we will outline how new technologies have affected the operation of the school library. Not all of these things happened in all school libraries, and they did not take place at the same pace in all school libraries. Furthermore, school librarians may not always have been the leaders in implementing these technologies. Larger academic librarians and some larger public librarians took the advantage of mainframe computers to do some of their management tasks. The development of minicomputer technology made computer technology less expensive to use for the management of the library. New, less expensive computers became available and affordable to more and more academic and public libraries and led to the development of networks that combined their catalogs of materials, upon which they began to share resources.

For many smaller school districts through the mid-1970s, total computing capability was leased computer time, perhaps one or two hours at a time, from a local college or industry to perform business functions. Larger school districts would have a mainframe, but school librarians did not have access to mainframe technology to house circulation data. Mainframes in school districts were used to schedule classes for students, create grade reports, handle budgets, and issue salary checks for teachers. School librarians really didn't need the same type of management systems for circulation of materials, for ordering materials, and for organizing them as their academic and public counterparts. Most did not have the expertise to automate the school library's circulation system. That had to wait for the proliferation of small computers into school libraries. With the development of PCs and simpler software for circulation systems, school librarians could begin to afford management technology.

Circulation Systems

Circulation has always been viewed as a repetitive task that some think could be accomplished by nonprofessionals. Academic libraries viewed the automation of circulation as being labor-saving and a natural outgrowth of using college computer systems. Automating circulation was generally the first library function in the school library, but it occurred considerably later than in academic libraries, because school libraries rarely had the in-house computer systems and expertise necessary to implement library circulation systems.

Security Systems

Many school librarians would not consider security systems to be technology in the most modern sense of the term, but a strong case can be made that a security system is technology. Not only is it technology, but it was the first technology that many school librarians had the opportunity to use. Security systems filled a practical purpose and were approved by school administrations and school boards for one simple reason—they saved money! As security systems became more prevalent in the 1970s, school librarians found that they were typically saving between 80 percent and 90 percent in lost book costs. School boards and administrators quickly saw the financial savings and became strong proponents of security systems.

Not all school libraries were designed to take best advantage of security systems. Some aesthetically pleasing features of school libraries, such as multiple entrances and exits, balconies, and outside access, can make school library security systems less effective, but their ability to reduce book losses continue to make them near must-haves in the 21st century school library.

CATALOGING, LIBRARY SYSTEMS, AND MARC

In pre-electronic technology days, with the latest technology the typewriter, the cataloging of materials was a major undertaking in the school library. Cataloging was laborious, and some school librarians with a bent toward cataloging would posit that there is artistry in cataloging. Most school librarians were not able to keep up with changing cataloging rules and did not have time to spend to spend cataloging materials. Cataloging was often an area that received less emphasis, because it took away from time needed to work with students and teachers.

One solution was to purchase preprinted catalog cards or to receive books from jobbers that included catalog cards. It was not always neat Library of Congress cataloging, but it fulfilled the primary purpose of cataloging—allowing books to be found on the shelves. Though the best possible cataloging was always the goal, sometimes less was acceptable if it got books in circulation and allowed them to be found on the shelves. In today's parlance, this would be the theory of "good enough."

The advent of technology that allowed for automated cataloging happened first in the academic arena for many of the reasons outlined above. Academic libraries generally took advantage of their on-campus computer systems to automate cataloging functions. Furthermore, they had the personnel with the cataloging expertise to make the system work, in contrast to the school library where even the best situation had perhaps two librarians to perform all functions in the school library from library instruction to readers advisory and assistance with research assignments. As with automated circulation systems, their proliferation had to wait for the widespread use of the personal computer.

Personal Computers

Computers have been with us since the 1940s. Early computers were invented to automate repetitive tasks, such as the formulation of artillery trajectories. The first practical computer that did just this was ENIAC, built at the University of Pennsylvania. These early computers operated using a combination of vacuum tubes and circuits to perform their calculations. Without going through a lengthy history of the development of the computer, keep in mind the evolution of a device that filled an entire building had less computing power than is in one of today's cell phones. As a matter of fact, the United States put men in space with less computing power than in an iPad has.

Two developments eventually brought us to the PC as we know it. The first was the development of the transistor at Bell Labs in 1947, for which William Shockley, John Bardeen, and Walter Brattain received a Nobel Prize. The second was the development of the silicon chip, which made the personal computer in its present incantation possible. We are not in the business of trying to determine the most significant inventions in history, but the personal computer would certainly have a high rank. This is equally true for its effect on the school library and the school librarian. As stated earlier, though automation in the school library was possible with mainframe and minicomputers, it was not practical. The personal computer made it possible.

As we move forward in our continuum of technology in the school library, we can recall the first standalone personal computers in a school district. They looked good, but what could be done on them? Many summer workshops were spent writing simple BASIC programs on these early personal computers that calculated such things as speeding fines for drivers' education classes. In those days, floppy disks were just that, and we used a paper punch to punch a notch on the disk to make it double sided, to increase capacity and to save money. For school librarians, the big advance was to be able to use an application program such as AppleWorks to actually automate some library functions.

One of the early goals of technology, not just in libraries, school libraries, or business, was to create what was optimistically known as a paperless society. This goal was as much a pipe dream as Thomas Watson's prediction about the need for computers. ("I think there is a world market for maybe five computers," said Thomas Watson, chairman of IBM, in 1943.) Not only do we not have a paperless society, but the explosion in the amount of information available has geometrically increased the amount of paper used.

The evolution of the PC suddenly made it possible for school libraries to automate functions such as circulation, cataloging, and use of the library catalog. Closely tied to these innovations was the invention of easy-to-use, easy-to-maintain networks. Without these networks, it would not have been possible to provide practical public online catalogs. It was wondrous to use that first library system in which one could see items in nearly real time when they were added to the system, using which one could search for all the books on a particular subject to see whether they were checked out. We are miles beyond that today, but in our minds, we still should see that school librarian who keeps the shelf list up to date because "the system might go down."

Audiovisual Equipment and Materials

Through the "bad old days" down to today, the school library has frequently been the home of audiovisual hardware and materials. For many years, this meant film projectors, filmstrip projectors, record players, cassette players, and perhaps even video tape equipment. In addition the school librarian maintained a store of spare parts and bulbs to answer that inevitable call: "This thing won't work." A certain level of repair expertise was often part of the job description. Though the media and the hardware have changed over the years, this function is generally still a part of the school librarian's duties.

Repairs

Today, instead of film projectors, school librarians distribute DVD players or instruct PC users in how to stream video to their computers. Computer projectors, located in most classrooms, are now used for streaming video available from commercial sources. As we look at different methods of delivery, it may well be what was formerly available in the school library or in a support facility may be available electronically. This is an area that has exploded, changing how school librarians can search for resources and make them available to their clients.

Internet and Electronic Resources

We have discussed the effect of the invention and proliferation of PCs on the school librarian. A logical outgrowth of the technology, and an innovation that has had a profound effect on the school library, is the Internet and the use of electronic resources. This is one of the easiest areas to contrast the past with the situation today. Before 1985, neither the Internet, to any practical degree, nor electronic resources existed.

Before the use of the Internet and electronic resources, resources available to students in the school library were simple: books and magazines. Books were located using the card catalog, and students took notes on the information needed or, if they were fortunate, were able to photocopy material. If they were using an encyclopedia and another student was using the volume needed, they simply had to wait. The use of magazines was also straightforward. A student would search the *Reader's Guide to Periodical Literature* for articles relating to their topic and then determine whether their library had the magazine. If not, it was back to the *Reader's Guide*.

Though disarmingly simple, the process was little changed since the advent of school libraries.

School librarians early recognized that this was an area that could be significantly improved by technology. One of the earliest attempts to use technology to improve student access to resources with a product named InfoTrac. This product allowed users to search a microfilm file supplied monthly to find magazine articles, viewing the article on microfiche. It was no longer necessary for the school library to have paper copies of all indexed magazines.

As revolutionary as this was, it was the introduction of online searching using services such as BRS or Dialog that really opened the availability of resources but on a commercial basis. These computer-based services were far from easy to use, and the searching remained the purview of librarians because of the charges for search time. In many cases, school librarians were required to take college courses in the searching techniques required to use these databases. The use of BRS and Dialog required the use of a database thesaurus and the use of the databases required per minute payment. This intermediate step led to . . .

The Internet! It is difficult to overestimate the impact and value the Internet has had on information-seeking behavior in the school library. From its earliest days as a terminal-based network using Mosaic to its ubiquitous graphical user interface, the Internet has simply changed the amounts and ease of data access. This significant change has not all been for the good. The huge amount of information available on the Internet has made it incumbent on the school librarian to thoroughly and completely teach how to evaluate information. Too often students use search engines using general search terms such as "World War II" or "Shakespeare" and then are flummoxed when the search yields 10 million or more results.

The nature of the Internet as an unmediated network has resulted in large numbers of webpages with invalid, incorrect, or biased information. Too often our students take this information at face value, saying, in effect, "If it is on the Internet, it must be correct." Though all school librarians support freedom of access to information, this proliferation of questionable websites has resulted in laws requiring the use of software that blocks access to certain websites in school libraries. In a perfect world blocking software would not be necessary, but unfortunately, this is not a perfect world.

Collateral to the Internet is the use of electronic databases. They use the Internet for access but provide information that is generally credible and, with training, allow users to find exactly the information they need. The databases can be general or extremely specialized. For example, many of the general periodical indexes allow users to access the full text of 2,000+ magazines dating back as far as ten years. This stands in stark contrast to the days of the *Reader's Guide* and hard-copy magazines.

Other databases are very narrow in their coverage. These are specialized databases that are designed specifically for college students while others are specifically for elementary school students. One of the major issues that school librarians face with relation to electronic databases is their cost. One of the innovations that will be discussed in more detail later in the book is such participatory databases as Wikipedia. Such free databases based on the contributions of users have had an impact on the school library.

INTERNET 2

The Internet 2 is a group of social networking applications that have since their inception been the purview of the students rather than the teachers. This seems to be changing as schools and school librarians are adapting such Internet 2 applications as blogs, wikis, podcasts, and virtual conferencing to educational use. In some ways, the most difficult task the school librarian faces when using these applications is convincing parents and school administration that there are educationally viable reasons for using these Internet 2 applications. The use of these applications will be discussed in much greater detail later in this book.

What is the future for school librarians and technology? Only time will tell but one fact is inescapable: School librarians must be leaders in educational technology if they are to remain viable in the schools of the future.

RESEARCH AND DISCUSSION QUESTION

In this chapter, a school board member was quoted as saying that school libraries do not need books, because everything is available on the Internet. That school board member also believed that everything on the Internet is free. Is that person correct in either statement? Why, or why not? Your response to this should be research-based, citing several sources for support.

REFERENCES

American Library Association. "AASL Information Power Action Research Project." AASL. www.ala.org/ala/mgrps/divs/aasl/aaslproftools/informationpower/information power.cfm.

Borgman, Christine. "From Acting Locally to Thinking Globally: A Brief History of Library Automation." *The Library Quarterly*, 67, 215–249.

Burke, John J. *Neal-Schuman Library Technology Companion: A Basic Guide for Library Staff*. New York: Neal-Schuman, 2004.

Doggett, Sandra L. *Beyond the Book: Technology Integration into the Secondary School Library Media Curriculum*. Englewood, CO: Libraries Unlimited, 2000.

Herrin, Mark. "10 Reasons Why the Internet is no Substitute for a Library." ALA. www.ala .org/ala/alonline/resources/selectedarticles/10reasonswhy.cfm.

Johnson, Doug. "Are Libraries (and Librarians) Headed toward Extinction?" *Teacher Librarian*, 2 (December 2003), 24–27.

Johnson, Doug. "Why Do We Need Libraries When We Have the Internet?" *Knowledge Quest* 27(1) (1998). www.doug-johnson.com/dougwri/why-do-we-libraries-when -we-have-the-internet.html.

Jurkowski, Odin L. *Technology and the School Library: A Comprehensive Guide for Media Specialists and Other Educators*. Lanham, MD: Scarecrow, 2006.

Kochtanek, Thomas R., and Joseph R. Matthews. *Library Information Systems: From Library Automation to Distributed Information Access Solutions*. Westport, CT: Libraries Unlimited, 2002.

Kohn, John M., Ann L. Kelsey, and Keith Michael Fields. *Planning for Integrated Systems and Technologies: A How-To-Do-It Manual for Librarians*. New York: Neal-Schuman, 2001.

Lance, Keith Curry. "What Research Tells Us about the Importance of School Libraries." White House Conference on School Libraries. www.imls.gov/news/events/white house_2.shtm#kcl.

"Library Technology Awareness Resources." Library Technology Awareness. www.users .muohio.edu/burkejj/techawareness.html.

Odlyzko, Andrew. "Silicon Dreams and Silicon Bricks: The Continuing Evolution of Libraries." http://hdl.handle.net/2142/8137.

Scheeren, William O. *Technology for the School Librarian: Theory and Practice*. Santa Barbara, CA: Libraries Unlimited, 2010.

"School Libraries History." Internet School Library Media Center (ISLMC) School Library History. http://falcon.jmu.edu/~ramseyil/libhistory.htm.

Williams, Brad. *We're Getting Wired, We're Going Mobile, What's Next? Fresh Ideas for Educational Technology Planning*. Eugene, OR: ISTE, 2004.

2

How It Is

Chapter 1 described the "bad old days" of school libraries and how the job as school librarian might disappear if we don't change our relation to technology. And those bad old days at the end of the last century are nothing compared to what is happening now. The even "badder" days are now. School librarian positions are being lost nationwide—a trend that seems to be continuing no matter how much is said about school librarians' being at the core of teaching and learning or about how much is being accomplished using technology. School library positions are among the first to go when budgets are sliced.

Just in the past two years in several western Pennsylvania school districts, the job of high school librarian has been combined with that of junior high librarian. The result? One librarian fewer and, at best, half-time library service in both the junior high school and the high school. In one school district undergoing renovation, the high school library was simply closed for a full school year, with no alternative made available. Other states are facing similar cuts.

In October 2013, the AASL Executive Summary NCES Schools and Staffing Survey for 2011–2012 provided some baseline data for schools nationwide:

1. 79,000 of 85,500 (92%) traditional public schools in the United States have a school library. This is a high percentage, but this figure leaves out the issue of staffing within school libraries.
2. 2,200 of 4,500 public charter schools have a school library. This is a much less satisfactory 49% and perhaps reflects priorities in one of the hottest educational trends in the United States, the charter school.
3. 67% of school libraries in traditional public schools have a full-time, paid, state-certified school librarian.

Too many librarians or dwindling positions

In October 2013, *Library Journal* published data concerning placement and salaries for 2012 library school graduates, and the results were stunning. The field is overcrowded, with not even half of 2012 library school graduates obtaining permanent professional positions. Only the southern and midwestern states have placements above 50 percent, with southwestern states not even placing a third of graduates in professional positions. Of even more concern is self-reporting from library schools, which describe 1,648 of 6,184 graduates' (27%) being employed. It is also noteworthy that the average starting salary for professional librarians—generally having a master's degree—declined 0.1% in 2012 (Maatta, 2013).

Now let's focus on school librarians, both nationwide and in Pennsylvania. The National Center for Educational Statistics showed a distinct downward trend in the number of school librarians from 2005 to 2012.

The survey noted that numbers of school librarians declined more than those of any other school staff during that period. Carl Harvey noted: "Cuts to school librarian positions betray an ignorance of the key role [that] school librarians play in a child's education, especially in this era of Google, when today's students are flooded with an unprecedented volume of information. . . . The value of school librarians has been measured in countless studies demonstrating that strong school library programs help students learn more and score higher on standardized achievement tests" (State of America's Libraries, 2013).

The complete results of this survey are noted in the references, but several items bear repeating here as well. In 2012, U.S. Secretary of Education Arne Duncan noted that over the next few years, textbooks would become obsolete, their place taken by eBooks. He noted a school in Minnesota that had done just that. Yet I find this notion just plain wrong-headed. Until there is much more digital equity among students, such an approach is not a viable solution. School districts would be required to provide students tablets or similar means of accessing electronic textbooks. As far as any supplementary resources, not all information is available online, and even that which is certainly not always free.

vast amount of tech info but students not digital literate

Two reports from the nation's school librarians reflect this. More than three-quarters of teachers surveyed said that Internet and digital search tools have had a "mostly positive" effect on their students' research work, but 87 percent complained that today's digital technologies "do more to distract students than to help them academically," the report said. "The [I]nternet has opened up a vast world of information for today's students, yet students' digital literacy skills have yet to catch up" (State of America's Libraries, 2013), says a summary of the study.

"Twenty-four percent of those surveyed said [that] students lack the ability to assess the quality and accuracy of information they find online, and another 33 percent reported that students lacked the ability to recognize bias in online content. Not surprisingly, almost half the teachers surveyed think courses and content focusing on digital literacy should be incorporated into every school's curriculum," (State of America's Libraries, 2013).

Let's now take a look at Pennsylvania. In 2012–2013, 126 professional school librarian positions were eliminated. Furthermore, 89 of 496 reporting school districts in Pennsylvania eliminated a school librarian. In 2012–2013, four school districts eliminated all certified school librarians—worse, eleven school districts have no certified school librarian at all. The numbers continued spiraling down in 2013–2014. A 4 percent decrease in school library positions was reported, with eighty-eight positions eliminated in forty-seven school districts. On a somber note, twenty-eight of these positions were in the school district of Philadelphia, which eliminated 32 percent of its school librarians. Now fifteen school districts in Pennsylvania have no certified school librarian at all—districts that together serve more than 16,000 students (PSLA).

If these numbers don't scare school library professionals, nothing will. However, being the center of education in the school and being the school (or school district) leader in technology can help make you indispensable to your school. *Make yourself indispensable & a tech leader* Sometimes that is enough, and it can be helped by implementation of the Common Core Standards. These standards note the importance of technology in instruction:

> New technologies have broadened and expanded the role that speaking and listening play in acquiring and sharing knowledge and have tightened their link to other forms of communication. The Internet has accelerated the speed at which connections between speaking, listening, reading, and writing can be made, requiring that students be ready to use these modalities nearly simultaneously. Technology itself is changing quickly, creating a new urgency for students to be adaptable in response for change. (Fredrick, 2012)

Elizabeth Crawford Reisz has noted that funding is of critical importance in the retention of school librarians and that school librarians who are able to integrate technology into the school library program and collaborate with other teachers are likelier to retain their positions. She noted also that if librarians are recognized more as guardians of book collections than as educators, then the essential skills that they teach—inquiry, critical thinking, digital citizenship, and technology—are lost. Digital resources alone will not help students research or read complex text.

Seven key points describe what it takes for a student to be college- and career-ready under CCS. Students must

- demonstrate independence
- build strong content knowledge
- respond to demands of audience, task, purpose, and discipline
- comprehend as well as critique
- value evidence
- use technology and digital media strategically and capably
- come to understand other perspectives and cultures (Nudging toward Inquiry)

This describes the heart of what school librarians do daily (Reisz, 2013).

Education Week published a lengthy article in its March 21, 2014, edition that discussed education in what it called the post-literate age. Many of this article's conclusions reflect on technology in the school library and the implications for school librarians. The author, Christopher Doyle, noted that books as we know them are no longer important—in students' minds. He also notes the need for information literacy instruction, having observed his students searching online using search engines, but not knowing the most efficient search terms to use.

To today's students, the traditional school library is a space they hardly even recognize. The space once dedicated to books is now often dedicated to computers and distance learning equipment. School librarians are often advised that the Internet is enough: It has all the information students could ever need—and it is all free! Some even suggested that the Internet allows students to teach themselves. The less said about that idea the better. In fact, research shows that students who most readily access new technologies become less independent.

Carol Kuhlthau, in her article "Guided Inquiry: School Libraries in the 21st Century," explicitly identifies the school librarian as the best agent for education in the 21st century. School libraries must be the hubs of learning, the dynamic learning centers, in Information Age schools. She posits that Information Age schools will teach by what is primarily known as the inquiry method. This constructivist method is certainly not a new concept. In the 1960s, Dr. Edwin Fenton of the then Carnegie Institute of Technology had already advocated the inquiry method for teaching Social Studies in high schools. According to this method, students would form a hypothesis, research to find information either supporting or refuting the hypothesis, and then form a conclusion. And such a method, as more closely defined by Kuhlthau, is ideal for the technology-centered school librarian.

She also notes five kinds of learning best accomplished using the inquiry method:

- Information literacy: Five criteria for evaluating information—expertise, accuracy, currency, perspective, and quality—apply for making good choices in the inquiry method.
- Learning how to learn: Using the stages of the information search process helps the learner become better aware of his or her own learning process.
- Curriculum content. If the library does not have a specific curriculum, one should be created.
- Learning competence: Students need to be able to understand informational text and be able to read to learn, rather than learning to read.
- Social skills: The inquiry method develops social skills by establishing a community of learners who can interact and collaborate with each other. (Kuhlthau, 2010)

THE IMPORTANCE AND NEW LOOK OF SCHOOL LIBRARIES

Debra E. Kachel and Keith Curry Lance noted in 2013 that a full-time school librarian makes a critical difference in student achievement. Their study simply reinforces conclusions that have been drawn nationwide about the importance of school librarians:

- High-quality school library programs significantly affect the most vulnerable students.
- An examination of PSSA scores in Pennsylvania found that reading and writing scores were consistently better for students who had a full-time certified school librarian.
- The school librarian's role in teaching affects writing scores even more positively than it does reading scores.
- Staffing of school librarians remains a key issue.

A final quote from this study is germane to the technology-savvy school librarian:

This study adds to the evidence that all K–12 students need and deserve quality school library programs with full-time certified staff. Students are more likely to succeed when they have library programs that are well staffed, well-funded, technologically well equipped, well stocked, and more accessible. And the neediest learners may benefit the most from trained librarians and quality library programs. (Kachel and Lance, 2013)

An article written by a school librarian for the *Harrisburg Patriot-News* noted how the school library should look in the 21st century. The author noted that the role of the school librarian is to help students find information both efficiently and ethically. In the past, school librarians were seen as the protectors and preservers of books, but if they are to survive, they must become the agents matching students with both print and digital resources that meet their information needs. In other words, the school library must be not only the hub of learning, but the hub of technology. Those who fail to get on board will not be happy in their positions—if they can retain them (Miller, 2012).

What are school libraries today? They are more than brick-and-mortar facilities that offer only print books and paper magazines. They are—or they should be—information centers that offer students and teachers a wide variety of technological solutions as well as traditional library materials. Perhaps the school librarian's most important job is to teach students to be informed information users. Students must know how to find the best information, how to determine whether information is useful to their research, and—perhaps most important—how to give credit not only for words, but also for ideas, using correct citing (Miller, 2012).

Glenn Miller, the executive director of the Pennsylvania Library Association, once said cutting school libraries has a "cascading negative effect. If kids are not instructed on how to research, the use of technology at an early age, and consistently through their school years, they come out of K–12 into the workforce or higher education ill-prepared" (Miller, 2012).

"Leadership is the ability to influence or inspire others to achieve shared goals. The school librarian's leadership is demonstrated daily via interaction with administrators, teachers, students, parent volunteers, and community partners. An active participant in curriculum reform, they may serve as the delivery person for new state standards. School librarians often are leaders in promoting new technology for teacher and student use. Knowing that reading is essential to learning, they seek to balance new ways to promote reading as a pleasurable, life-long habit. School librarians collaborate and share instructional responsibilities with fellow teachers" (Dees et al., 2007). Leadership opportunities abound in our profession today for those willing to hit the ground running. And that is what you must do. If you don't, there is little hope that our profession will survive as we know it now.

RESEARCH AND DISCUSSION QUESTIONS

Your principal has notified you that your job as the high school librarian has been recommended for elimination. Research the value of school librarians and prepare two items for the principal:

1. A paper, at least ten pages long, documenting the essential role of the school librarian in academic achievement. (Keith Curry Lance's studies would be a good place to start.)
2. A presentation, suitable for display to the school board, summarizing your findings. As an alternative, you may prepare a podcast or a YouTube video relating your findings. (Doing so would also exhibit your technological skills.)

REFERENCES

"AASL Executive Summary: NCES Schools and Staffing Survey 2011-2012." www.ala.org/aasl/sites/ala.org.aasl/files/content/researchandstatistics/AASL_ExecSummary_NCES-SASS_2011-12.pdf.

Barack, Lauren. "The League of Extraordinary Librarians: SLJ's Latest Tech Survey Shows That Media Specialists Are Leading the Way." *School Library Journal* (November 4, 2012). www.thedigitalshift.com/2012/11/k-12/the-league-of-extraordinary-librarians-sljs-latest-tech-survey-shows-that-media-specialists-are-leading-the-way/.

Dees, Dianne C., Kristi Alexander, Rachel Besara, Robb Cambisios, Teresa Kent, and Jodie Plaer Delgado. (January 2007). "Today School Library Media Specialist Leader." *Library Media Connection.* https://learn.eku.edu/bbcswebdav/courses/LIB800_14288_F12/LIB800_14288_F12_ImportedContent_20120808022316/Modules/Module%2014%20%20Evaluation%20Module%2014%20SoftChalk%20Product/Today's%20school%20library%20media%20leader_1.pdf.

Doyle, Christopher L. (April 2, 2014). "K–12 Education in a Post-Literature Age." *Education Week.* www.edweek.org/ew/articles/2014/04/02/27doyle_ep.h33.html.

Fredrick, Kathy. (May–June 2012). "Fostering Media-Literate Students. *School Library Monthly.*

Kachel, Debra E., and Keith Curry Lance. (2013.) "Latest Study: A Full-Time School Librarian Makes a Critical Difference in Boosting Student Achievement." www.slj.com/2013/03/research/librarian-required-a-new-study-shows-that-a-full-time-school-librarian-makes-a-critical-difference-in-boosting-student-achievement/#_.

Kuhlthau, Carol Collier. (January 2010). "Guided Inquiry: School Libraries in the 21st Century." *School Libraries Worldwide.* https://comminfo.rutgers.edu/~kuhlthau/docs/GI-School-Librarians-in-the-21-Century.pdf.

Maatta, Stephanie L. "Placements and Salaries 2013: Explore All the Data." *Library Journal* (October 15, 2013). http://lj.libraryjournal.com/2013/10/placements-and-salaries/2013-survey/explore-all-the-data-2013/.

Martin, Ann M. "School Libraries Renewed." *District Administration* (October 2008). www.districtadministration.com/article/school-libraries-renewed.

Miller, Barbara. (September 16, 2012). "School Libraries Are Still about Teaching Students 'to Use Information Efficiently and Ethically.'" *The Patriot News*. www.pennlive. com/midstate/index.ssf/2012/09/school_libraries_are_still_abo.html.

"Nudging toward Inquiry: Common Core Standards." (September/October 2011). *School Library Monthly* 49–50.

"Outdated School Libraries: What Can You Do to Update Yours?" www.educationworld. com/a_admin/admin/admin181.shtml.

Reisz, Elizabeth Crawford. (winter/spring 2013). "Critical Issues in K–12 School Libraries." *Maine Policy Review*. http://digitalcommons.library.umaine.edu/cgi/viewcontent. cgi?article=1597&context=mpr.

"School Librarians Bear the Brunt of Staff Reductions." www.ala.org/news/ state-americas-libraries-report-2013/school-libraries.

"State of America's Libraries." www.ala.org/news/sites/ala.org.news/files/content/2013- State-of-Americas-Libraries-Report.pdf.

"Survey of Library Staffing in PA Public School Districts, 2012–2013." www.psla.org/assets/ Documents/Publications/PSLA-Publications/Staffing-Survey-Results20122013. pdf.

"Survey of Library Staffing in PA Public School Districts, 2013–2014." www.psla.org/assets/ Documents/Publications/PSLA-Publications/Staffing-Survey-Results20132014. pdf.

"Survey of Professional Library Staffing in PA School Districts, 2012–2013." Data by Intermediate Units. www.psla.org/assets/Documents/Publications/PSLA-Publications/ Staffing-By-IU13113.pdf.

3

Technology Skills for School Librarians

Determining what technology skills a school librarian should possess is one of the most important measures in assessing how effective the school library will be in the 21st century. It is important not only to determine the skills, but also to plan how the skills are acquired, maintained, and updated.

Two erroneous statements about the preparation of school librarians are that (1) they bring all the technology skills they will need into library school because they are digital natives, and (2) the coursework provided in library school will provide them all the technology skills they need. Both statements are inaccurate, not least because not all students in library school are digital natives. Those who are considered digital natives and do possess many technology skills may have technology skills that are eclectic at best. They can create Facebook accounts and download music, but they cannot organize files in the Windows environment. They can use digital and cell phone cameras and download pictures to their computers and mobile devices, but they cannot set up headers and footers in a word processing program. These digital natives can program a cell phone or a VCR but have no idea how to create formulas that will unleash the power of a spreadsheet program. This may be the hodgepodge of technology skills that digital natives who are prospective school librarians bring with them to library school.

The second erroneous statement is that library school will provide prospective school librarians all the technology skills they will need. If this were true, it would solve this entire issue. Unfortunately, however, the technology skills taught to prospective school librarians vary as widely as the technology skills the students bring with them to library school. Very few school library programs have discrete courses dealing with technology, and if they do, they deal with specific applications or provide a general introduction to productivity software.

Even some digital native librarians are lacking in tech skills

Is this bad? Not in itself when compared with other programs that provide instruction in technology only within the parameters of other courses. Instruction in specific software or in the use of productivity software only scratches the surface of the software skills that will be required of school librarians in the 21st century. A broader approach is essential.

The preparation programs that will prepare school librarians to work in the schools of the future must prepare as thoroughly in technology as in the skills traditionally required of school librarians. To fail to do so does a great disservice not only to the school librarians, but also to the students they will work with in their schools. Furthermore, school districts looking forward to meet the needs of their students will not employ school librarians who do not have the necessary level of technology skills.

THE ROLE OF THE SCHOOL LIBRARIAN

The issue of the technology skills required of the school librarian was analyzed by Carrie Love in an online publication from 2001. The author posits that librarians are the original information specialists or information managers. This remains as true today as it did in 2001. This position cannot be overemphasized in a world where this definition is opposed, even by some librarians themselves. For them, the word *librarian* is sufficient, and using the word *information* denigrates the role and idea of the person. Unfortunately for some, the word *librarian* or *school librarian* best describes the "traditional" someone who selects and distributes books and reads to the students, helping them find answers to their questions and helping them locate something to help write their research papers. This is the perception that allows the administrator to ask for parent volunteers to run the library and even to have a library clerk take on the title "librarian." A school library instructional program provides a myriad of information skills that are critically important to the student. Adapting these information skills requirements define the role of the school librarian.

In 1997, University of Nebraska researcher Gary Hartzell recognized the importance of information and technology skills to define the role of the school librarian. He saw the failure of the school librarian to be a participant in the decisions that affected technology not only at the district or building level, but even in the school library itself. He also found that few, if any, schools of education focused on the importance of the library and of information in the learning process. Is it any wonder, in light of these findings, that the school librarian can become superfluous and, when budget cutting occurs, unemployed?

Hartzell's results with regard to school librarians and technology, even at that early date, had great implications for the "traditional" school librarian.

Though not denying the value of books and other print material, he emphasized the role of the school librarian as information manager or specialist and as educator. This research also presented what Hartzell called "guiding principles" for the school librarian as we move further into the 21st century. Each of these principles presented has implications for the level and type of technology skills that will be required for the school librarian to be a viable force in American education.

1. There are no walls associated with school libraries. The power of technology has made this true. Once limited by a collection within four walls, technology has increased expectations. Students expect, and deserve, access to library materials twenty-four hours a day, seven days a week, from any location. The means that the technology-savvy school librarian must provide patrons access to library resources from home. Anything less is not acceptable.

2. Even more than in previous years, the school librarian must be flexible. This is not just Hartzell's view; it was put forth in the ALA Publication *Information Power: Building Partnerships for Learning*. The reality of the situation is that if you are not the most flexible person in your building, you are not flexible enough. You must be able to move seamlessly among roles as teacher, instructional planner, information specialist, and program administrator.

3. You must ensure that your students are effective users of information. There can be no question that our society is information-based. For better or worse, we are no longer a society that makes things. What are the implications for our students as we move from a production-based to an information-based society? It means that all students must be able to manipulate and use information, because the manufacturing jobs that did not require the use of information simply no longer exist. One has only to travel through the northeast and Midwest "rust belts" to see the truth of this. This now is the essence of the school librarian's task: to ensure that students are ready for these information challenges.

4. Information is everywhere, and as already mentioned, it is central in our lives. Sometimes we, as well as our students, are short-sighted about this concept. Doing research is as important in the job search process as when researching a topic in the library. The whole concept that information is everywhere is key in the quest to ensure that our students are effective users of information.

Contrary to popular opinion, the proliferation of information in our society and the use of technology in our schools emphasize the need for library and technology in all our schools for all of our, students whether in an affluent neighborhood or the inner city. This statement brings us face-to-face with administrators or school board members who believe that technology and the Internet obviate the need for school libraries and librarians. This attitude further divides the world of the haves from the world of the have-nots in our nation.

More than fifteen years ago, the term "intermediation" was coined. The idea was that as technology became more advanced, users would require less assistance to use it. As we have seen, this is patently untrue. As technology has become more advanced, users require more, not less, assistance. One has only to observe student searches for information to see this. Students believe that googling for information is the be-all and end-all of information seeking, regardless of the millions of matches the most basic search yields. Furthermore, without extensive mediation, students are unable to discriminate between good and bad sources. Rather than students' requiring less assistance using more advanced technology, more assistance is required.

This brings us back to the skills related to technology that are required of the school librarian. These are still general, but as we move forward, you will be able to see the meshing of these with more specific skills.

1. Learn about technology. See what technology can do for your library, and see how you can use the technology. This learning process must be ongoing and be an integral part of your professional development.
2. Be involved with technology in your school. Be on the technology committee. Be on the strategic planning committee. It is not practical to make excuses for why you can't, because you need to do these things and be a leader on these committees.

These steps are no longer optional. Failure to do these things is not only a disservice to your students, but also could cost you and others in your district, and others in neighboring districts, a job.

COMPUTER SKILLS IN CONTEXT

When examining the technology skills a school librarian must have, consideration must be given to the context in which the skills will be used. For many years, school librarians have worked continuously to avoid teaching library skills in isolation. Nothing was more deadly for students than coming to the library to "learn how to use the Reader's Guide" no matter whether the students were doing research at that time or not. The ability of the school librarian to plan and work with the classroom teacher to integrate information skills into the curriculum has eased this issue to a considerable degree, at least in secondary schools. This will be discussed in greater detail in chapter 11.

The advent of technology has brought these issues to the table again. In some cases, we have not even determined the role of technology or, more specifically, the role of the computer in education. Early on, use of computers involved programming and, as time passed, use of productivity software. School librarians became more empowered through the integration of library skills into the curriculum, and they will be more empowered still as they integrate the use of technology and information skills into the curriculum. The computer is still useful as a mechanism to create reports, but it is much more.

[handwritten: What is the role of tech in ed.?]

As the use of technology has advanced, some of the most involved have been business education teachers, mathematics teachers, and technology education teachers as well as librarians. These others all have some vested interest in the use of technology in education, but they are not specifically trained as persons to teach students the use and integration of information through technology into education. What technology competencies might be relevant to the school librarian?

1. Knowing the basic operation, terminology, and first-echelon maintenance for technology equipment.
2. Knowledge of computer-assisted programs.
3. Knowledge of the effects of technology on careers, society, and our culture.
4. Computer programming. This last skill has waxed and waned as time has passed. Though often requiring specific and high-level skills, it remains one of those skills that if taught to students can produce employment.

[handwritten: Tech relevant to School librarian]

SCHOOL LIBRARIES: AN UNDER-RESOURCED RESOURCE

A study completed in Canada in 2005 by David Coish echoed many of the conclusions reached earlier and reemphasized the need for technological proficient school librarians in order for students to move forward in our information based society. Some interesting highlights of the study included that 75 percent of school principals felt that a majority of their teachers and school librarians had enough skill with technology to use computers for administrative purposes. Left unsaid was what the principals viewed as administrative tasks. Conversely, less than half the principals felt the majority of their teachers had the skills to effectively integrate computer applications into their instruction or to teach students how to use computers.

Coish found that as the number of school librarians in a school increased, the likelihood of technology applications incorporated into instruction increased. The implication here is that there is a strong correlation between having school librarians in schools and the use of specialized technology applications in instruction. It appears that if school librarians are thoroughly trained in the use of technology, they not only perform a valuable role in the educational process of students, but also can act as mentors for their fellow teachers, helping them become more proficient in using technology. The survey of the role of the school librarian and the technology skills they must possess is necessarily theoretical—necessarily because a lack of a theoretical framework makes any conclusions about technology and the school library and the technology skills necessary for the 21st-century school librarian questionable.

GENERAL TECHNOLOGY SKILLS

When we consider the technology skills needed by school librarians, be they general or specific, we have to consider where these librarians will learn these technology skills. As alluded to in chapter 1 and earlier in this chapter, it is obvious that technology skills are not being taught to preservice school librarians. Why is this so when it is, again, obvious that technology skills are widely required for any school library position? Perhaps one or two explanations can be advanced. First, many library schools perpetuate some difference between "library science" and "information science." Library science concentrates on management, reference, and organization of materials, whereas information science covers computer construction and software building. Second, many view the library, especially the school library, as one of the last bastions of traditional print-oriented skills. It takes great courage to throw aside the concept of spending a large percentage of time on reading guidance to one where the object is to prepare the student for the next step on the academic ladder or into the world of work. If any librarian's reason for entering the profession had to do with loving books and reading, they probably need to find a job in a bookstore, because a love for reading is not a key skill for many librarians, and it certainly isn't for school librarians.

The skills that are essential for librarians and especially for school librarians are discussed below. It may take a concentrated effort to make sure that library and information science programs are providing these for their librarians.

BASIC TECHNOLOGY SKILLS

The first skill is a rather generic skill that is applied here to technology. However, a school librarian's reaction to change may be a good indication of that librarian's potential success in the school environment.

1. *Embrace Change*. This is a basic corollary for school librarians. If you do not embrace change, particularly as it relates to technology, you will become as much of an anachronism as buggy whip manufacturers became with the advent of the automobile. This is not to say that all school librarians need to be on the so-called "bleeding edge" of technology all the time, but the meaning is clear: You must move forward with technology. If you don't have a computer or an iPad at home, get one. So many people today have a cell phone and use them, but adults need to learn how to send text messages and even use the cell phone as a computing device. Get and use a Facebook account. Automate every task in your library that can be automated. Be able to use the most advanced media technologies, and learn to use each new one as soon as it surfaces.

2. *Be Comfortable Online*. Being comfortable online seems so basic that some might question whether this is worthy of mention. It does, however, get right to the base of today's technology in the school library. Not only must a librarian be able to use cataloging software and search databases, but the technologically savvy school librarian also must know and be able to use search engines more effectively than just using one-word general searches in Google. You must be able to evaluate the resources you find online. We all know that there are widespread bias and outright falsehoods on the Internet; you must be able to evaluate this mass of information. You must be able to work with email much more than just sending a joke a day to your colleagues. Use text messaging. Today's students are much more apt to communicate via text messaging than by email. You must overcome the fear that students' emailing and texting in school is bad and accept that there are good, cogent reasons for students to be able to communicate electronically in real time. To be more succinct, you must be as comfortable online as your students are.

3. *Be Able to Fix Things, or Anoint a Fix-It Team*. A long-existing fable in the myths of information technology about the help desk rep at (Dell, Apple—take your choice) was that the desk was contacted by a computer user who could not get their computer to turn on. The user and the help desk rep went through numerous checklists and steps to determine why the computer would not turn on, to no avail. Becoming progressively more frustrated, the help desk rep, on a whim, asked the user whether the computer was plugged in. When the response was "ah, no," the exasperated help desk rep responded, "Then you are too **** dumb to use a computer."

Apocryphal? Probably, but what the military would call first-echelon maintenance should be core skills for school librarians. When an entire bank of computers goes black right in the middle of the OPAC lesson, the first place you will want to look is at the power cable that has mysteriously been unplugged. The second place to look is for those pesky network cables that magically become unplugged. Sometimes these things happen maliciously, but much more often, students will test you. Nothing deflates a sixth-grade jokester more rapidly than just plugging the plug back in and going on with the lesson.

It is true that there will be a limited number of IT personnel available to maintain technology. In fact, school districts often have fewer than 10 percent of the number of personnel that industry would have to maintain the same number of computers. Furthermore, there is constant turnover in school district IT personnel because of the low pay. A second truism is that school districts will pay their head of IT less than a teacher even though that individual would make more than the superintendent if he or she were in industry. It is very frustrating for these underpaid and overworked people to receive a call from a harried school librarian reporting that all the computers in the library have gone down only to arrive in the library and discover that a playful student has pulled a plug or two. But what should a school librarian reasonably be expected to do?

A school librarian should be able to put paper in printers and clear paper jams. In other words, be comfortable doing basic maintenance on the technology in your library. Know how to use a wide variety of storage devices. If you are frustrated with the amount of maintenance you might find yourself doing, you might try recruiting students to help. Long years ago, students were taught to load 16mm films onto projectors. Their grandchildren are very able to help with technology glitches, quickly and seemingly effortlessly. It does take a certain amount of willingness to trust those students, but having a geek squad available on call when that overworked IT person can save much of your time.

This is an area that is in a state of flux. As more and more school districts go to Bring Your Own Device (BYOD) programs, the task gets that much harder for school librarians. Certainly no school librarian can know the detailed ins and outs of every device, but at the same time, you should be able to recognize most computing devices the students use and how they function.

One service you might offer your teachers is a "fair" where you put all the technologies available in your library on show for an afternoon and teachers can come in and try them. It would be a good time to have students there to demonstrate.

4. *Be willing and able to learn new technologies.* If you are to be a technology leader in your school, you must learn new technologies and be eager to do so. When your school adopts a new technology and you haven't been a

part in the selection, you should be right there to learn about it, regardless of whether it will be specifically housed or used in the library. How you learn to use the technology is not important. Some people learn better by sitting down with the documentation and learning systematically, whereas others are more eclectic learners and would rather play with and experiment with the technology to learn how to use it. There is a bit of a caveat with this latter method—sometimes experimenters do not realize all the features or do not use all of the features of technology in the most effective way. Some school librarians simply ask a student to demonstrate the piece of technology.

Perhaps one of the best ways to sharpen your skills with new technology is to do a workshop or training session for other librarians or teachers on either new hardware or software. This puts them in a nonthreatening environment in which they can thoroughly learn new technology and you can verify in your own mind your knowledge of the technology. Training is wonderful! Unfortunately, many school districts seem to think that teachers can learn about technology without training. They are reminiscent of the characters in the movie *Field of Dreams*: "Build it and they will come." Only they believe that if you provide the technology, teachers will somehow sense or automatically know how to use it. If I were to list the five biggest fallacies about technology in education, this would be near the top of the list. You can provide all the new technology in the world, but if teachers are not trained in how to use it and an added reason for using it, they will not use it. It is a strange commentary when school districts will provide the technology but not train educators to use it.

5. *Keep up with new ideas in technology*. This seems like such a basic idea that perhaps it does not need to be written down, but it is important. For some reason, education and school librarianship seem to be professions where getting the degree or certification is the turn off the "learning light" for many. This whole idea of keeping up with new ideas in technology can, in fact, be expanded to keeping up with new ideas in school librarianship. Very few school districts provide tangible rewards for those who keep up with new ideas, but it is certainly part of your professional responsibility to do so. We keep coming back to it, but failing to keep up with new ideas in either technology or librarianship is doing a disservice to your students. This is a tough requirement, but you have to make the time to at least keep up with technology innovations through your professional reading.

ADDITIONAL TECHNOLOGY SKILLS

The skills just discussed are key technology skills for the school librarian. There really is no room for negotiation: You must have these skills.

Following are six other areas of technology skills that, though important, are not as key as the previous five.

1. *Managing library technology projects.* One of the skills we all must use as school librarians is the ability to manage library technology projects. Ideas are wonderful when one implements technology, whether it is upgrading your OPAC or a major project such as providing a computer, Internet access, and a workspace to every user in your library. If you want to see these good ideas come to fruition, you had better be able to plan and manage the project, because it is going to be done, it will be your responsibility. Plan carefully so that if your plan is approved you are ready to move right into the implementation phase. Be sure you have answers to questions that might be asked, as well as alternative plans. Several good planning models are available. Select the one you like best, and follow it.

2. *Determine why you do things in your library, and setting policies.* This is a long title for a single word: Question. Why do you do what you do in your library? Too often we do things or set policies that do not benefit anyone but ourselves, or we have policies that seem to be outmoded. This again relates not just to technology, but to library policies as well. With relation to technology, one policy nearly every school library and even school district seems to have in force is forbidding the use of cell phones by students in school. There are many reasons for this prohibition: Cell phones can be disruptive. Cell phones can be used to cheat on examinations. Cell phones can be used to communicate with others surreptitiously. These are all true. However, by banning the use of cell phones we are prohibiting a very powerful piece of new technology—one that not only has communication capabilities, but one that can be used to gather information. Androids and iPhones are not just telephones, but sophisticated computing devices having good, cogent educational uses. Perhaps in light of this, one might want to revisit a policy that bans cell phones completely. Many school districts are beginning to see light on this and overcome the issues that muddy the waters.

3. *Be able to determine who needs what.* When you are planning for technology, it is crucial that you see which of your constituencies needs what. Consider what students need, what teachers need, what the school administration needs, and what parents need. Also, and equally important, consider what the library staff needs. In this hierarchy of things, what you need generally falls last. When you consider the needs of these different constituent groups, the group that should be satisfied first is the students. We are in the business of educating and providing information to them. Ignore their needs at your peril!

One other constituent group's needs must considered—the library staff's. You may have great ideas about technology, but you must make sure that your staff is on board with whatever technology plans you have.

4. *Translate traditional library services into an online medium.* As we move forward into the 21st century, it is becoming evident that education is increasingly delivered to students in nontraditional ways, with digital schools leading the way. Online education has been growing for the past twenty years, but until recently, the focus has been on postsecondary education. As a matter of fact, a for-profit, primarily online institution, the University of Phoenix, is now the largest university in the United States, with over 400,000 students.

This movement to online education is spreading into the K–12 education arena as well with the spread of digital schools and cyberschools. Who are the students in these schools? It varies, but the typical cyberschool students generally fall into three categories. First are students who are being home schooled. Using cyberschools takes much of the burden off the parents of homeschoolers. Second are those students who for health or legal reasons are not able to attend traditional schools. The third category is those students who select only certain courses to take through the cyberschool. An example of this would be a student whose high school offers only a limited number of Advanced Placement or higher-level courses. The student can attend the cyberschool to make up these needs.

When students are involved in a cyberschool, it is incumbent on the school librarian to provide a digital library to these students. The entire issue of digital libraries will be discussed in a later chapter, but the tech-savvy school librarian must be able to convert traditional library services such as reference and instruction to an online medium. It is just not enough to make sure your online students have access to the Internet; they must also have access to sophisticated library services.

5. *Be critical of technology.* This competency seems to be a dichotomy, because we have emphasized so much the need to understand and use technology—and here we are saying to be critical of technology. Accepting all technology unquestioningly is as bad as not having any technology at all. A term Farkas uses is "technolust"—wanting to have everything just because it is technology, regardless of its application.

A school librarian has so many legitimate uses for technology that it is really necessary to select the best of every new technology. Part of the task is to evaluate the best technology for a particular task and whether, in fact, technology is needed at all. Technology is not a panacea for all your needs in the school library. You must be critical of technology, both hardware and software, and be sure that it can be integrated into the school library. Use of Web 2.0 social networking can really appeal to your students, but if you cannot integrate it into your library's program, you should not be using it.

Though you may want all the technology, if you are to maintain your credibility with your administration, you will have to be judicious in the technology you implement. Use technology to fill a need, not just because it is nice to have.

6. *Be able to sell technology in the library.* Few of us signed on to be school librarians in order to be salespeople, but it is such an essential part of the job that it simply cannot be overlooked. After you plan for the technology you want in your school library, you have to sell its value to your building teachers and principal, as well as to district administration. Many school districts have begun dividing budget requests into needs and wants categories. Your technology plans and requests must fall into the needs category rather than the wants category to increase the chances of being funded as budgets become tighter and tighter. It is always easier to emphasize a "need" if teachers and even parents can support the technology as a "need."

This is not all the selling that has to be done, however. You must be able to sell your technology ideas to your faculty so that they appreciate its usefulness and want to use it. You must be the cheerleader for your library program and be able to convince your faculty that it is an integral part of the school. If you cannot, or if you will not, you will soon become superfluous.

TECHNOLOGY SKILLS FOR SCHOOL LIBRARIANS: A RECAP

Surprisingly little has been written about the technology skills that school librarians will need to be successful. It is, again, almost as though we, as school librarians, are expected to know about technology through osmosis, without any training at all. Following are a number of technology skills needed by school librarians, with more detailed explanation of what is included in the skills. The first list is based on material prepared by the Colorado Department of Education in 1999. The second group of competencies was prepared by a commercial concern in 2005. Others have been developed in the past few years. There are overlaps among the lists but significant differences as well. Note that many of the skills from these earlier lists remain valuable to today's school librarian.

Colorado Technology Skills

These skills, formulated more than ten years ago, are detailed and break the skills into three areas:

1. Basic computer and technology operations and concepts. These would be skills that provide school librarians with the basic ability to operate a computer and other technology tools. Included in this basic area would be the following:

   a. Computer operations
- Assemble a computer system and be able to start up and shut down the computer and its peripherals.
- Identify and use basic parts of the workspace, including icons, separate windows, and menus.
- Start an application and prepare output from that application.
- Use the operating system to name, save, find, retrieve, and revise output from applications
- Set up, add, delete, and use different types of printers.
- Use storage devices, including hard drives, flash drives, cloud storage, CD-ROMs, and DVDs.
- Use the operating system to copy files among and between different storage mediums.
- Use the operating system to save, open, and put documents in subfolders and directories.
- Multitask; open and use more than one application at a time.
- Use more than one platform effectively. Ideally this would be several versions of Windows and the Macintosh and various tablet and cell phone computing devices.
- Initialize and name and rename the storage devices described above.
- Create, name, and rename folders and subdirectories within your operating system.
- Run programs from the cloud, networks, or CDs and DVDs.

   b. Maintenance and troubleshooting
- Care for computer hardware and storage media.
- Prepare backups of documents, files, and the system.
- Keep printers supplied with paper, toner, and ink cartridges, as appropriate.
- Perform first-echelon maintenance on computers, peripheral devices, and local network connections.
- Prepare and follow troubleshooting checklists and procedures for computers, peripheral devices, and networks.
- Address environmental issues when planning areas for computers and peripherals in your library.
- Protect your technology from computer viruses and data breaches.
- Know the steps to follow to obtain next-level technical assistance.

2. Personal and professional use of technology in the school library means the skills that allow you to apply technology tools for productivity in the school library and for the school librarians' personal use. Included in this area are the following:

  a. Word processing and desktop publishing
- Create and edit text.
- Use the cut, copy, and paste functions, including their extended capabilities.
- Format and style documents, including fonts and font size, margins, line spacing, tabs, and bullets and numbering.
- Spell- and grammar-check documents.
- Create, edit, and copy headers and footers.
- Insert, edit, and move date, time, and page numbers in documents.
- Add columns to documents and manipulate section breaks to change column setup.
- Insert, populate, and edit tables in a document.
- Insert, edit, and change all types of graphics in a document.
- Create and change mail merges.
- Create and apply styles and templates.
- Import and insert data from other applications.
- Create PDF and HTML documents from word processing documents.

  b. Spreadsheets and charting
- Plan and interpret a spreadsheet.
- Change or modify existing spreadsheets, including formatting and appearance.
- Create a new spreadsheet with appropriate rows, columns, and headings.
- Create and copy formulas to calculate within a spreadsheet.
- Use functions within a spreadsheet to simplify formulas and calculation.
- Understand and use correctly, relative, absolute, and mixed cell references.
- Create appropriate charts from spreadsheet data.
- Sort spreadsheet data.
- Use spreadsheet data to create reports.
- Create PDF and HTML documents from charts and spreadsheet data.

  c. Databases
- Interpret and effectively communicate database information.
- Add, delete, and modify records in a database.
- Use specific fields to sort a database.
- Extract data that meets specific criteria.

d. Networks
- Use local area networks to connect, log on and log off, open a program, retrieve a document, and save a document.
- Use the network to share files with other users.
- Understand network terminology including local area network (LAN), wide area network (WAN), access rights, security, passwords, file server, and zone.
- Use the cloud to connect, log-on and log-off, open a program, retrieve a document, and save a document.

e. Telecommunications
- Use both local and network connections to connect to the Internet.
- Understand the difference among Internet search engines, and use the appropriate search engine.
- Use different web browsers and locate resources quickly and effectively.
- Download and print online resources in different formats.
- Use the social networking features of Web 2.0, including, blogs, wikis, Facebook, Twitter, podcasting, and virtual conferencing.
- Effectively locate data and information on the hidden web.
- Manage bookmarks or their equivalent in all browsers.
- Access and use resources from appropriate states' databases for books and electronic data.
- Use email tools, including compose, send, retrieve, read, reply, forward, delete, and archive.
- Create email accounts.
- Attach different types of files to email.
- Retrieve and view, read, save, and print attachments in different formats.
- Create and use contacts and groups using the address book feature of email.
- Use email, websites, and other types of discussion media to collaborate with professional colleagues.
- Create websites and webpages to be posted to the World Wide Web.
- Connect to the Internet using all types of connections, understanding the limitations of each type of connection.
- Use Internet resources when not online.
- Install, configure, and use telecommunications software.
- Configure and use an FTP program to communicate with remote computer sites.
- Use technology for instructional purposes including distance learning and desktop video conferencing.

f. Media communications use
- Prepare and operate video media, including VCRs, DVD players, LaserDisc players, and streaming video.
- Set up large-screen displays connected to computers and other video sources.
- Use paint, draw, and authoring tools to enhance other electronic media.
- Use multimedia presentation software to plan, create, and use both linear and nonlinear presentations.
- Use imaging devices such as digital cameras, video cameras, or scanners with computer systems and software.
- Produce and edit a video and then digitize it.
- Know when and how to use file compression utilities.
- Add digitized sound from audio sources to presentations.
- Apply animation techniques to presentations and webpages.

3. *Integrate technology into the curriculum.* The technology skills at this level are becoming more sophisticated. This level moves us past simple technology skills to integration and synthesis of technology skills with curriculum planning. These are essential technology skills, because the use of technology or teaching technology skills to students out of context lessens transfer learning and eliminates ties to the curriculum. The technology skills included in this area include the following:

a. Curriculum
- Create learning experiences for students that are appropriate to the curriculum, relevant to different learning styles, and based on principles of effective learning and teaching, incorporating media and technology when appropriate, using a variety of media communication tools.
- Use literacy instruction to guide students in accessing, synthesizing, evaluating, and using information resources.
- Consider students' technical skills when developing and using lesson plans.
- Use the Internet and other telecommunications channels to gain access to educational resources for planning and instruction.
- Use all technology resources to assist in locating, evaluating, and selecting appropriate teaching and learning resources and curriculum resources for content and target audiences.

b. Design and management of learning environments and resources
- Develop tasks that will require students to locate, analyze, and draw conclusions about information and use a variety of media to communicate their findings.

- Collect information about student learning using computers and other technology media appropriately and effectively.
- Communicate a variety of information about student learning to colleagues, parents, and others using computers and other technology.
- Recognize and create physical settings that support student involvement, inquiry, and collaboration.
- Create and implement organizational and management strategies that support student involvement, inquiry, and collaboration.
- Ensure that all types of technology resources are available.

c. Child development, learning, and diversity
- Address differences in children's learning, learning styles, and performance using media and technology.
- Support learning for special-needs children using media and technology.
- Use a variety of media and technology to support learning for children whose primary language is not English.
- Use all levels of services or resources, local, state, and national, to meet a variety of learning needs through technology.
- Modify computers and input and output devices to enable all students, regardless of disabilities, to create, manipulate, store, and distribute information.

d. Social, legal, and ethical issues
- Know and enforce school district policies and procedures and federal law concerning copyright law and fair-use guidelines.
- Be responsible, ethical, and legal when using technical information and software resources.
- Provide equal access to media and technology resources regardless of students' race, ethnicity, sex, religion, or socioeconomic status.

4. *Building-level technical support.* These skills may seem strange to see on a list of technology skills a school librarian should possess, but as we have discussed earlier, a generally low level of technology staffing in public schools makes many of these skills necessary for the efficient use of technology. You can't just put an Out of Order sign on technology that is not working and wait for someone to come and fix it. Pretty soon you will have all signs and no technology. Among the required skills are the following:

- Set up computer systems and correctly attach peripheral devices.
- Clean computer components and printers. Keep a big supply of canned air and alcohol wipes on hand.
- Install, reinstall, and update system software and printer drivers.
- Make memory available by manipulating system software.

- Diagnose and correct common basic hardware and printing problems using self-help resources.
- Understand and troubleshoot basic computer configurations.
- Add users and assign passwords on the network server.
- Maintain the local area network (LAN).
- Install, reinstall, and update application software.
- Understand the design and configuration of your local area network.
- Add users and assign passwords on the network server.
- Maintain the local area network.
- Install, reinstall, and update application software.
- Understand the design and configuration of your local area network. (Colorado)

As time has passed, there has not been much research done with regard to the technology skills that are required for the school librarian. Often the literature expands to address technology skills for educators, and that is all right, because school librarians are, at the heart of the matter, educators. Four authors have addressed this issue.

A 2011 article titled "Technology Skills for New Librarians" listed two levels of technology skills that are needed by school librarians. It is shown here as a checklist to see how your skills match those listed here:

BASIC SKILLS

- Computer operating system
  - Downloading and installing programs
  - Connecting an auxiliary device to a computer, such as a printer or scanner
  - Understanding the system settings
- How to troubleshoot anything
  - Knowing what to ask a library user who reports a technology-related problem to find out whether it's a hardware or software issue
  - Knowing how to replicate a problem
  - Knowing how to research a solution online
- How electronic resources work
  - Understanding what a persistent URL is and being able to tell whether a URL is persistent or not
  - Knowing what authentication and proxy mean in the library setting
  - Understanding how an electronic resource is set up for access from a trial to the link placed in different library systems such as OPAC (Open Public Access Catalog), ERMS (Electronic Resources Management System), Open URL Link Resolver, and the library website

- Knowing how to troubleshoot remote access issues to electronic resources
- Systems
  - Knowing what different library systems do and how they work together to provide users with access to information resources (e.g., Integrated Library System [ILS], OPAC, discovery service, open URL link resolver, ERMS, digital repository system, content management system, proxy server)
- Web
  - Proficiency in research tools available online
  - Knowing how to properly use the WYSWYG editor in a blog or any content management system
  - Understanding the difference between HTML and Word documents
  - Understanding what a web browser does
  - Knowing how to make screencasts (video tutorials) and podcasts
  - Knowing how to create and edit images and video for the web
  - Knowing what usability is and how it applies to a library
  - Knowing how to write for the web
  - Knowing how to use social media such as Facebook and Twitter
  - Understanding the mobile devices and related technology that are applicable to a library

MORE ADVANCED SKILLS

Here is a random selection of cool technology skills one may want to check out: (Don't be overwhelmed. This is by no means a list of required skills.)

- Markup languages such as HTML, CSS, XML, and XSLT
- Programming and scripting languages such as JavaScript, PHP, Python, Perl, and Ruby
- JQuery and other similar JavaScript libraries
- Relational databases and SQL
- Unix
- Open-source CMS (e.g., Drupal, WordPress, Joomla) installation, customization, upkeep, etc.
- Proprietary ILS systems
- Open-source digital repository and indexing systems
- APIs and mashups
- Semantic web and linked data
- Web analytics and statistics
- Data mining and data visualization (Tech Skills)

Back in 2005, Laura Turner published a list of the twenty technology skills that educators should have. It could serve as a list of the topics you might cover in your staff development plan to help teachers:

- Word processing
- Spreadsheet calculation
- Database use
- Electronic presentation
- World Wide Web navigation
- Web design
- Email management
- Digital camera use
- Network knowledge applicable to your organization
- File management and Windows Explorer use
- Downloading software (including ebooks)
- Installing software onto a computer system
- WebCT or Blackboard teaching
- Videoconferencing
- Computer-related storage
- Scanner use
- Mobile computing
- Deep or hidden web
- Educational copyright
- Computer security

In 2014, Thompson noted that the Turner article had generated the most hits, and he conducted a survey to see whether these were applicable almost ten years later. His list included the following;

- Searching efficiently
- Mastering Microsoft Office and basic word processing
- Being willing to learn new technology
- Connecting with social media
- Sharing and collaborating via YouTube and blogging
- Unlocking the potential of mobile devices
- Reaching out with email
- Making your point with presentation software
- Googling it
- Getting ahead in the cloud

These remain an excellent list of potential staff development topics for many school librarians to offer to their teachers.

WHAT CAN LIBRARY SCHOOLS DO?

The answer to this should be obvious: library schools must offer more courses that relate to technology in the school library. Simply offering courses in application software is not enough. Courses related to webpage design, telecommunications, and integration of traditional library services into technology would be a good starting place. Perhaps even more important is providing the school librarian with the skills and attitudes to adapt and change with technology. All types of technology will change as time goes by. If school librarians have the ability to adapt as technology changes, they will be successful.

After introducing school libraries without technology and the importance of technology to the school librarian, we have moved in this chapter to a detailed examination of the technology skills that are required for the school librarian is to be a vital and viable force. We have moved from a theoretical look at technology skills to lists of important technology skills for the school librarian and for the school librarian to use to plan staff development for teachers. This sets the stage for forthcoming chapters that will examine in detail all issues related to technology and the school librarian.

RESEARCH AND DISCUSSION QUESTION

The lists of technology skills and competencies for educators and school librarians are necessarily dated as of the writing of this book. In order to bring these lists up to date, research the topic "Technology Skills for School Librarians." Compare what you found with the lists included in this chapter, discussing any changes or additions you found. Be sure to comment on items or skills that are no longer considered crucial.

REFERENCES

American Library Association. "AASL Information Power Action Research Project." AASL. www.ala.org/ala/mgrps/divs/aasl/aaslproftools/informationpower/infor mationpower.cfm.

Burke, John J. *Neal-Schuman Library Technology Companion: A Basic Guide for Library Staff.* New York: Neal-Schuman, 2004.

"Colorado Technology Competency Guidelines for Classroom Teachers and School Library Media Specialists." www.eric.ed.gov/ERICWebPortal/custom/portlets/ recordDetails/detailmini.jsp?_nfpb=true&_&ERICExtSearch_SearchValue_0=ED 433020&ERICExtSearch_SearchType_0=no&accno=ED433020.

Credaro, A.B. "Skill Sets for School Librarians." Warrior Librarian Weekly. http:// warriorlibrarian.com/FOUND/skillset.html.

Doggett, Sandra L. *Beyond the Book: Technology Integration into the Secondary School Library Media Curriculum.* Englewood, CO: Libraries Unlimited, 2000.

Eisenberg, Michael, and Doug Johnson. "Learning and Teaching Information Technology Computer Skills in Context." www.libraryinstruction.com/info-tech.html.

Farkas, Meredith. "Skills for the 21st Century Librarian." http://meredith.wolfwater.com/wordpress/2006/07/17/skills-for-the-21st-century-librarian/.

Holzweiss, Kristina A. "Using Tech Tools for Learning with Standards." www.schoollibrarymonthly.com/articles/Holzweiss2014-v30n4p13.html.

Jurkowski, Odin L. *Technology and the School Library: A Comprehensive Guide for Media Specialists and Other Educators.* Lanham, MD: Scarecrow, 2006.

Kochtanek, Thomas R., and Joseph R. Matthews. *Library Information Systems: From Library Automation to Distributed Information Access Solutions.* Westport, CT: Libraries Unlimited, 2002.

Kohn, John M., Ann L. Kelsey, and Keith Michael Fields. *Planning for Integrated Systems and Technologies: A How-To-Do-It Manual for Librarians.* New York: Neal-Schuman, 2001.

Lowe, Carrie. "The Role of the School Library Media Specialist in the 21st Century." Eric Digest. www.ericdigests.org/2001-3/21st.htm.

NCLIS. (2008). "School Libraries Work." http://www2.scholastic.com/content/collateral_resources/pdf/s/slw3_2008.pdf.

"School Libraries—an Under-Resourced Resource?" www.statcan.gc.ca/pub/81-004-x/2005002/8051-eng.htm.

"Tech Skills for New Librarians." www.bohyunkim.net/blog/archives/1319.

Thompson, Greg, "10 Technology Skills Every Educator Should Have." http://thejournal.com/articles/2014/01/22/10-tech-skills-every-educator-should-have-aspx.

Turner, Laura. "20 Technology Skills Every Educator Should Have." www.instructor.aviation.ca/content/view/133/71.

Williams, Brad. *We're Getting Wired, We're Going Mobile, What's Next? Fresh Ideas for Educational Technology Planning.* Eugene, OR: ISTE, 2004.

4

Networks, Hardware, and Software for School Libraries

In chapter 3, we discussed the technology skills all school librarians should possess. In this chapter, we will discuss networks, hardware, and software that school librarians should be familiar with if they are to be technology leaders in their schools. Not all schools will have all these things, and not all school librarians will work with all these aspects of networking, all these hardware devices, or all these types of software. This chapter is merely an introduction to these things for school librarians, providing an outline of networking concepts and terminology, along with a discussion of different types of computer hardware and computer software. The aim is to provide the school librarian with some base of knowledge upon which to can build as different aspects of technology enter the library.

TRENDS IN LIBRARY TECHNOLOGY

As was mentioned in chapter 1, most school librarians are at a particular level of technology acceptance: the bleeding edge, the leading edge, in the wedge, or in the trailing edge. (You may want to go back and review the levels before you continue.)

No matter the level of technology acceptance, it is essential that school librarians be able to intelligently evaluate technology choices before they make any purchases. Several criteria are available, but the one part put forth by Moore is quite appropriate. When evaluating technology choices, one should consider the following:

- Is it suitable? In other words, does it meet the need for which the technology was designed? This is an area that those on the bleeding edge often ignore, because they are ready for all new technologies.

- Is the technology nearing obsolescence? This is a hard area for school librarians to judge, but they should not hesitate to ask whether something newer is close to introduction. What makes this a difficult issue is uncertainty about how obsolete the will technology become. As an example, Windows 8 has been available for several years but an earlier operating system, Windows XP, is still used in many schools even though Microsoft no longer supports Windows XP. Issues like this have significant financial implications for schools and school libraries because not all can afford to upgrade even if some technology is no longer supported.

- How durable is the technology? For school librarians, this is almost a no-brainer. The technology purchased for schools must withstand the wear, tear, and rough use that students will give it. If it cannot, do not buy it.

- Does the technology fit in the library environment? It is incumbent on the school librarian to determine whether technology really fits the needs of their library and also whether it works in the physical footprint of the school library. Always keep in mind that the "latest and greatest" may not fit the needs of the library.

- Are there training implications for the technology? You have to determine whether the learning curve for technology is high or low. Some pieces of hardware and software are not intuitive and have steep learning curves. Those types of technology might not be appropriate for all school library situations.

- Does the technology have maintenance, updating, or upgrading requirements? Almost all technology today does, but you must determine whether it is so onerous as to pose a significant barrier. Determine whether these things are easy to do or whether they require outside intervention. Are maintenance agreements available? Determine whether the upgrades, updating, and maintenance agreements have costs associated with them. In today's technology arena, be particularly careful of maintenance agreements. The cost for many kinds of technology, particularly computers, has dropped so drastically that maintenance agreements are rarely cost-effective.

- Is there support available if there are problems with the technology? This is closely related to the previous point: No one wants to spend extended periods on the telephone with a help center. Help must be affordable and easily obtainable.

- Is the technology cost-effective? In these days of decreasing school library budgets, this is an essential element. Do other technologies do almost the same thing for less money, or is the technology unique?

- Is the technology the most appropriate way to provide the service? This is where the rubber meets the road for the school librarian. Just because there is technology available to accomplish a particular task does not mean that using it is the best way to do things. The truth is that sometimes a pen and paper is the best, most cost-effective technology to accomplish a task.

In a recent article, Marshall Breeding discussed some technology trends in school libraries and in some cases how they relate to public libraries. This article and the next one discussed by Lenovo should give school librarians food for thought as they consider what technology is right for their library.

SCHOOL LIBRARY AUTOMATION

School libraries are different but have many shared characteristics. An "automation system for these libraries must include features to identify materials by grade level, in support of selection and management of materials and in its search or discovery features presented to students" (Breeding, 2013).

LARGE NUMBERS OF SCHOOL LIBRARIES

"School libraries tend to be quite small compared to a typical public library, but the number of facilities is very large. According to a 2013 American Library Association (ALA) fact sheet, there are 99,180 K–12 school libraries in the United States, compared to 16,417 public libraries" (Breeding).

During the course of the last decade or so, there has been a shift toward implementing library automation systems centrally through the district rather than for each school library individually. This district-wide approach yields much more efficiency and flexibility compared to the early days of school library automation where a PC-based system was installed in each library. Centralized web-based systems eliminates the need to install software in each school, provide better tools for managing the resources throughout the district, and expand the body of materials available to the students. (Breeding)

SPECIALIZED FUNCTIONALITY

School libraries need functionality out of a library automation system designed to accommodate their operational needs (Breeding). A recent Lenovo article identified fourteen questions that educators and school librarians should ask to identify the right technology solutions for schools.

Though some certainly are self-evident, as you are looking at technology for your school library, carefully consider each of these to get the best and most suitable technology for your school library.

1. **Student Grade Levels**: Younger students may need computing devices with greater durability and ease of use, as well as different levels of security. They may be better served by external rather than on-screen touch keyboards, depending on your teaching and learning objectives. Older students, in contrast, will probably need the power and performance to run more sophisticated applications and multimedia programs.

2. **Portability**: How much wireless mobility is needed for successful implementation? Mobility should be one of your top priorities, and it is important to determine the right mix of PCs, laptops, and tablets. Consider whether you still need to support some computer labs with desktops or even high-powered workstations, depending on the requirements of your school and grade levels.

3. **Durability**: What are your expectations for ruggedness in devices? Students—and teachers—can be tough on computers. Ask your vendors to provide you with evidence of devices' durability. Find out whether the devices have withstood rigorous durability tests such as the MIL-SPEC military specification testing. In light of the potential for drops, dings, and spills in a school setting, evaluate warranty and service options to minimize replacement and repair costs.

4. **Operating System**: Which is better for your environment? Many schools already rely on the Windows computing platform, whereas others rely on tools and applications from Apple and Google for both traditional (Mac OS, Google Chrome) and PC Plus (Apple iOS, Google Android) needs. Windows and Android choices are growing in popularity with users and IT teams thanks to their flexibility and easy app customization, in contrast to the Apple system, which relies exclusively on the iTunes store. Remember that operating system will also influence your data storage choices, so make sure you factor in server versus cloud storage preferences. Last, be sure to consider issues of existing network compatibility and security—Windows devices currently more easily integrate with your existing security and management tools than Android or Apple devices.

5. **Size**: What is the appropriate mix? The larger screens of desktops and all-in-ones give students more real estate to work with, whereas laptops, notebooks, and tablets offer a wide range of screen sizes. Consider factors such as portability, durability, and the need for multimedia graphics when determining the appropriate mix of screen sizes for your environment.

6. **Connection Ports**: Which peripherals will your students and teachers need? Which external devices will your users need to plug into their computers? How many USB or HDMI ports will be necessary? Desktops and laptops typically offer more options than tablets, and some consumer-focused tablets, such as the iPad, lack USB support. For maximum flexibility, look for devices with built-in HDMI ports that can connect to projectors, large screens, and other multimedia devices, as well as SD card slots for fast and easy file transfers.

7. **Multimedia**: What capabilities do you need? Do you want to enable robust student interaction, group collaboration, or distance learning? Do you need laptops with the power and memory to support video editing and gaming? No matter your needs, make sure your hardware choices have the graphical capabilities, cameras, speakers, displays, audio technology, and processing ability you need to meet your objectives.

8. **Connectivity**: What do your students and teachers need to access? Even with Wi-Fi available on most devices and in many schools, you often need to go one step farther. If your students require access where there is no connectivity—at home or in the community—you may need to add a wireless WAN.

9. **Battery Life**: How long should devices work between charges? Some mobile devices have batteries that last six hours, while other batteries last eight or nine hours or even longer. Although this may appear sufficient, battery life problems can become a major disruption, so plan accordingly. Consider whether you have enough electrical outlets per classroom and if external power sources or surge protectors are needed. Mobile carts also offer portable charging, and new device innovations, such as RapidRecharge, can extend student productivity.

10. **IT Management**: How much control do you need over your devices? If you need to maintain strict control over deployment and maintenance, look for devices and services that support zero-touch configuration and easy remote management. Powerful Microsoft and Intel tools, along with solutions such as webNetwork from Stoneware, help IT deliver good end-user productivity without compromising security or manageability.

11. **Security**: How much security do you need to protect your data and devices? To protect your investment, look for comprehensive security tools that include secure components and advanced security features. Windows 8.1 Pro comes with robust BitLocker disk encryption built right in, and fingerprint readers protect data and anti-theft options such as Absolute Software's Computrace can aid in recovery if a device is stolen or lost. New

ideas such as webNetwork also let you unify important applications and resources inside a secure single sign-on cloud platform.

12. **Energy Savings**: How does energy usage affect your operating costs? To drive down energy consumption and operating costs, select technologies that meet Energy Star requirements. Also look for device utilities that shut down and boot devices on a set schedule.

13. **Warranties**: Is extra protection really necessary? In making this decision, consider the availability of your tech support staff and their ability to service current and future purchases. Also bear in mind that extended warranties negotiated before you buy are extremely effective in the long run. Schools that demand a lot from their computers may want opt for a three-year extended warranty, particularly on mobile devices.

14. **Price Points**: How can you maximize your computer budget? First, carefully compare prices and features. Then consider total cost of ownership, looking beyond the initial price to issues like durability and projected uptime that dramatically affect long-term costs. Always take advantage of prenegotiated contracts, and carefully compare costs when you are looking at general service contracts. Public schools should find out whether vendors participate in any state contracts such as WCSA and take advantage of the available discounts, whereas independent schools should consider banding together for volume purchasing.

WHAT IS A NETWORK?

As the use of computers has increased in school libraries, so, too, has the use of networked computers. In the early days of PCs, computers were typically standalone. All applications were contained on each computer, and information could only be shared by using storage devices such as floppy disks. Most home computers are still standalone machines because of the cost and technical skills required to have a network in the home.

As time passed it became more and more necessary for computers to be networked. Standalone machines do not meet the requirements of computing and technology in the school library. In simplest terms, a network is a group of connected computers. Expanding this definition a bit, a network is a group of connected computers that can exchange information with each other.

Home Network

Most networks can be defined as home networks, local area networks (LAN), or wide area networks (WAN). Home networks are just what the name implies, a network within one's home. A home network may be either a wired network or a wireless network, and although data sharing may be a goal of a home network, it is most often used as a single path to the Internet. With a home network, each computer can work through a router and single modem to connect to the Internet.

Local Area Networks

A local area network (LAN) is a computer network that serves or covers a small geographical area. Based on this definition, a home network could be a LAN, but more typically a LAN covers a building or group of buildings, such as a school, campus, or office. In contrast to wide area networks (WAN), a LAN is usually characterized by higher data transmission rates, smaller physical areas covered, and not having a need for leased or purchased telecommunication lines. As noted earlier, the use of a network allows users to share data and information, but there are some very cogent reasons why a LAN is to be favored over stand-alone computers in a school library:

1. Fewer peripheral devices are needed, because they can be shared by LAN users. No longer does each computer need to have its own printer.
2. All types of information can be shared.
3. Software programs can be shared.
4. Users have access to resources when needed, minimizing downtime.
5. If devices on the network are not functioning, they can be bypassed and other devices used.
6. Telecommunication costs can be minimized.
7. Licensed databases can be shared within the school library.
8. Moving and sharing data is accomplished electronically rather than physically.
9. Resources can be added incrementally.

Although you as the school librarian will probably not get involved in the wiring of a building LAN unless you are also the technology coordinator, you need to be aware of the components of the LAN, including wiring, network topology, access method, and network design. The type of wiring used in the construction of the LAN determines the bandwidth and the data rate of the network. In prior years, these were considerations most related to cost, but as sound and video have become much more common, the size of the pipeline and how fast data can be moved have become even more important aspects. There are three general types of communications media. The cheapest is twisted pair cable. This has a data rate of 10 Mbps (megabits per second) and a bandwidth of 500 KHz. Twisted pair cable has typically been used for telephone voice communications and for data transmission. Of the three communications media, twisted pair is the cheapest and easiest to work with, but is also has the smallest capacity and is the slowest.

Coaxial cable is the second type of communications media. Its data rate is 500 Mbps and its bandwidth is 550 KHz. Often coaxial cable, which is most commonly used for television cable, will be the backbone of a LAN, with twisted pair cable branching from the backbone cable. Coaxial cable is less vulnerable to interference and has much more bandwidth than twisted pair cable.

By far the fastest is fiber optic cable. Along with this much greater capability is an extremely high cost. For school districts, the high cost of fiber makes it impractical for purchase, but recently consortiums have negotiated group prices for fiber, bringing it within the budget of school districts.

Wide Area Networks

A wide area network is one that covers a wider geographic area than does a local area network. A couple of examples should help clarify this point. The city of Philadelphia has a wireless network that allows all of its residents to connect to the Internet. Although this is technically a metropolitan area network (MAN), it is also an example of a wide-area network. Although some might consider a network that connects all the facilities of a school district as still being a local area network, for our purposes it would be considered a wide area network, because it allows the local area network in each school facility to be connected. The largest, and by far best known, wide area network is the Internet.

Many wide area networks are proprietary and are for use by a particular entity. Typically these types of networks require authentication for entry to the network. Other wide area networks are constructed by Internet service providers, such as Comcast or Verizon, and are used to provide connections from individual computers or local area networks to the Internet.

LANS VERSUS WANS IN THE SCHOOL LIBRARY

If the school library has its own local area network, all library-related software is housed on the library's server and the library does not share any tasks or even records with other school libraries in the district. In other words, each school library has its own local area network that does not connect to other school libraries. On the other hand, in a wide area network environment library software is stored on a network server in a central location and all of the school libraries share their resources. Although the latter is overwhelmingly the environment used by most school districts, there are some advantages and disadvantages to each.

Local Area-Based Configurations

Advantages	Disadvantages
1. Faster access to the collection, because access is local	1. Limited collection available, because only local holdings are seen
2. Easier and faster diagnosis of problems and hardware troubleshooting	2. Local control over the database
3. If web server is maintained, school library's OPAC can be available on	
4. Only local holdings visible (many would also consider this a disadvantage)	

Wide Area Configurations

Advantages	Disadvantages
1. Access the holdings of multiple school libraries	1. Access may be slower because of high traffic levels
2. Consistency through centralized cataloging	2. Server malfunctions affect entire system, not just one school library
3. Wide area network software more economical than local area network software	3. Steep learning curve

NETWORK TOPOLOGY

Just as your school library has a floor plan that was developed to allow the most efficient use of resources and facilities, so networks have different blueprints for their layouts. Network topology refers to the physical arrangement of computers, cabling, and other network components. The three most common network topologies are bus, ring, and star. The type of topology used for a network helps determine the network's performance. Just as one plan may not be satisfactory for all school libraries, not all network topologies are equally efficient.

Bus Topology

In a bus topology network, all computers and peripherals are connected in sequence. The bus topology is most often used on a peer-to-peer (P2P) network and rarely on a client-server network. In the bus topology network, each computer can communicate with every other computer. Advantages of bus topology networks are their simple design and low cost. Furthermore, no server is required. This topology has several disadvantages, many of which mitigate against the proliferation and growth of bus topology networks. First, if there is a break in the cable, the computers are cut off from one another, and the network is effectively disabled. Second, as the distance of the cabling and number of nodes on the network increases, performance is degraded. Early AppleTalk networks used the bus topology.

Ring Topology

In a ring topology, often called a loop topology, the nodes on the ring, whether computers or peripherals, are in a circular configuration. Data flows around this circle and is passed from computer to computer until it reaches the computer for which it is intended. Ring topologies are sometimes called token ring networks, because the data is transmitted using a special data packet called a token. The primary advantage of the ring topology is that even with large numbers of nodes, the performance is at an acceptable level. As with the bus topology, the ring topology network is stopped if one computer in the ring fails. Furthermore, problems on a ring can be hard to find or diagnose.

Star Topology

The star topology is the most widely used client/server network topology used today. This topology is called a star because the network nodes connect to a central communications device called a switch. The Ethernet is the communications protocol, the set of rules for the exchange of communication, used by many star networks. A star network has several advantages. First, if one computer fails, the performance of the network is not affected. Second, the addition of nodes to a star network typically does not degrade network performance. Third, the diagnosis of network problems is easier. The major disadvantages of a star network are the complexity of the cabling and the relatively high cost.

These descriptions of different network topologies lead to one question: What is the best network topology? As networks have evolved over the years, it has become obvious that the star topology is the network design to use in school libraries. Although they can be relatively pricey, versatility and flexibility make the star topology the network design of choice. Just as you will rarely find a peer-to-peer network outside the home environment, the same is true for any network topology other than a star.

WI-FI NETWORKS

The past few year have seen a proliferation of Wi-Fi networks that are taking the place of wired networks. Nearly all schools now have Wi-Fi networks that have taken the place of our wired networks.

"Wi-Fi is the standard way computers connect to wireless networks. Nearly all modern computers have built-in Wi-Fi chips that allows users to find and connect to wireless routers. Most mobile devices, video game systems, and other standalone devices also support Wi-Fi, enabling them to connect to wireless networks as well. When a device establishes a Wi-Fi connection with a router, it can communicate with the router and other devices on the network. However, the router must be connected to the Internet (via a DSL or cable modem) in order to provide Internet access to connected devices. Therefore, it is possible to have a Wi-Fi connection, but no Internet access." (Wi-Fi).

Nearly all computing devices in use today have Wi-Fi capability, including the newest smartphones. This allows them to connect directly to the Internet. Many people have installed wireless networks in their homes so that they are no longer tethered to their wired connections. This allows computing using the Internet to take place all over their homes and even outside, within some distance restrictions. When one is using a wireless network, security can easily be compromised if one is not careful and using encrypted technology. If this is not used, it is easy for someone just driving by to access a wireless network.

Advantages of Wi-Fi Networks

Using a Wi-Fi network is generally less expensive than using a wired network. Wi-Fi networks are very handy when working outside or in areas that do not have wired network connections.

1. Manufacturers are building wireless network adapters into most laptops. The price of chipsets for Wi-Fi continues to drop, making it an economical networking option included in even more devices.
2. Different competitive brands of access points and client network-interfaces can interoperate at a basic level of service. Products designated as "Wi-Fi Certified" by the Wi-Fi Alliance are backward compatible. Unlike mobile phones, any standard Wi-Fi device will work.

NETWORKING BASICS

Network basics will describe network architecture, network components, transmission media, network adapters, network navigation, and networking software. Understanding these basics allows you to talk to network technicians understanding their vocabulary.

Network Architecture

A network's architecture refers to how a network is designed, how networks are controlled, and the distance between network nodes. When you hear

people discuss how a network is administered or controlled, they are refer-
ring to either local control or central control. A peer-to-peer network is the
most common type of locally administered network, whereas a client/server
network is the most commonly encountered type of centrally administered
network. The most common type of home network is a peer-to-peer network. This type of network may even be effectively used in a small school;
most networks with ten or more nodes are client/server networks. Of course,
all bets are off when the home or the school is using a Wi-Fi network.

A client/server network comprises "two types of computers, clients and
servers. The client is the computer that users use to complete tasks. The
server is the computer that provides information or resources to the clients
on the network" (Johnson). The server also provides the control, or central
administration for the network. In addition to being a wide area network, the
Internet is a type of client/server network. When connected to the Internet,
your own computer is a client and your Internet Service Provider (ISP) the
service that allows you to access the Internet.

Network Components

To operate, all networks must have a way for the nodes to connect to the
network. This may be either cable or wireless. Furthermore, devices that
allow the nodes to communicate and send data and software that control the
network's operation are required.

Transmission Media

All the nodes of a network, both "computers and peripherals, connect to
each other and to the network using a transmission media" (Johnson), such
as existing wiring, additional cabling, or wireless technology. The additional
cabling used to connect network nodes can be "twisted pair cable, coaxial
cable, or fiber optic cable" (Johnson). These cabling options were discussed
earlier in this chapter. Radio waves are used by wireless networks to connect
network nodes rather than wiring or cable.

The different types of transmission media transmit data through networks
at different speeds. The bandwidth, which is also called the data transfer
rate, measures the maximum speed data can be sent. "The throughput is
the actual speed of data transfer" (Johnson) and is generally slower than the
data transfer rate. The bandwidth and the throughput are measured in megabits per second (Mbps), which represents one million bits.

Network Adapters

"Devices installed in or connected to network nodes that allow the nodes
to communicate with each other or get to the network are called network

adapters" (Johnson). They may be external devices but are much more likely to be installed in the nodes and are known as network interface cards (NICs). For Wi-Fi access, nearly all modern computing devices have wireless cards installed.

Network Navigation

Data sent over transmission media in a network is often bundled and called packets. Network navigation devices such as routers and switches facilitate this data flow. When data packets are transferred between two or more networks, routers are used. This is the process that allows data to be transferred from the Internet to a computer. Switches are like traffic lights on a network. They receive the packets of data and direct them to the correct nodes on the same network.

Networking Software

All client/server networks are controlled by specialized network operating software (NOS) such as Windows Server 2012 or SUSE Linux Enterprise. Network operating software handles requests for data, access to the Internet, and "the use of peripherals for the entire network" (Johnson).

CONNECTING TO THE INTERNET

It is estimated that more than 2 billion people around the world are connected to the Internet. The truth is that if you are not providing your students and staff with Internet access in your library, you are overlooking a service that is expected in today's school library. When we began experimenting with the Internet nearly twenty years ago, the connection was dial-up using a modem and standard telephone lines. As time passed, broadband connections became the best way to connect to the Internet and the preferred Internet connection method in school libraries. Broadband Internet connections include cable, satellite, and digital subscriber line (DSL).

Dial-Up Connections

Although rapidly being replaced by broadband Internet connection, dial-up connections are still in use. All that is required to connect to the Internet is a telephone line that connects to an ISP and a dial-up modem in or attached to the computer. Owing to the proliferation of broadband connections, new computers no longer have built-in modems; these have been replaced with network interface cards and wireless network access cards.

At one time, we could say that a dial-up connection was enough for the casual Internet user. That is no longer true; today's casual users are interested in downloading music and videos and in gaming, three things for which a dial-up connection is insufficient. This is the main disadvantage of a dial-up connection: It is too slow to do the things with the Internet that your students and staff will want to do.

Broadband Connections

Broadband Internet connections are the connections of choice today for your library. As mentioned earlier, there are several types of broadband connections but not all are available in all geographic locations. Furthermore, not all these broadband services are necessarily available to school districts. At any rate, if your school district has not moved forward to a broadband Internet connection, it needs to do so as soon as possible.

The first broadband connection to the Internet is a cable connection. The connection to the Internet is made using a standard coaxial cable. To use a cable connection, you will have to have a cable modem and a network interface card. Although a cable connection is faster than a dial-up connection, there can be speed degradation during peak usage times.

A DSL, or digital subscriber line, connection to the Internet uses a dedicated telephone line to connect to the Internet. If you are using a DSL connection you must have a DSL modem that connects the computer to the DSL line. One of the primary strengths of a DSL connection is that it is not affected by busy times and by numerous users' sharing the same line. The main drawback of a DSL connection is that you must be in relative proximity to the telephone company central offices, because the signal seriously degrades beyond 18,000 feet (about three-and-a-half miles).

Fiber-Optic Internet Connections

Fiber-optic connections use fiber-optic cable to receive the Internet data. This connection is also called FiOS. The primary advantage of a FiOS connection is its very high speed. That speed, however, comes with a substantial financial cost. Furthermore, fiber-optic cable is so costly to install that it is only available in certain areas of the country.

Satellite Connections

Schools that do not have other high-speed Internet options may elect to access the Internet via satellite. Schools need a satellite dish and cable to connect the dish to their network. Although the speed is relatively high, the signal from the satellite to the disk can be affected by interference or adverse weather conditions. The use of satellite can also be affected by mountains and other physical obstacles such as tall buildings. Generally speaking, this type of connection is line of sight.

We previously discussed the use of wireless networks to transmit data. Similarly, a school district can use a combination of a broadband Internet connection and a wireless network to access the Internet. In this situation, the district must have line-of-sight connections with the facility where the Internet signal is received. That data is then transmitted wirelessly to the various facilities within the school district. This is becoming the Internet connection of choice for many school districts, but it does present significant security issues.

FAT AND THIN CLIENTS

When you are deciding what types of computers to place on your network you may want to decide whether thin clients would be appropriate. A thin client is not a full-service computer, but rather almost a terminal accessing a server for nearly all software requirements. In contrast, a fat client is a full-service computer, even though it may still be attached to a network. Libraries are prime candidates for the use of thin clients, because library users very often do not need all the power of a full-service computer. Furthermore, significant cost savings can be realized if thin clients are used. Some advantages to consider when evaluating thin or fat clients include the following:

Advantages — Thin Clients	Advantages — Fat Clients
1. IT costs are lower, because thin clients are managed through the server.	1. Fewer server requirements.
2. Thin clients are easier to secure, because data generally does not reside on them.	2. Better multimedia performance.
3. Better data security—again, because the data resides on the server, not the thin client.	3. More flexibility.
4. Lower hardware costs, because thin clients do not have a disk, application memory, or a powerful processor.	4. Better peripheral support.
5. Lower energy consumption.	
6. Easier failure management; a thin client is generally just swapped out if it fails.	
7. Less value to thieves.	
8. Operable in dusty and dirty environments, because they have far fewer moving parts.	
9. Less network bandwidth required.	
10. Simple hardware upgrades. Often obsolete full-service computers can be used as replacements for thin clients.	
11. Lower noise levels.	
12. Less wasted hardware.	

These are issues that school librarians must consider if they are thinking about using thin clients on a network rather than full-service computers. The thing that makes thin clients the most attractive is the cost savings. You can get a lot of bang for your buck using thin clients, but cost economics are sometimes outweighed by other factors.

COMPUTER HARDWARE

The next items to consider are computer hardware. This category includes the computer itself and what is inside the computer box, as well as peripherals such as storage devices, monitors, mice, sound devices, printers, and scanners. The current trend is items that were not originally thought of as computing devices, such as smartphones and tablet computing devices. This is not an all-inclusive list, because new items considered computer hardware are developed almost daily. As a corollary to the development of new hardware is the seemingly geometric increase in computing power.

The cofounder of Intel, one of the large chip manufactures, Gordon Moore, posited a trend in computing hardware in 1958 that has been borne out for more than fifty years. He stated that the number of transistors inside the CPU (central processing unit) of a computer would increase so quickly that CPU capacity, and thus computing capacity, would double every eighteen months. The performance of the computer industry since Moore published his findings has borne this out, and his conclusions are now known as Moore's law. What are the real implications of Moore's law for school districts and school libraries? It means that unless you or your district have an unlimited supply of money, you will not always have the newest, best, and most powerful computers. Hard decisions will have to be made about when to purchase an upgrade, what to purchase or upgrade, and whether to purchase or lease computer hardware.

In an ideal world, we would be able to add new technology as it becomes available, but we know the ideal world does not exist. The school librarian has a few considerations when purchasing computer hardware. First, always try the technology before you commit to buying or leasing it. Sometimes this may require a trip to a library that has the technology you are considering, but it will be a trip that will pay for itself if you find what you are looking for. Second, always compare models and technologies. Though you may not want hardware at the bleeding edge, neither do you want hardware that is inadequate for your needs or that will soon become obsolete.

Third, you have to know when you have to stop looking and start buying. Sometimes we get so tied up in comparing and analyzing options that we cannot actually pull the trigger and buy. This is known as "paralysis by analysis." Finally, do not get caught in the trap of being influenced by any of the computer myths out there, including the myth that you should wait to purchase, because computer prices will stabilize. This has not happened for 50 years; why would it happen now? Another myth is that you should wait to purchase because the prices will drop. There may be some truth to this, but it is reminiscent of a person who is known as a great shot. The problem is that he never takes a shot, because he is always waiting for the perfect shot. If you keep waiting for that price to drop just a bit more, you will never purchase anything. The third myth is that delaying purchasing will allow current technology to become obsolete and new technology to become available. The question here is how long to wait. Finally, you should never fall for the myth that just because technology is available and here, it can be used. That is how schools end up with closets full of technology that is never used.

TYPES OF COMPUTERS

As described in chapter 1, the computer has evolved from a massive tube-operated machine with a very limited computing capacity to handheld computing devices such as smartphones or tablet computing devices. For the purpose of our discussion, we will consider three basic types of computers.

The Supercomputer

Only a few supercomputers exist in the world, and they are used to perform very complex calculations very rapidly. They are typically used where very intense mathematical calculations are required. Supercomputers are often shared by two or more universities. In geographic areas where there are supercomputers, their excess capability is often offered to students.

The Mainframe or Minicomputer

The second basic type of computer is called a mainframe computer and is designed to support a large number of computer users at the same time. A mainframe computer is able to execute many different computer programs at the same time. Depending on its capacity, it may also be called a minicomputer. School districts have moved forward to the point that many of them now own or lease mainframe computers. They are typically used for business applications in the school district or to host the school district's school management software. The school district's mainframe computer is often part of a school district network so that functions such as grade book applications can be linked to the school district management software.

The Microcomputer

The third basic type of computer is the ubiquitous microcomputer. It comes in many brands and has many levels of capability, but it remains the computing backbone in school districts and school libraries. It comes in a variety of configurations, from the desktop to the tablet.

The term "desktop" may be a misnomer, with most people stowing computer towers under or beside their desk, leaving only the connected mouse, keyboard, and monitor on the desktop. A desktop case houses only the computer itself, leaving the user to use either included peripherals or third-party products. The most customizable form factor, desktops offer easy access to RAM slots, hard drives, interface cards, and even processors, enabling tinkerers to build and customize their machines for a specific use. This upgradability and capacity makes desktops the computers of choice for many gamers and those using professional video or CAD software. Of course, portability is not an option for a desktop user, but a well-equipped desktop can act as a server or backup station for a home network, enabling you to access files or stream your music or video remotely to a laptop. Although a desktop box can be inexpensive compared to a laptop with similar capabilities, make sure to include the price of a monitor in your calculations.

In 2005, laptops overtook desktop computers in overall popularity, and many of today's laptops offer features and versatility that used to be the exclusive realm of desktop models. With high-resolution integrated displays, full-size keyboards and multicore processors, laptops are usually powerful enough to run most applications as quickly as a desktop. The portability of a laptop enables you to work from wherever you want, and virtually all today's laptops include Wi-Fi. Sizes and capabilities vary widely, however. Compact "netbooks" offer inexpensive, lightweight, Internet-capable computers but may skimp on storage, processing power and even screen and keyboard size. Larger "desktop replacement" models include screens as large as 17 inches, interfaces for connecting peripherals and additional monitors, and processors suitable for gaming, but also carry a much higher price tag and shorter battery life. Even "middle-of-the-road" models with 13- to 15-inch screens offer varying capabilities. With such a broad range, there's a laptop for almost every need and budget.

All-in-one computers are represented by the iconic Macintosh. It was the first widely accepted all-in-one computer: a desktop machine with an integrated screen. Apple reinvented its flagship all-in-one in 1999 with the iMac, and today it and others, like the Acer Veriton and HP Omni, have similar form factors: The "works" of the computer hide behind its screen for a sleek look. USB connections offer you a choice of mouse and keyboard, and newer models such as the HP TouchSmart include touchscreens as well.

The downside of an all-in-one computer is that it lacks the portability of a laptop as well as the upgradability of a desktop tower. However, if you want an unobtrusive computer for your home or a machine for a small space or kitchen, you may find an all-in-one to be your best option.

Tablets are taking over the market. This newest computer form became popular in 2010, when Apple introduced the iPad. The lightest, most portable computer design, a tablet uses a touch screen as its primary interface, although external keyboards are available for most models. Some, like the Asus Transformer, connect with a keyboard and track pad to mimic a laptop. Most tablet brands offer 3G or 4G LTE connectivity as an option, with Wi-Fi only on their base models. The low-power processor in a tablet means longer battery life than á laptop, and a tablet can be ideal for connecting to email, making notes on the road, reading e-books, or giving presentations around a table. Although most tablets are limited by their Android, iOS, or Windows RT operating systems and the tablet-optimized apps available from dedicated app stores, Microsoft's Surface Pro adds the ability to run the full Windows operating system. Like laptops, tablets' form factors vary, from the Surface's 10.6-inch display to the iPad's 9.7-inch screen and the Kindle Fire's 7-inch screen. Storage in most tablets is fixed, though some feature memory-card slots for expansion. As with other form factors, tablet prices vary widely depending on capabilities, operating system and connectivity, but you can find basic tablets running Android for less than $200 (Cox).

Smartphone Computing

The fourth type of computing device is not, strictly speaking, a computer. Nearly every student and teacher has a smartphone. What are the implications for the school library?

First, you, the school librarian, should be proficient in the use of each of these forms of computing as well as the smart phone. Though many may not like the idea of the smartphone as a computing device, it appears that this is the future of computing right now. Second, you must be able to find apps and have students use them in the library. Many schools are now preloading all textbooks onto either a smartphone or a table computing device, obviating the need for hard-copy textbooks.

Today's school district buyer has such a wide array of options that it's almost hard to believe that until very recently, the choice was simple for most: a desktop or laptop. However, with the popular adoption of netbooks and touchscreen tablets, there's a computer with a form factor for everyone. Whether you want massive screen real estate, high-powered processors, great industrial design, or the ability to check your email while you walk down the street, there are computers available for all levels of usage.

INSIDE THE COMPUTER

Simply put, a computer is a data processing device with four functions: (1) It gathers data, (2) it processes data into information, (3) it outputs data or information, and (4) it stores data or information. Let's look at what is in the computer case, be it a desktop, notebook computer, or alternative computing device. The main thing that is in the computer case is the central processing unit, or CPU. This is really what makes the computer compute. The CPU performs calculations and is responsible for processing input data into information. The CPU is located on the motherboard, the main circuit board in a computer. A number of different processors are available and include Pentium Dual Core, Centrino, and AMD processors. As a school librarian, it is not always necessary to know all the technical specifics of the CPU, but there is a big question you should be prepared to answer: How fast should the CPU be in the computers you use? The simple answer, and perhaps it is an oversimplification, is that the CPU should be fast enough to meet the requirements of the hardware and software you use. What often happens is as you add new components to the system, the requirements on the CPU increase. Sooner or later your system will not support the new components, and you will have to upgrade.

In addition to the CPU and motherboard, the computer case contains different circuit boards that perform functions for the computer. They generally are able to connect to other devices and are called expansion cards. Typical expansion cards might include sound cards, video cards, modem cards, wireless cards, and network interface cards. The computer case also contains the power supply for the computer and the memory modules, also called RAM. RAM, or random access memory, is the storage space for data and commands used by the CPU. There is a saying in technology that you can never have too much memory. The more memory your computer system has, the faster and more powerful it will be. The case of a computer will also contain a hard disk drive. Although a hard drive is in fact a storage device, it is considered here because it is physically located in the computer case. It is the most efficient and fastest type of storage available and usually holds the system software, application software, as well as data and information. This brings us back to the question posed with reference to RAM: How big a hard drive is appropriate? Again, technology experts would say that you can never have too big a hard drive. The bigger the hard drive, the more applications and data you can store. Many alternative computing devices do not have internal hard drives. Rather, data and information are saved to the cloud.

COMPUTER PERIPHERALS

Computer peripherals can be divided into two categories—input devices and output devices. Input devices include keyboards, mice, digital cameras, camcorders, webcams, and microphones. Also, specialized input devices are available to be used by physically challenged individuals. Output devices include monitors, printers, and speakers. In addition to input and output devices listed above, computer peripherals also include storage devices and scanners.

STORAGE DEVICES

Several different types of storage devices can be used with computer systems. We have mentioned hard drives contained in the computer case, but external hard drives are becoming more common as their price decreases. The advantage of an external hard drive is the speed at which it can be accessed and the high storage capacity. External hard drives connect to the computer through a Universal Serial Bus (USB) port.

In the early days, the only real practical storage device was the floppy disk. In the earliest computers, they were truly floppy, but as the computer evolved, floppy disks standardized on 3.5-inch plastic disks. Today, very rarely do computers have floppy disk drives. The capacity of these early storage devices just is not large enough to hold meaningful amounts of information and computers with floppy disk drives often have to be especially ordered. Similar to floppy disks are zip disks. A zip disk storage system has a higher storage capacity than a floppy disk, but the special zip disk requirements and the cost of the zip disks themselves hindered the widespread adoption of the zip disk system.

In most popular kinds of storage devices today are flash memory cards, flash drives, CD-ROMs, and DVDs. For day-to-day use, flash memory cards and flash drives are the most common. Flash memory cards are most often used with digital cameras, though information from flash memory cards is easily downloaded to computer systems. Flash drives are the most common type of mass storage used. The price of flash drives is dropping rapidly, and their capacity is increasing rapidly. Flash drives connect to computer systems through USB ports.

CD-ROMs and DVDs are examples of optical storage devices on which bits of information are etched using lasers, readable by optical disc drives for download to computer systems. In terms of speed, DVDs are faster than CD-ROMs, and BluRay discs are the fastest of all. Both DVDs and CD-ROMs can be either R or RW. DVD-R or CD-ROM-R means read-only; data cannot be written to this type of DVD or CD-ROM. DVD and CD-RWs can not only contain data, but data and information can be written to them by the user.

MONITORS

While monitors may be slowly disappearing, they still need to be considered. For desktop computers, the two most common types of monitors are cathode ray tube displays (CRTs) or liquid crystal displays (LCDs). LCD monitors are also referred to as flat-panel monitors. LCD monitors have taken the CRT out of the monitor market. LCD monitors are lighter and have a smaller footprint than CRT monitors. Furthermore, they use less energy and are cheaper than CRT monitors. Keep in mind that either of these types of monitors can be attached to a notebook computer. CRT monitors are similar to a regular television set. You may be asked what the optimum size is for a monitor for a computer system. As a general rule, monitors should not measure less than 17 inches. There are 15-inch monitors, but they are very difficult for students to read.

SOUND DEVICES

One of the things your students will want to do is listen to sound from their computer systems. This can range from music to streaming video to podcasts. In a home computer system, a set of speakers provides sound output. Depending on the needs of the system user, the speaker system can be very sophisticated. In a school library situation, however, you will probably want to use headphones with any sound system. If the system is used in a classroom or larger area, an amplifier may be required.

PRINTERS

Printers have always have been the primary output devices for computer systems. As mentioned earlier, one of the early goals of technology and computer systems was to achieve some sort of paperless system. We know now this goal has failed; we print more than we ever have, and that includes only the intentional printing of documents, printing that was meant to be done. All too often printers are the weakest part of a computer system, and our students prove it every day. If they send a print command and no paper comes out, do they think something is wrong? No, they just continue to send print commends. When whatever issue the printer had is fixed, out come multiple copies of the same thing. What a waste of paper!

For our purposes we will consider three types of printers: impact printers, inkjet printers, and laser printers. Impact printers, more commonly known as dot-matrix printers, have become legacy items except in business offices where large masses of printing must be done. Impact printers are still the cheapest way to print, but they do either not print graphics or print them very crudely.

The printer of choice in home computer systems, for considerations of both cost and quality, is the inkjet printer. Inkjet printers vary widely in both price and print quality. Inkjet printers have decreased in cost to the point that it is not cost-effective to repair them; they are just discarded and replaced. The major expense associated with inkjet printers is the cost of ink cartridges. Inkjet printers are often not the best choice for school libraries because of their cartridge cost and because they often turn into color photo-copiers, with users producing multiple color copies at will.

The most efficient type of printer available for the school library is the laser printer. Although the initial cost for high-quality laser printers is greater than for inkjet or dot matrix printers, the cost in lifespan of toner cartridges makes laser printers the best solution for heavy-duty library printing. Laser printers use laser beams and static electricity to place an image on paper. Laser printers are quick, quiet, and produce high-quality printouts.

When you are deciding what printers you want in your school library, there are several points to consider—first, the speed of the printer. Print speeds generally range from eight to thirty pages per minute. Always remember that printing text is faster than printing graphics. The second considera-tion is the printers' resolution. This is the printed characters' clarity and is measured in dots per inch (dpi). As a general rule, the higher the resolution, the more expensive and slower the printer. Think about what your library's printers will be used for when considering the acceptable resolution. The third consideration is color output. If you are committed to having at least some color printing capability in your library, you will have to decide if you want an inkjet capability or a color laser printer. Printers need internal memory to print. You must determine what your printers will be used for when determining how much memory is required. Inkjet printers can slow to a crawl if they do not have enough memory, whereas laser printers simply will not print if they do not have enough memory. Look carefully at your printing needs. If you are printing mostly text documents, a laser printer is probably the best choice. If you have a requirement for high-quality color graphics, then an inkjet printer is probably the best choice. The final consid-eration when evaluating printers is the cost of consumables.

A type of printer gaining popularity with home computer users is the all-in-one printer. An all-in-one printer combines the functions of a printer, scanner, copier, and fax into one machine. They can be valuable in the library offices because they save space, but they should be used with cau-tion in the public areas of the school library, because they have capabilities you may not want to make available.

One final concept of printing needs to be considered—centralized print-ing. As discussed earlier, much paper can be wasted in a school library through a lack of awareness about malfunctions of printers. A way to solve this is to centralize printing. This allows monitoring of printers and, it is hoped, a minimum of wasted paper. Though it often takes a dedicated worker to monitor the centralized printing, this cost can be matched by the savings from paper that is not wasted.

One way to attack the cost of printing is to charge a nominal fee for printing. This is more common in public libraries but can be effective in school libraries. It does challenge students, however, who have little money to pay for a school lunch.

SCANNERS

At one time, it was thought scanners and the scanning process would become one of the primary input modes for computers. For several reasons, this has not proved true. Scanning can be a complicated process and often does not yield results or the quality desired. Scanners can scan graphics and text. When you scan graphics, they can then be manipulated using graphics or drawing programs. Text can be scanned and then converted using optical character recognition (OCR) software. OCR software is designed to simplify the conversion of text material for use with a word processing program. However, this is a complicated process. If the user does not have a nearly perfect copy of the text, cleaning up after the scan can take an inordinate amount of time. A skilled typist can enter text more rapidly than OCR software can accurately convert text if the copy is flawed. It is true that scanners have become less expensive and a bit easier to use, but the most commonly used application for scanners is in large-scale digitization projects, such as the Google Books digitization project.

This introduction to computer peripherals is basic but provides school librarians with some fundamental knowledge that will be valuable. There are other computer peripherals out there, but the ones described here are the most commonly used. By the time you are reading this, there could well be several other types of computer peripherals available.

STUDENT COMPUTERS

Trying to determine what kind of computers available for students in the school library, how many are needed, and determining how they will be financed are key questions the school librarian must address. Later in the chapter, we will discuss the different types of computers available for student use and discuss in some detail the technical specifications for the "ideal" student computer. Another issue affecting what computers should be available for students is the concept of Bring Your Own Device (BYOD) that is becoming much more common in schools. This concept will be discussed in more detail in chapter 12.

When trying to decide how many computers are the ideal for your school library, the driving force is how much money is available. You always have to take into consideration the dollars. In an ideal world, each user of a school library would have a computer with an Internet connection and a work area. But reality is often less than that, even to the point of having only one computer in the school library. Much literature discusses how one computer can be effectively used in a school library. You will have to determine what your situation will bear.

One of the aspects you will have to resolve is whether you will use library budget or whether your district will purchase computers or lease them. This will depend to a great degree on the source of funds for technology. If the funds are one-time or will be bonded, it may make the most sense to purchase computers; otherwise, leasing is a viable option. This is not a decision that should be made precipitously, because purchasing means a large initial outlay for computers that will all become outdated and need to be replaced at one time, creating the need for another large outlay.

Leasing provides you with some flexibility with computer procurement, but it requires a constant funding stream, because there will be payments required each year. The advantage to leasing is that you can plan for phased replacement of computers each year with a less substantial outlay of funds. In summary, then, if you have one-time funding, purchasing computers is probably the best option; if you have a steady funding stream, leasing is a smarter option.

Types of computers have already been discussed in terms of hardware. Here they are presented in terms of student use. Students will use a variety of types, including desktops, laptops, tablets, notebooks, handheld computing devices, and netbooks. Each one of these computers has varying degrees of power and a wide variety of uses. In general, there are two basic computer platforms—Windows computers and Macintosh computers. At one time Apple computers were preeminent in the field of education, but that has changed over the past fifteen years with Windows-based computers now the overall leader. Though Lenovo and Hewlett Packard are the leading manufacturers of Windows-based computers, no one manufacturer is predominant in the field.

Desktop Computers

Desktop computers of some kind have been the most common computers used in education, no matter whether elementary school or college. There were several reasons for this. First, when considering the capability and power of computers, desktop computers are the most economical. The same power that you might find in a desktop computer, if in a notebook computer, be significantly more expensive. Second, desktop computers are easy to expand and update. Expansion and upgrades for a desktop computer are relatively unlimited compared to other types of computers. Desktops easily accept peripheral devices and are, as mentioned before, relatively cost-effective. A drawback when using desktop computers in a school library is that they are more difficult to move easily if you want to quickly change the configuration of the library.

Laptop Computers

Laptop computers put the computer CPU, monitor, mouse, and keyboard in one unit, giving users a large amount of flexibility as to where they will compute. As laptop computers have evolved over the years, they have become lighter and more compact yet at the same time more powerful. Another factor that has made laptop computers more popular is the proliferation of wireless networks. Instead of being tied to a desktop computer with a wired network connection, a notebook with a wireless network connection allows a student to work where he or she wants as long as the battery in the notebook lasts and the computer is in range of the wireless network.

Notebook and Tablet Computers

The differentiation between these two has to do with the capability of each. Initiatives in several states and many school districts give each school student a notebook computer. One of the first school districts to successfully implement a notebook giveaway program was the Greater Latrobe School District in Latrobe, Pennsylvania. In several of these programs, the notebook computers given to the students were not as capable as laptops and had some limits to their capability. Though programs of this sort can be very costly, they do overcome the issue of equity that can occur when there is a great deal of computer software and information for student use but not every student has access to a computer.

When weighing the use of notebook computers in the school library, there are a few drawbacks. The first is cost. On a per-unit basis, notebook computers are significantly more expensive than desktop computers. Second, their very portability makes them vulnerable when they fall out of backpacks.

Tablet computers make up a rapidly increasing part of the computers sold. Tablet computers are in effect a notebook computer with the additional user capability of interacting with software using a stylus or one's finger to tap on the tablet screen. Tablet computers also have the software capability to convert what is written on the tablet to word processed text. This capability has existed in other hardware for some time, but tablet computers are a step forward in sophistication.

Handheld Computing Devices

As we move forward into the 21st century, the use of handheld computing devices is becoming much more common, and it may be the answer to every student having a computer. Handheld devices are generally a smartphone, such as the Apple iPhone. In each case, the device allows access to the Internet and e-mail and also provides a utility program similar to MS Office and a basic operating system. It is well to keep in mind that today's handheld computing device has more computing power than NASA did when it put a man on the moon.

Netbooks

The final computer to consider is the netbook or subnotebook, as it is also called. A netbook is a small computer about a third the size of a notebook computer that provides nearly as much computer capability as a full-size notebook computer. A netbook normally sells for less than $300 but provides full access to the Internet and to email. They typically use Linux instead of Windows for their operating system and Open Office, rather than Microsoft Office, for their productivity suite. Netbooks are very prevalent in Europe and Asia and are just beginning to catch on in the United States.

SPECIFICATIONS FOR STUDENT COMPUTERS

It is a challenge to include typical specifications for student computers, because as soon as one reads them they are out of date. Nevertheless, two sets of specifications for student computers are suggested, a minimum set and the preferred set.

Computer Specifications

Feature	Minimum	Recommended
Processor	Intel 1.66 GHz	Intel 2.4 GHz
Memory	2 GB	4 GB
Hard Disk	80 GB	250 GB
Optical Drive	CD-RW/DVD	DVD-R
Network	Built in LAN 10/100 Wireless for laptops	Built in LAN Gigabit Wireless for laptops
Video Ram	128 MB	256 MB
Operating System	Windows 8 Mac OS X	Windows 8 Mac OS X
Software	Microsoft Office	Microsoft Office

SOFTWARE

Several different categories of software for the library computers are discussed in this chapter. These categories include operating systems, productivity software, browser software, web development software, antivirus software, and spyware. All these categories of software are of importance to the school librarian, but every application does not have to be on every computer with the exception of operating system software. As you examine this list of categories of software, you may notice two categories missing. The first is educational software, such as drill and practice and simulations. Though this book is attempting to be as comprehensive as possible, the topic of educational software used primarily in the classroom is beyond its scope. The second category of software not described in this chapter is library management software. This category will be discussed in much greater detail in a subsequent chapter. Software changes almost as rapidly as hardware. Though we may be inclined to always have the newest and most powerful software, it is not always necessary.

OPERATING SYSTEMS

The operating system of a computer controls how a user interacts with the computer. Its functions include the management of the computer hardware, computer software, and the computer peripherals. In the early days of personal computers in school libraries, the type of computer or platform used determined which operating system was used. This remains the case today. Again, in the early days of computing, if you were using Apple computers in your school library, you were using some version of the Apple operating system. If you had IBM or compatible computers, you used DOS, or the Disk Operating System. The DOS system resembled a terminal-based operating system; as commands were typed in at a prompt, which caused operations to occur. What we will discuss here are graphic user interface (GUI) operating systems, the ones we are now generally familiar with. We will examine Microsoft Windows, Mac OS, and Linux.

Microsoft Windows

Microsoft Windows is the base operating system for most non-Apple Macintosh computers used in school libraries. Windows has gone through many upgrades and improvements since its introduction as Windows 1.01 in 1985. The most current version of Windows is Windows 10, introduced to replace Windows 8.1.

Mac OS

The Mac OS functions only on Apple Macintosh computers. There is no compatibility between Windows and Apple computers, but the operating systems are very similar in appearance and functionality. In 1984, the Mac OS was introduced with the Macintosh computer. The Mac OS was the first commercially available operating system with a graphic user interface, or GUI. This allowed users to have a point-and-click interface not available with DOS operating system computers. It took the introduction of Microsoft Windows to achieve this same point-and-click graphical user interface on other types of computers. Over the years, the Macintosh with the Mac OS has become a niche machine, generally used for graphics applications. Mac OS users are a loyal group and point to the system's greater system reliability. Furthermore, the Mac OS is nearly invulnerable to viruses. However, because the Macintosh is a niche machine, far fewer software applications are available.

Linux

As users—business, education, and home—have become less satisfied with Microsoft Windows and Mac OS, more have turned to the Linux operating system. Linux is an example of open-source software that is available for developers to use or modify. The reputation of Linux is that it is more stable than other operating systems and far less apt to crash. Because it is open-source software, it is easy to change or modify to meet any developments in operating systems. Linux is an operating system that in its basic form can be downloaded for free. Other versions of Linux do have charges and fees associated with them, but they also provide support and other features not available with free versions of Linux.

PRODUCTIVITY SOFTWARE

Productivity software is the real core of computing for many users. It is, in the educational arena, software used to produce research papers, create grade books, produce attractive presentations, and allow for the creation and manipulation of databases. More specifically, productivity software generally includes word processing software, spreadsheet software, presentation software, and database software. Each type of application is available from several manufacturers and for all computer platforms. All these applications have their genesis in mainframe computer applications and have evolved for the personal computer.

As time passed, users looked for productivity software that integrated all of these pieces into one software package, called a "suite" of software.

The first integrated software suite available to the educational user was Appleworks, which was developed for the Apple II family of computers. Since then there have been many software suites developed, but the most commonly used productivity software suite today is Microsoft Office. It is widely used in education and is the standard productivity software. It is taught in nearly all educational institutions and is widely used in educational administration. Microsoft Office, in its most popular configuration, consists of Microsoft Word for word processing, Microsoft Excel as the spreadsheet component, Microsoft PowerPoint as the presentation software component, and Microsoft Access as the package's relational database. The interface of these components is so tightly interwoven that, for example, if an Excel chart is placed in a Word document, when the Excel data is changed, so is the data in the chart placed in Word. At once praised and criticized, Microsoft Office really tries to be all things to all users. This, in turn, has created an extremely powerful program, but one for which the average computer user will only scratch the surface of its power.

Two other software suites that deserve mention are Microsoft Works and WordPerfect Suite. Both have shipped preloaded on personal computers at different times and were billed as lower-cost alternatives to Microsoft Office. Microsoft Works was widely used in education because of its lower cost and simplicity of use. Though having fewer features than Microsoft Office, Microsoft Works was generally viewed as easier to use. There was one major drawback to Microsoft Works, however, and that was a nearly total lack of compatibility between Microsoft Office and Microsoft Works. It was not, for example possible to open a Works word processor document in Word. Databases created in Works could not be opened in Access. This lack of compatibility was a major drawback for the Microsoft Works user.

The other productivity suite mentioned was Word Perfect Suite, software based on the Word Perfect interface and shipped at no additional cost on many personal computers. Though the software is robust and user-friendly, Word Perfect Suite has the same drawback as does Microsoft Works: It is not compatible with Microsoft Office, an absolute requirement when Microsoft Office is the standard.

A third productivity suite is Open Office. Like Linux, Open Office is open source software and can be downloaded for free from the Internet. Open Office has a great deal of compatibility with Microsoft Office, but it takes a relatively experienced computer user to get the compatibility right. Open Office can be used with Windows, Mac OS, or Linux.

COMMUNICATION SOFTWARE

Three types of communication software will be discussed—IM or instant messaging software, chat software, and email software. Actually IM is not software, but a service that allows communication with others online at the same time as you are. Rather than allowing relatively unfiltered communications as chat software does, IM requires a predefined list of contacts before you can send or receive messages.

Chat rooms, which use chat software, are a type of synchronous (real-time) communication that occurs when conversation occurs in real time and all parts of the conversation are visible to everyone else in the chat room. Although not a hard and fast rule, chat rooms are generally organized around a single theme or topic. It was felt at one time that the concept of chat and chat rooms would just be a computing fad that would be popular for a short period of time and then disappear. This has not proved to be the case, as the topicality of chat has helped it remain popular.

Before moving to email software, some discussion of the pros and cons of chat and IM, synchronous communications in the library or education setting is in order. As a rule, schools rarely permit either IM or chat anywhere on school networks. Districts feel there is too much risk and too much wasted time when they are permitted. In truth, there can be cogent educational reasons to allow synchronous communications, particularly chat, if there is close teacher or librarian supervision. An example of using chat in an educational setting is the formation of study groups for AP courses. Again, it must be directed and supervised by a teacher or school librarian.

Today in schools and libraries, the first thing we want to do when we sit down at a computer is check our email. Email is a type of Internet-based communication whereby people correspond. Email is an example of asynchronous communication: The sender and receiver of email need not be available at the same time to correspond. Email has achieved great popularity because it is fast and convenient and saves postage and phone bills. A recent survey showed that 80 percent of Americans who use the Internet use it primarily for email.

Two different methods of using email are client-based email, which requires local installation of email software, and web-based email, which only requires a web browser. Most email used in schools and school libraries is client-based email; the email software resides on all district computers. In many cases, school district email users can also access their email from home and school through web-based email. The big advantage to using web-based email is that you can access your mail from any computer any time.

If you are using client-based email, chances are good your email software is Microsoft Outlook. Microsoft Outlook is a powerful email software package that also includes a robust calendaring and scheduling feature. Versions of Microsoft Windows prior to Windows Vista included a more basic email package called Outlook Express. For many email users, this was all the capability they needed for email.

Before leaving the topic of email, all school librarians, teachers—in fact, all email users—need to understand that there is no inherent right to privacy with email. The courts have found that email does not carry with it the same right to privacy as the U.S. Mail, particularly when an employer's email system is used. All email users must be aware of this and be wary when using email.

ANTIVIRUS SOFTWARE

Antivirus software is software designed to detect viruses that are attempting to attack a computer and protect the computer and its files from harm. Other than the operating system, which allows the computer to function, no other type of software is as necessary as antivirus software. No computer in your school library should be without antivirus software, and it is essential to keep it up-to-date as new viruses are circulated every day.

A virus is a computer program, generally brought in through the Internet, which attaches itself to other computer programs and attempts to spread to other computers when files are exchanged. A very few viruses can be harmless, but the vast majority want to harm a computer or computer files. For example, a virus that you download might erase the hard drive of your computer. Having antivirus software on your computer, keeping it updated, and regularly scanning your computer system for viruses is essential.

GRAPHICS SOFTWARE

The growth in the different types of graphics software made available in the last fifteen years has been great. If you want to make graphics software available on your computers in the library, you will want to consider a drawing software program and a photo editing program. A number of good drawing programs are available, so you will want to consult with the art department in your school to determine their preference.

As far as photo editing is concerned, one of the most commonly used pieces of software is Photoshop. The full version of Photoshop has a very steep learning curve and is quite expensive, so you might want to consider its less robust version, Photoshop Elements. If you are going to provide an environment in your school library where students are going to work on projects, then graphics software is a must.

INTERNET BROWSERS

Two things are required for the computers in your school library to connect to the Internet: an Internet Service Provider (ISP) and browser software.

Web browser software allows users to locate items online and to navigate the World Wide Web. The most common browsers in use today are Microsoft Internet Explorer, Mozilla Firefox, and a relatively new entry in the arena, Google Chrome. Each of these browsers has its proponents and its detractors. School districts generally standardize on one browser, so other than providing opinion and input you may not be able to make the final decision. When you are working with Internet browsers, there are a couple of things to keep in mind: First, the same webpage may display differently in different browsers and second, monitor settings can also affect how webpages display.

WEB DEVELOPMENT SOFTWARE

Three approaches are available for creating webpages. The first is to use Hypertext Markup Language (HTML) to create pages. For more experienced web developers, this is the method of choice, because it provides absolute control over the appearance of a webpage. The second approach to creating webpages, particularly for just one or a few, when there is no need for a full-blown website, is to create documents in different applications such as Microsoft Word, then convert the documents to webpages.

Falling somewhere between these two approaches is the use of webpage authoring software. The use of webpage software eliminates the need for programming skills when creating webpages but at the same time allows for the creation of complex websites relatively easily. This type of software generally includes wizards, reference pages, and templates that will help the user in creating webpages and websites. The most widely used web development software packages are Adobe Dreamweaver and Microsoft Expression Web. Expression Web has replaced Microsoft FrontPage, though you will still find FrontPage in many education environments. Although these software packages do make the creation of webpages and websites easier, they both have high learning curves and are not particularly intuitive.

SPYWARE REMOVAL SOFTWARE

Spyware is generally not particularly dangerous when it is downloaded to your computer, but it can be very bothersome. Spyware is a program that is downloaded from the Internet to your computer along with software you have meant to download. Many spyware programs use cookies to collect information on what is used on your computer, whereas other spyware records keystrokes with the aim of stealing login credentials or credit card information. To keep spyware off your computer, you will want to install anti-spyware software. No matter your operating system, there are anti-spyware programs that you can and should install. Because there is new spyware created daily, you should keep your anti-spyware up to date and run it frequently.

RESEARCH AND DISCUSSION QUESTION

Chapter 3 discussed several reasons for having your school library networked. The alternative is standalone machines. Please explain why it is a good plan for the school library to be part of both a local area network and a wide area network. Are there any drawbacks? Incorporate the latest research into your response.

REFERENCES

American Library Association. "AASL Information Power Action Research Project." ALA. www.ala.org/ala/mgrps/divs/aasl/aaslproftools/informationpower/informationpower.cfm (accessed January 11, 2009).

Bilal, Dania. *Automating Media Centers and Small Libraries: A Microcomputer-Based Approach.* Greenwood Village, CO: Libraries Unlimited, 2002.

Breeding, Marshall. "Tech Trends and Challenges for K–12 School Libraries." *Computers in* Libraries. September 2013. http://search.proquest.com/docview/1440137000?accountid=35812.

Burke, John J. *Neal-Schuman Library Technology Companion: A Basic Guide for Library Staff.* New York: Neal-Schuman, 2004.

Cohn, John M., Ann L. Kelsey, and Keith Michael Fields. *Planning for Integrated Systems and Technologies: A How-To-Do-It Manual for Librarians.* New York: Neal-Schuman, 2001.

"Colorado Technology Competency Guidelines for Classroom Teachers and School Library Media Specialists." ERIC. www.eric.ed.gov/ERICWebPortal/custom/portlets/recordDetails/detailmini.jsp?_nfpb=true&_&ERICExtSearch_SearchValue_0=ED433020&ERICExtSearch_SearchType_0=no&accno=ED433020.

Cox, Michael. "Types of Computers and Their Differences, Advantages, Disadvantages and Characteristics." http://techchannel.radioshack.com/types-computers-differences-advantages-disadvantages-characteristics-2162.html.

Doggett, Sandra L. *Beyond the Book: Technology Integration into the Secondary School Library Media Curriculum.* Englewood, CO: Libraries Unlimited, 2000.

Evans, Alan, Kendall Martin, and Mary Ann Poatsy. *Go! Technology in Action.* Upper Saddle River, NJ: Prentice Hall, 2010.

Farkas, Meredith. "Skills for the 21st Century Librarian." http://meredith.wolfwater.com/wordpress/2006/07/17/skills-for-the-21st-century-librarian/.

"Identifying the Right Technology Solutions: An IT procurement checklist for K–12 schools." www.eschoolnews.com/2014/06/24/finding-right-k-12-solutions-procurement-checklist/.

Johnson, Don. "Lecture—Unit 8." www.slideshare.net/JohnsonDon/lecture-unit-8.

Jurkowski, Odin L. *Technology and the School Library: A Comprehensive Guide for Media Specialists and Other Educators*. Lanham, MD: Scarecrow, 2006.

Kochtanek, Thomas R., and Joseph R. Matthews. *Library Information Systems: From Library Automation to Distributed Information Access Solutions*. Westport, CT: Libraries Unlimited, 2002.

Lowe, Carrie. "The Role of the School Library Media Specialist in the 21st Century." Eric Digest. www.ericdigests.org/2001-3/21st.htm.

NCLIS. "School Libraries Work." http://www2.scholastic.com/content/collateral_resources/pdf/s/slw3_2008.pdf.

Turner, Laura. "20 Technology Skills Every Educator Should Have." www.instructor.aviation.ca/content/view/133/71.

"Wi-Fi." http://techterms.com/definition/wi-fi.

Williams, Brad. *We're Getting Wired, We're Going Mobile, What's Next? Fresh Ideas for Educational Technology Planning*. Eugene, OR: ISTE, 2004.

5

Computing in the Cloud

Cloud computing has been on technology radar screens for some time. Many definitions are in place to explain this new technology. According to the National Institute of Standards and Technology (NIST), "[C]loud computing is a model for enabling ubiquitous, convenient, on-demand network access to a shared pool of configurable computing resources (e.g., networks, servers, storage, applications, and services) that can be rapidly provisioned and released with minimal management effort or service provider interaction. This cloud model is composed of five essential characteristics, three service models, and four deployment models—e.g., networks, servers, storage, applications, and services that can be rapidly provisioned and released with minimal management effort or service provider interaction" (NIST). The major cloud computing providers are IBM, Intel, Amazon, and Google.

In this chapter, cloud computing is examined with a broader view. Then the chapter moves to the possible uses of the cloud in education and, finally, the potential effect of the cloud in school libraries.

A BROAD VIEW OF CLOUD COMPUTING

Most of the literature dealing with the theoretical aspects of cloud computing has been in existence for some time. *InfoWorld* has categorized cloud computing in several areas:

1. SaaS delivers applications to users through what is called a multitenant architecture.
2. Utility computing provides remote IT services.
3. Web services in the cloud are a closely related service to SaaS.
4. Platform as a service allows applications to be developed on a provider's servers.

5. MSP (managed service protocols)
6. Service commerce platforms offer a service hub that users interact with.
7. Internet integration (Knorr 2008)

Michael Miller, in his 2008 online book *Cloud Computing: Web-Based Applications That Change the Way You Work and Collaborate Online*, discussed in detail many aspects of what cloud computing is and how it works. He suggests that cloud computing changes what you do from being on your local computing device to it all being web-based. Many cloud computing applications are already being used, such as email or calendaring functions, but one thing that most emphasizes the use of the cloud is in collaboration, which is most useful for education applications.

The *International Journal of Information Management* defines cloud computing as "clusters of distributed computers (largely vast data centers and server farms) which provide on-demand resources and servers over a networked medium (usually the Internet)" (Sultan). Furthermore, it discusses three main kinds of services that may be offered through the cloud:

1. Infrastructure as a Service (IaaS). This is generally the full computer infrastructure.
2. Platform as a Service (PaaS). This application of cloud computing provides centrally managed operating system, hardware, and other items that are typically managed by the IT department.
3. Software as a Service (SaaS). Applications are provided through a medium such as the Internet rather than being loaded on an individual computing device.

This all sounds very good, but in the effort to save money, one must remember that few, if any, cloud solutions are apt to work straight out of the box. As early as 2009, it was recognized that the main things to be delivered by cloud computing were to be the economic advantages, simplification, and convenience of how computer related services are delivered.

If your school district and you are considering moving to the cloud, everyone needs to consider the pluses and minuses associated. It is not all sweetness and light; cloud computing presents some challenges. However, cloud computing positives include the following:

1. Low cost of computers for users. With the cloud, it is no longer necessary for all computers to be the latest and greatest, as software will reside in the cloud along with the files saved.

2. Improved performance. Computer performance is improved when apps are run from the cloud rather than from the computer itself.

3. Lower IT infrastructure costs. Using remote servers from the cloud allows the IT department to invest in things other than servers.

4. Fewer maintenance issues. Less hardware and less software maintenance saves here. Without cloud computing, a software upgrade generally requires each computer to be touched; not so with the cloud.

5. Lower software costs. In essence, the cloud allows for software to be leased and not purchased, reducing software costs.

6. Instant software updates. The update happens automatically in the cloud and is available as soon as it is released.

7. Increased computing power. The user is not limited by the power of the computer he or she is using, but rather has the entire cloud.

8. Unlimited storage capacity. See item 7.

9. Increased data safety. Note that I did not say security, but safety. The issue of hard disk crashes and the like is eliminated.

10. Compatibility between operating systems. Using a Mac? A Linux system? With cloud computing, operating systems do not matter.

11. Better document format capability. It used to be that the version of the software you were running mattered when you moved to other computers. This is not so with the cloud.

12. Easier collaboration. The sharing of documents leads to better collaboration. Of course, everyone must participate in the collaboration.

13. Universal access to documents. If it is in the cloud, you can get it anywhere. No more forgetting that pesky flash drive.

14. Latest version availability. This is seamless and up to date in the cloud. Your IT department no longer has to touch each computer for updates.

15. Not linked to specific devices. When you have created a document on your laptop, you can access it on your phone, your tablet—whatever computing device you are using.

The benefits listed above make a strong case for using the cloud. However, cloud computing negatives include the following.

1. Internet. For cloud computing you always must be connected to the Internet.

2. Low-speed internet connections. The cloud does not generally work at all with dial-up Internet connections, and slower "high-speed" connections can be problematic.

3. Speed. This relates to item 2, above.

4. Limited features. If you are using a cloud service from Google or Microsoft, the web-based applications may not have all the features that regular software may have. Microsoft Office 365 has addressed this problem.
5. Data security. This is a significant issue with cloud computing that has not been addressed to everyone's satisfaction.

Four types of users really benefit from cloud computing:

1. Collaborators. This is one of strongest features of the cloud.
2. Travelers. Any document is available, no matter where, if there is a reliable Internet connection.
3. Cost-conscious school districts and IT departments.
4. Users with increased computing needs. This is another area where cost savings come into play.

The cloud may not be helpful for others:

1. Users who are not comfortable using the Internet.
2. Offline workers. Remember that the cloud requires the user to be online.
3. Those concerned about data security.
4. Anyone so pleased with an application such as Microsoft Office that he or she does not feel comfortable with other applications.

SCHOOL DISTRICT USES OF CLOUD COMPUTING

Though some of the issues related to a broader view of the use of cloud computer, other issues are more directly related to the use of the cloud in school district use. *District Administration* magazine published an article as far back as 2009 that recognized the possible value of cloud computing to school districts. It was posited that cloud computing held a large promise of increased efficiency and cost savings, particularly in school district administrative tasks. Among the functions that were envisioned for increased efficiency and cost savings were the following:

1. Data backup
2. Mass notification
3. Assorted computing devices
4. Surveillance
5. Websites and email

"A recent survey shows that nearly 90% of K–12 educational institutions are using one or more cloud applications" (Johnson, "Computing in the

Clouds"). They are using them because of the cost savings and the educations potential. "In contrast to costly and complex learning-management systems implemented onsite, schools can now turn to providers who deliver these learning support, tracking and management capabilities instantly in the cloud. What's more, these platforms and their capabilities are perpetually updated, refined and improved, reflecting a faster pace of product innovation than traditional software vendors could deliver" (Johnson, "Computing in the Clouds"). The key factors that IT departments can make when justifying cloud computing are as follow:

1. Increased efficiency
2. Greater flexibility
3. Better customer service
4. Ongoing innovation (What IT Leaders)

The NIST "describes two basic types of cloud infrastructures: internal and external. In an internal cloud, servers, software resources, and IT expertise are used inside the school system to build a scalable infrastructure that meets cloud computing requirements. In an external cloud, service providers sell on-demand, shared services to a school. IT support, services, and expertise are included in the package; the school needs to run only the provided applications and services" (NIST). The article also listed six reasons why school districts should go to the cloud.

1. "Provides a flexible, scalable, cost effective model that does not tie schools to out-of-date infrastructure or application investments
2. Offers the flexibility to meet rapidly changing software requirements for today's and tomorrow's teachers and students
3. Allows software standardization, a shared pool of applications for use school- or district-wide, and easier maintenance through centralized licensing and updates
4. Enables rapid development and deployment of complex solutions without the need for in-house expertise
5. Can eliminate the upfront financial burden of deploying new technologies through a pay-as-you-go model
6. Supports multiple client platforms both inside and outside the school infrastructure" (NIST)

A final examination of cloud computing and education was in a September 2010 policy brief. In this document they offered five characteristics of cloud computing.

1. Remote data centers. Data is not kept on site and thus does not require local servers to a great extent.
2. Pooling of resources. All services are shared. This means you do not have to plan capacity for peak usage that is then not used at other times.
3. Infinite scalability. This addresses sudden peaks.
4. Customers pay only for the services they use.
5. Web 2.0 can be looked as an application, whereas the cloud is looked at as a method by which applications and data are hosted and delivered.

Let us review again the benefits of cloud computing for educations institutions and for their teachers and students as well as administration:

1. Economics
2. Elasticity
3. Enhanced availability
4. Lower power needs
5. Concentration on the core job—education
6. End user satisfaction

Noted risks are again delineated here. They are important enough to be viewed again.

1. Data security
2. Unsolicited advertising
3. Locking in to a particular company

To close the section on the use of the cloud in education, one example of the economics that drive cloud computing is offered. The Pike County schools in Kentucky used cloud computing to convert 1,400 old computers that only had value as doorstops or boat anchors into functional virtual machines. No other economy could be so telling (Sultan).

IMPACT OF CLOUD COMPUTING AND THE SCHOOL LIBRARY

The final portion of the chapter dealing with cloud computing will examine the impact the cloud may have on the school library. Cloud computing has only become an issue for school librarians as districts have been faced with severe, even draconian, budget cuts.

The *International Journal of Information* Management discussed the cloud as a possible chance for school districts strapped for cash to save money. This also applies to the use of the cloud by the school librarian.

From a technological and access standpoint, a large portion of what school librarians do could be done in the cloud, freeing their time for other pursuits. The most obvious cloud based application for the school librarian is access to the library's collection through the online public access catalog.

For the school librarian, the one category that he or she will most frequently encounter is described by Doug Johnson in an article in the May/ June 2009 issue of *Library Media Connection* simplifying the definition of cloud computing as it generally relates to librarians. Johnson said, "Cloud computing relies on applications and file storage that reside on a network, usually the Internet itself, with minimal resources stored on local computers' hard drives" (Johnson). This definition has hit home in many school districts in my home state, Pennsylvania, as all educational institutions are looking at moving their technology functions to the cloud. This would mean no in-house data storage, no more need to purchase upgrades for software such as Microsoft Office, no requirement for constant upgrading of computers in the school, anywhere anyplace access to files and collaboration, and, most important, a reduction in technology costs as functions formerly done in house are moved to the cloud.

Among the things school librarians will see when computing moves to the cloud will be the use of applications such as Google Docs or Google Apps that allow students and staff to use applications from a remote server through the cloud. They are similar to Microsoft Office and allow files to be exported back and forth between Office and the Google cloud. Other vendors are offering similar services to schools, but Google appears to have the lead, because their services are free.

Johnson continues to discuss cloud computing, noting advantages and how librarians can take advantage of cloud computing:

1. One can work on any file anywhere, regardless of the computer being used. No more moving files on flash drives or other storage media.
2. Cloud applications such as GoogleDocs and apps allow files to be easily worked on collaboratively.
3. No cost, or low cost, for applications.
4. A full computer is not required for most tasks. Even a smartphone or any mobile computing device can work in the cloud. This is important to students and staff as the proliferation of mobile computing devices continues (Johnson).

In the time since Johnson wrote his article, the face of cloud computing has changed. This is indicative of the rapid changes that accompany any new technology until it is made obsolete by another technology. However, at

present, the areas that librarians can use to take advantage of cloud computing remain:

1. Use of less than full featured computers—save money here.
2. Use of email, such as Gmail accounts.
3. Use of cloud tools for online searching.
4. Using GoogleDocs instead of Microsoft Office for productivity tasks.
    Most people only scratch the surface of Microsoft Office's capabilities.
5. Webpage editing. Putting your library catalog and circulation system
    in the cloud (Johnson).

In 2011, Johnson updated his discussion of the cloud and the school
library. He was blunt in his assessment of what the K–12 technology leader
should consider when dealing with the cloud.

1. Forget about IT as you know it today;
2. Get ready to outsource IT;
3. Let go of the desire to control;
4. Embrace diversity in the IT environment;
5. Blow the lid off of storage limits; and
6. Quit saying things like, "A wired network infrastructure will always be
    necessary because wireless will never be fast enough for everything."
    (Johnson)

He also listed several ways school librarians could take advantage of
cloud computing:

Library Advantages

1. Use of any computing device rather than a desktop computer. This fits
    right in with the students using any computing devices they want.
2. Email. Many school districts are moving to mail systems such as
    Gmail. ← How?
3. Web searching and bookmarking
4. Use of alternatives to Microsoft Office.
5. Storing photos and editing them in the cloud
6. Creating and editing webpages.
7. OPACs

Future considerations for cloud based computing in the school library

1. Does your school have a policy about student-owned devices that can
    be used to access the resources you provide in the cloud? (Parents will
    not allow a simple ban on them, any more than most did not allow
    schools to ban cell phones.)

2. Does your school have the reliable, adequate, and secure wireless infrastructure to support dozens, if not hundreds, of student-owned computing devices designed to take advantage of cloud-based applications?

3. Is your library helping your teachers and students receive the training, resources, and strategies to use the cloud?

4. Is your district exploring cloud-based enterprise solutions such as Google Apps Education Edition or Microsoft's Office365?

5. Is your library using cloud-based applications to lower its operating costs?

6. Might libraries repurpose those general-use computer labs, providing instead a combination of lots of wireless netbooks that can be used anywhere in and out of the library and fewer, but more powerful media production computers in common labs?" (Johnson).

Cloud computing has some disadvantages, most of which have already been presented. If the Internet is down, then the cloud cannot be used. Security is an acknowledged issue with cloud computing; all school technology directors would think long and hard before they would do payroll and place personal records in the cloud. Finally, it requires school librarians and technology leaders to rethink how technology is handled and what we want our students to learn. All that said, it certainly appears that cloud computing is here, alive, and well; it is incumbent on us to be ready for it if we are not currently aware, ready to help our school district administrators implement its use. As with any new technology, the school librarian stands ready to explain to, teach with, and collaborate with teachers and students to expand their technology horizons.

REFERENCES

Corrado, Edward M., and Heather Lea Moulaison. "The Library Cloud Pros and Cons." www.thedigitalshift.com/2012/03/software/the-library-cloud-pros-and-cons/.

Dyrli, Kurt O. "The Start of a Tech Revolution." *District Administration* (May 2009). www.districtadministration.com/article/start-tech-revolution.

"IITE Policy Brief: Cloud Computing in Education." http://iite.unesco.org/pics/publications/en/files/3214674.pdf.

Johnson, Doug. "Computing in the Clouds." *Learning and Leading with Technology*. www.learningandleading-digital.com/learning_leading/200912#pg18.

Johnson, Doug. "Libraries in the Cloud." *LMC*. www.doug-johnson.com/dougwri/libraries-in-the-clouds.html.

Knorr, Eric, and Galen Gruman. "What Cloud Computing Really Means." *InfoWorld*. www.infoworld.com/d/cloud-computing/what-cloud-computing-really-means-031.

Miller, Michael. *Cloud Computing: Web-Based Applications That Change the Way You Work and Collaborate Online*. New York: Que, 2008.

"The NIST Definition of Cloud Computing." http://csrc.nist.gov/publications/nistpubs/800-145/SP800-145.pdf.

"Schools, IT, and Cloud Computing: The Agility for 21st Century eLearning." www.intel.com/content/dam/doc/case-study/cloud-computing-education-21st-century-e-learning-study.pdf.

Sultan, Nabil. "Cloud Computing for Education: A New Dawn?" *International Journal of Information Management* (2010). www.sciencedirect.com/science/article/pii/S0268401209001170.

"What IT Leaders in K–12 Need to Know about Cloud Computing." www.enpointe.com/images/pdf/what-it-leaders-in-k-12-need-to-know-about-cloud-computing.pdf.

6

Planning for and Funding Technology in the School Library

In chapters 3 and 4, we discussed the technology skills that the 21st-century school librarian should possess and have provided an overview of hardware and software that may be appropriate to use in the school library. In chapter 5, the economy of cloud computing was outlined. In this chapter, the technology planning process that should be used in the school library is described, because it directly relates to securing funding for that technology.

The need for technology is so obvious that planning for it and justifying its purchase is critical. It requires detailed planning and full justification for purchasing, because hardware, software, and computer applications change so rapidly that planning ahead seems impossible. School librarians need to be on the cutting edge of technology, and because they are so knowledgeable, they are on the district and their school's planning committees.

These committees have a very big responsibility. They must ensure that any technology is implemented and the needed components purchased after complete and thorough planning. The specific reasons or purposes for technology implementation apply from the largest school district to the smallest school library.

In many states, justification of the planning process is required by state mandate. Even if the technology planning is not mandated, it remains critical. Two things make this essential. First, as has been stated previously, no superintendent or school board ever recognizes the need to spend money without prior planning and justification. This is their assignment for their positions in the process of providing education for students. Second, the more thorough and transparent the planning process, the more likely it is the technology plan will be approved.

The technology planning process may take one of three approaches. It may be a part of the formal strategic planning process completed periodically to meet a state's requirements and follow general guidelines. The requirement for a formal technology plan is currently required in Pennsylvania. Other states have adopted an electronic "cookie-cutter" approach to technology planning. In these cases, everyone's technology plan is based on a predesigned template, so all technology plans look essentially alike.

Not all states require a technology plan and in those states, the development of the plan is in the hands of the school district. Regardless of whether your state requires a formal plan, a technology plan is essential to your district's and your library's technology future. It is also essential for those outside agencies who require a plan for requests for funding such as applying for the E-Rate.

THE SCHOOL LIBRARIAN IN THE TECHNOLOGY PLANNING PROCESS

What is your responsibility as a school librarian in the technology planning process? If you expect to have technology in your library, you had better be right in the middle of the process. It is easy for us to say that planning for technology is someone else's responsibility, but that is a sure recipe not to have any technology in your library or to have technology that you discover isn't as useful as another kind would have been. You are in the forefront of the planning process, and you can make sure that the district's technology plan includes the infrastructure that will accommodate the library's needs, the procurement of electronic content, the creation of electronic content, and any requirements from outside sources of funds where the agency needs to see your technology plan. The infrastructure must include support for instruction, library office needs, and IT and networking issues. It must include funding for the purchase of electronic content, such as electronic curriculum databases and access to electronic reference sources such as periodicals, dictionaries, and encyclopedias, because these, though they may be available in hard copy, are not used by teachers or students. Funds for the creation of electronic content for the school library would include the creation of descriptive cataloging and the creation of digital collections.

As stated above, among the outside agencies that might ask to see your school library technology plan would be to apply for E-Rate funds, so consideration must be given to how the technology plan will be used. Nearly all procurement of funds such as E-Rate and state and federal funds require that a technology plan be approved and be on file to obtain the funding.

A school library technology plan can take one of three forms. First, and most typical in school districts, it is part of a larger organization technology plan such as the school district's technology plan. Second, it can be part of the library's overall plan. This most often occurs in school districts with multiple libraries and a library department chair or supervisor. Third, the library's technology plan can stand alone, because the first two options do not exist. Whether it is to be a part of the district plan, the plan for school libraries in the district, or only for the single school library, the process has many requirements. If you are a part of the first option, here are some guidelines for the development of an effective technology plan.

EFFECTIVE TECHNOLOGY PLANNING

An idea for effective technology planning often begins with some questions you or one of your teachers may ask. These questions can be the starting point for technology planning and can frame the technology perceptions of teachers, administrators, and students:

1. Have you ever thought there has to be an easier way to do this?
2. Have you ever thought I could do this faster if only . . . ?
3. Have you ever thought I wish I had someone to help me do this?
4. Have you ever thought I wish I had a computer or other device so I could . . . ?
5. Have you ever thought I wish I or my students could contact someone right now to tell them . . . ?
6. Have you ever thought I wish I or my students could contact someone right now to find out . . . ?
7. Have you ever thought I wish my students had computers or other technological resources available so they could . . . ?
8. Have you ever thought I wish my students had improved computers or other technological resources available so they could . . . ?
9. Have you ever thought I wish my students had more computers or other technological resources so they could . . . ?

The answers to these questions are key to constructing the technology plan.

CONSTRUCTING THE TECHNOLOGY PLAN

When one is working with a technology plan, be it for the entire school district, a school, or a school library, there are some other steps to implement. Though they may not be considered requirements in the strictest sense of the term, they do indicate show that the planning process has been carefully reviewed:

1. The committee should include more than one or two persons and should be made up of stakeholders in the process, some very technology-savvy and some less so, to make sure all needs recognized are met as much as possible.

2.   The committee should develop a needs assessment to determine the level of technology available in the school district. An inventory of the actual equipment may be readily available. What may more be more difficult to obtain will be the perceived needs of teachers for technology.

3.   The committee should plan to prepare one or more progress reports. The first should discuss where the school or library currently stands with relation to technology. This is the starting point for the technology plan. One or more progress reports during the planning process are also valuable, because they keep stakeholders posted as to progress in the technology planning process.

4.   Subdivide the responsibilities among all members of the committee. It goes without saying that there must be a chairperson, but that chair cannot do everything. Duties must be given to committee members based on their interests and their areas of expertise. If an assignment requires some level of expertise, one committee member who is very adept with technology should be paired with one having less expertise. Hopefully all the committee members are there because of their interest and willingness to serve. By subdividing the committee responsibilities, each member has a feeling of ownership and pride in the final technology plan. One other challenge may be the committee member with a single type of technology, such as personal network computers, who considers this the ultimate solution to solve all technology needs and doesn't want to discuss any other.

5.   Establish time frames and due dates for tasks. It is important that time frames and due dates be established for the report itself and for the subparts of the plan. In addition, there must be realistic, not some "pie in the sky" time frame. When time frames have been established, it is incumbent on the chairperson to ensure they are met. This is a responsibility that some chairpersons find disagreeable, but it is necessary if the technology plan is to be completed in a timely manner.

6.   Build consensus. If there is no consensus among all stakeholders on the final technology plan, it will be very difficult to make that plan work. It may be difficult to get it approved by the appropriate administrator(s). This sounds alarmist, but it is true. A technology plan approved by only a small but aggressive group of the stakeholders will cause strife and disagreement not just on the committee, but in the school district as a whole. In this regard, consensus among taxpayers is an absolute necessity. They are the bill payers and must agree to the plan.

7.   Ensure that the evaluation portion of the technology plan is formal and includes all stakeholders who helped develop the plan. Evaluation is key for the plan to be effective and if it is to be taken seriously within the community.

These are critical to beginning the process. To continue, Matthews's seminal work dealing with library technology planning uses the acronym "SMART" to define what a technology plan should be. In his view, a technology plan must be the following:

- Specific
- Measurable
- Aggressive but attainable
- Results-oriented
- Time-bound

If you are using an existing template, being SMART may be the best you can achieve. However, you should try to do as many of the items stated below unless they are beyond your control. However, as much as possible, the following items are essential:

1. Effective technology plans are for the short term, not the long term. If your school district administration wants a five-year technology plan, resist it! Remember Moore's Law: Few, if any, can predict what technology will be available in one year, much less five. For this reason, you tie your technology plan to phases, not years. If your school district insists on a time frame tied to the technology plan, you must explain that three years would be the absolute maximum.

If the three-year maximum does not work, correlate the plan with the district's budget process. Review the technology plan each year during the budget process to make sure you are able to buy new and cutting-edge technology. It is important in this regard to keep in mind that a technology plan should be dynamic and thinking of future applications.

2. Effective technology plans are based on applications of technology, not the technology itself. It seems counterintuitive to say that a technology plan is not based on technology, but it is true. Rather than your technology plan's being a lengthy list of hardware and software you want, the plan should say what you want your stakeholders to be able to do with technology and then let the objectives and outcomes determine what and how much technology will be required to meet the goals.

Often when technology plans are presented to school boards, the first question the board will ask is how the technology will be used. If the plan is written addressing what students and teachers will be able to do with the technology, the question is answered within the plan itself. Having the technology plan focus on technology outcomes can also help defuse debates about standardizing on a particular brand or platform. Though some standardization can be positive and cost-effective, the hardware and applications purchased should be driven by what will most effectively meet the objectives specified in the technology plan. The whole issue of standardization should not be a major issue today as modern networks can easily work with different platforms.

3.   The technology plan should definitely be used to enhance the curriculum, but it must move beyond this. The real goal of the technology plan is to allow the stakeholders to work easier, not harder. No technology plan should be written that the purpose of technology is to teach about technology. This has happened in schools with "computer classes" taught by a "computer teacher." It is unlikely that these persons do more than teach basic use technology, when students need to move beyond finding reference or resource material that meets their needs. In the second decade of the 21st century, a great many students have already been placing their fingers on some be some electronic device. If the purpose of computer classes is to teach keyboarding, a better solution might be typewriters stored in the district awaiting disposal. These could be used to teach keyboarding. It is no more effective to teach every application of a software package when the student needs only one than it was to teach finding information in the online catalog with no assignment to find information.

4.   Remember that there is more to technology than just desktop or laptop computers. The most effective technology plans deal with the entire gamut of technology, including photography equipment, television equipment, video-conferencing equipment and the software to support the equipment as well as social media. When the technology plan is completed, it must include all types of technology.

5.   Integration of technology into the curriculum makes a technology plan more effective. This relates closely to the third point. Teachers and librarians often rightly ask why they have to stop teaching their subjects to teach technology. As stated in the third point, technology is a tool used to assist learning, not the objective of the learning itself. Often when we teach technology, students will work with a piece of software to learn all the capabilities of the software. If you are integrating the use of the software into another lesson, isn't it enough to teach the students only what they need to know about the software to complete the lesson, not the complete software package? Think of this as "just in time" instruction.

6.   It is imperative that technology plans be closely tied to staff development plans. If they are not, they are doomed to fail. For many years, the solution to provide technology for teachers was to wheel it in and leave it—with no training. Apparently teachers are expected to learn to use technology by osmosis. What occurs when this is the case is to create very expensive door stops.

Staff development or training can be looked at as four steps: awareness, application, integration, and refinement. In many cases teachers are rarely beyond the awareness level as in "yes, that is a computer, but how can my students learn to spell their spelling words?" The goal of an effective technology plan is to attempt to move those at the awareness level as far up the continuum as possible. Not everyone will be able to move to the refinement level, but that should be the goal. Too often the conversation between two teachers at the refinement level causes those at the awareness level to just roll their eyes as a sign of not understanding. Perhaps a new approach to training is also necessary. Although schools have the general responsibility for staff development and training, the school librarian must take some responsibility for helping teachers learn. The critical need arrives with the purchase of a new technology. Teachers feel that their needs are being ignored when given a new technology and they are not trained in its use. Teachers should be given the opportunity to take any new technology home and, after a little explanation by the school librarian, learn that new application or software. Use the prep period to actually prep in the use of a new technology. It is more than just as social time. Is this a new paradigm? Yes. Is it needed? Yes. If you, the school librarian, mastered the new technology, you are responsible for teaching your teachers.

7.   Technology plans make technology the cost of doing business. When money and time are available for technology, some savings can happen. For example, is it necessary for every student to have a hard copy of a textbook? Would it be possible to only purchase classroom sets of textbooks and use the money that remains to purchase instructional resources for the school library? Is it possible for textbooks to be eBooks and be available to be downloaded to their computer devices? Let's take this a step farther: Is a textbook necessary at all? For example, would it be possible to move to a resource-based learning system and eliminate textbooks altogether?

8.   Attributes of the technology plan should be based on research. It is easy to write a technology plan based on intuition or gut feelings. It is harder, but more valid, to base the conclusions in a technology plan on research. The school librarian is the best person to locate the research needed to help others develop this plan.

9.   The users of a technology plan should be those who wrote it. Many times technology plans are developed by administrators or IT personnel who will not actually use much of the technology. From personal experience, I confirm that one of the most effective technology initiatives happens with a shared technology proposal process. Staff members who wanted technology were required to write a proposal for what they wanted. The proposals

were reviewed by the school district technology committee and then ranked. Technology proposals were then voted on, and those approved were funded.

10. Focus on a vision. All good technology plans have a vision for technology. It is an integral part of the technology plan, because it states the aim and focus of technology in the district. You must have a vision for technology in your school library that is powerful and accounts for both teaching and learning. Many times, when a technology plan is constructed, the vision statement is just an afterthought, something put together in a short period. This is really backward. The vision should be carefully and thoughtfully constructed so it is a true vision of what technology should be used for. All stakeholders should accept the vision, and it should guide all elements of the technology plan. Some schools go so far as to post the technology vision throughout the school.

This part of the plan becomes a measure of the achievement to meet the vision. The committee and the district personnel must never lose sight of the vision, and it may surprise everyone how much progress is being made with technology.

11. The technology planning process should help in managing the budget. Budget planning is a more cerebral process than many writing the plan, including school librarians, think. Budgeting is a matter of figuring out what the needs are and determining what is only "nice to have." At times you will be able to get both; other times, you will be able only to meet your needs. Unfortunately, there will also be times when you will not be able to get either your needs or your wants. The technology planning process should reflect budget trends and realities.

12. Current technology strengths and weaknesses can be easily identified through the technology planning process. One of the most important parts of the needs assessment is analyzing what is good about your current technology and what is bad. Only then can you begin to analyze what you need.

13. New technology is always coming on the market, and sales personnel will be the first to tell you how much you need the new technology. The technology planning process will help you determine what new technology you need and how to prioritize your needs for new technology. This process can be used to show how a new technology can be used effectively. One of the very important parts of the process is to illustrate exemplary uses of technology in the school and in the school library.

14. One piece of the technology planning process that is often overlooked is creating a fundraising plan. We always have a budget in technology plans, but we frequently do not indicate where the funds will come from. From this standpoint, a fundraising plan is essential.

The first part of the chapter has outlined the process for creating an effective technology plan. For a more complete description of the actual plan, please see later this chapter, under "Structure of the School Library Technology Plan."

In this planning process, some challenges may arise that will result in a much less successful plan. Following are some ways to miss completing an effective process.

CHALLENGES TO CREATING A TECHNOLOGY PLAN

Although there are many, many ways to create a successful technology plan, there are also some things done in the name of technology planning that will inevitably lead to shortcomings in it. These are the things you should not do.

1.   Having one, or at the most, two people write the technology plan. As stated earlier, a technology plan should never be created by one or two people. It should always be prepared by a committee representing all of the stakeholders. The plan should be a collaborative effort with the committee having a wide-range of constituencies represented. It should include not only those teachers and administrators who are in favor of technology, but also include those who are less enthusiastic about technology, and in particular, it should include parents and students.

2.   Doing the plan in a short period of time. Writing a technology plan the night before it is due is a certain recipe for disaster.

3.   Having the technology coordinator responsible for the planning. This person has more than enough work to do in his or her day-to-day routine to even think about taking charge of the planning. Furthermore, this person's expertise is generally hardware or networking, not the broader perspective of technology in education or in the library. Often you, the school librarian, are the ideal choice to be in charge of the technology plan process.

4.   Keeping the plan secret, never sharing it with anyone outside the one or two writers, or even the committee. It is kept from others in the district and in the community until it is completed. This is a cardinal sin, because a plan without support will not be successful, and support cannot be garnered if some constituencies do not know what is in the plan before it is finalized. You, the school librarian, remain the leader in communication and collaboration among stakeholders. You have made sure the plan was not developed by one or two persons alone, and you will make sure it is shared with everyone involved in technology, including parents and students. Keeping the plan a secret until the very last meeting of the committee or until it is presented to the appropriate administrators will make it that much more difficult to gain wide-ranging acceptance for the plan. Getting suggestions

for improvements along the way guarantees support and advocacy for the implementation at the end of the process. It could even result in a large attendance of stakeholders when the plan is presented at the meeting of the persons responsible for accepting the plan.

5.   Making the technology plan just a shopping list of technology. All this does is force your administration or school board to ask how the technology will be used. Anticipate this, and tie your technology plan to how teachers can improve learning and how students will have higher levels of achievement with technology.

6.   Not taking the needs of administrators, teachers, and librarians into consideration. This may happen if the technology coordinator prepares the plan. Often the coordinator is a technical person and not an educator. The plan must pay attention to what district staff want and need.

7.   Making no accommodation for technology support. This is a fatal and very frustrating problem. School districts will rarely have the level of technology support found in industry, but not having a plan for technology support will lead to very high levels of frustration and closets full of unused, broken or damaged equipment. The school librarian can offer much support, but the school district should not expect one technology person to serve a large number of schools.

8.   Making hardware, not curriculum integration, the focus of the technology plan. This relates to the shopping list concept described above. The plan must not focus on the technology itself but on how the technology will be used. If the technology cannot be tied to specific curriculum or library use, rethink what you are asking for. Rather than saying the school library needs thirty laptop computers, it should state that to allow equity of access, so students can research using electronic databases, the school library needs more computers.

9.   Leaving students out of the plan. Your students are your customers. You need to explain how technology is being used to support their needs. The plan must go beyond explaining how administrators, teachers, and librarians are using technology to explaining how students are using it. When the superintendent, the school board and your principals ask, the planning committee should ready to respond.

10.   Filling the technology plan so full of technology "nerdspeak" and educational jargon that it is unreadable by anyone except those with as much technical expertise as those who wrote it. Too often this makes those who attempt to read it wary of what is there, because they cannot understand it. The technology plan should be written in clear, understandable English for

the nontechnical readers, which will include most of your audience, among them members of the community.

11. Not including all important or pertinent information in the technology plan. If you are asking for technology that students can use to research using electronic databases and you do not define what kind of technology (computers, tablets, or cell phones) is needed and what kind of databases (commercial or free) they will use, then you are not providing all important and pertinent information.

The foregoing points outline some things guaranteed to keep a technology plan from being successful. These ideas are comprehensive and must be addressed.

GUIDELINES FOR TECHNOLOGY PLANNING

We have discussed in some depth what can make a technology plan bad or ineffective. In this section, we will discuss some guidelines—perhaps rules—for successful technology planning. These are probably not rules in the accepted sense of the word, but they will make technology planning easier and more effective. It would be easy to say that these should never be violated, but they are here to help you, the school librarian, in your role as member or leader of a technology plan committee:

1. The technology plan should clearly resemble the technological maturity of the school or school district personnel, teachers and students. What is meant by this? It means that when you develop a technology plan, you have to consider the technology needs of every teacher and student, not just those who are technologically proficient. If all teachers and students had a high degree of technological proficiency, creating the plan would be easier. Unfortunately, not all have the same high level of proficiency. Think carefully about why the nonusers of technology in the school are nonusers. In other words, look at the weakest and plan for them rather than planning for the strongest. If you do not do this, you will have parts of the school moving forward with technology, while other parts are technology-resistant. Keep this in mind as you go through the technology planning process: having the newest and best hardware and software does not necessarily indicate a technologically mature school. High-quality educational opportunities using technology at all levels do.

2. The technology plan reflects the economic level of the community. If the school is located in an affluent neighborhood, most students will have access to most technologies in their homes. If it is a mixed community, the plan must take into consideration those students who do not

have technology in their homes. In a lower economic community, few students will have technology in their homes, and most will not have access to the Internet outside the school unless they can go to a nearby public library.

3. Technology hardware and software require support! This is emphasized repeatedly because it is so important in the technology planning process for the school and then the school library. Many times, technology plans are not thorough. Providing computers and software with full explanations of the educational necessity for these things in the plan won't work if you have not provided for furniture for the computers in the classrooms or in the library. Again, the need for training on the new technology is essential and if the school librarian is not a part of staff development, who will accomplish this. This is a sure formula for any technology to be misused or not used at all. Similarly, if the committee is planning for increasing the amount of technology in the school district and in the school libraries in the district and the IT department has only one person to maintain all of the computers in the school, it is a formula for failure. The point is, make sure adequate support is there for what is in the plan or include the cost of additional support in the plan.

4. Do not confuse movement with change. Putting a new technology on a teacher's desk is movement; getting that teacher to use that that technology as a part of the educational process is change. In a similar manner, teachers and students can know how to use email as a signal of movement, but it is not until they are using email for conferencing with people across the globe that you will see change. Change will not occur magically or instantly. At the same time be sure to include measures of change in the plan and allow sufficient time for change to occur.

MAKING TECHNOLOGY PLANNING WORTHWHILE

The technology plan is worthwhile if it achieves the goals set forth in the plan and it is focused on the learning and not just on the hardware and software. It is worthwhile if it establishes a connection between the learning taking place in the classroom and school library and the hardware and software. If the plan is to be worthwhile, it must be embraced by all the stakeholders in the school. With all of this said, there are still challenges to meet for the technology planning to be successful.

It is important that the planning committee provide an established technology plan that is part of the overall improvement process in the school or school library. The technology plan is part of the assessment phase of the improvement program. The technology plan in this regard:

1. Assesses the current technology in use.
2. Communicates recommendations regarding technology.
3. Describes the projects and procedures that will implement the technology plan.
4. Indicates what resources will be needed to implement the technology plan.
5. Define the technology capabilities that support learning.

In the formulation phase of the improvement program, detailed specifications for the part of the technology plan are developed. At this point, the planning may go beyond the technical expertise within the school district, and it may be necessary to consult with outside experts to ensure the plan is feasible as written. Perhaps such assistance is available at the regional or state level or might be found in a nearby institution of higher education.

PRESENTING THE PLAN TO THE APPROPRIATE ADMINISTRATORS

At this point, the technology plan is submitted to the appropriate administrators or the governing body for approval. The governing body will, it is hoped, approve the plan and then set priorities and establish a funding stream for the plan. If it is a building or district technology plan, it will go to the school board. If it is only your library technology plan, it may go to the district technology committee or to your principal.

After the plan has been approved by the appropriate persons, the implementation phase begins. This is where the rubber meets the road and where the expertise of the school librarian becomes the catalyst for success in the use of technology in the district can be ensured.

IMPLEMENTING THE TECHNOLOGY PLAN

The implementation phase is when the technology plan is actually carried forth to reality. The specifications developed in the formulation phase are the guides for the implementation of the technology plan.

At this point, one returns to the reality in the process that the district must have or must build the necessary support systems for the technology. This was discussed at some length previously, but it cannot be overemphasized. One person in an IT department cannot be expected to be responsible for more than 1,500 computers in the district. This is simply an impossible task. Finding IT directors can be daunting. A school district was attempting to hire a new director of IT and was quite impressed with an individual who was a network manager for a Fortune 500 company. This individual was eager to leave corporate life and move into an educational environment until two questions were asked: First question: In your current job situation, how many people would be required to support 2,000+ computers? The answer— at least 20. Second question: How much money would take to bring you to XYZ School District? The answer was a figure higher than what the super- intendent was paid. This may seem extreme, but lack of technical support is more likely than adequate support in too many school districts. If this is the case in your district, changes have to be made or technology will continue to be looked at as a tool that uses too much and delivers too little. It may be that you will become the partial solution to this situation.

Your training has prepared you so that you know how to use technology— not how to repair it, but how to integrate it into the curriculum. Teachers also want to know how to use hardware and software so they can integrate it into the curriculum. They are not interested in the technology works, either. They just care that it does work, and they want to know all the ins and outs of making it effective in the curriculum. Forget the bits and bytes; you need only tell them how use it in the classroom. Your ability to carry out this assignment ensures your place in your school and continues the provision of library services to your students and their equal access to information.

INDICATIONS OF SUCCESSFUL TECHNOLOGY PLANNING

Your checklist of five criteria that are the core elements for a technology plan to be approved for E-Rate funding can be used to determine the prob- able success of your plan:

1. The plan should establish clear goals and a realistic strategy for using technology to improve instruction and administration in the education organization.
2. The plan should include an assessment of the hardware, software, net- working, human resources, and financial resources needed to improve education services.
3. The plan should provide for a sufficient budget and schedule to acquire, maintain, and secure the hardware, software, and related issues (e.g., training) needed to implement the strategy.
4. The plan should have a professional development strategy to ensure that staff members know how to use these new technologies to improve education services.
5. The plan should include an evaluation process that enables the organi- zation to monitor progress toward the specified goals and make mid- course corrections in response to new developments and opportunities as they arise.

Furthermore, successful technology plans should address all or most of the following major areas:

- Current technology status and needs assessment
- Technology vision statements
- Equity issues
- Appropriate technology standards
- Integration into the curriculum
- Pilot program activities
- Infrastructure and support for infrastructure, including such facilities-related needs as air conditioning/cooling and asbestos abatement
- Review of current "state of the art" technology for options in design of infrastructure
- Current capabilities of hardware and software
- Projections of "next generation" capabilities and features
- Long-range goals
- Inventory control issues, such as maintenance and replacement cycle
- Budget projections and funding sources for initial installation, hardware, software, maintenance, security, and training
- Staff training
- Benchmarking standards
- Quality control components
- Security planning
- Evaluation planning
- Review cycles

SCHOOL LIBRARY TECHNOLOGY PLANS

From this point on, the discussion of technology plans is exclusively for the school library or the school library department. The place where most school library technology planning will begin is with the definition of the current state of library services and technology in the school library. The technology plan depicts what the school library offers with technology and the plans for any new technology. As mentioned earlier, the aim should be how the technology will be integrated into the curriculum rather than just listing what is wanted without specifying how it will be used. As a matter of fact, few school districts will fund anything if they do not know how it will be used.

Next consider access to the content of local resources. Are students able to access them as needed, not just when they have a permit to come to the library? If electronic resources are to be accessed when needed, there must be remote access to them from their classrooms and beyond the school building. In other words, can the students access the electronic resources easily from home? This is a battle that the school librarian may well have to fight with the technology coordinator. IT personnel generally do not want to allow access through firewalls, and that is a requirement for home access to resources. The IT department would often like to say this is impossible, but it is not, and it must be done. Are some resources restricted in use? These types of questions must be answered so that issues of access can be dealt with.

Does the library have a portal to allow access to remote resources? One of the issues that will be discussed both later in this chapter and later in this book is the issue of the school library's web presence and the quality of its webpage. The school librarian must have the skills to work with a webpage and perhaps to have one or two students who can be trusted with this task.

Administrators, teachers, and students must have access to human assistance. This holds true even if these persons are trying to access resources electronically and remotely. It may require a help desk setup with students trained and willing to help as often as possible. It may require staff to have flexible work hours, or a willingness to be called at times other than during the school day. Having access to human assistance is very important.

BUILDING THE TECHNOLOGY ENVIRONMENT

Building and improving the infrastructure, the environment, for technology in the school library is a very important but often overlooked aspect of the technology planning process in the school library. Technology cannot be ordered without appropriate furniture and certainly adequate electrical outlets. Among the issues to be considered are:

1.   Electricity. This is the whole gamut of electric issues. Are there enough outlets? Is the wiring adequate for the increased load? Can the power company provide upgrades, if needed, on a timely basis? The electrical items are basic. Technology runs on electricity.

2.   HVAC. While not as crucial as it was some time ago, technology requires a controlled environment. In particular, the area housing some technologies still requires air conditioning. Furthermore, the air conditioning system should be forced air, not water-based. A water based system puts too much moisture in the air for efficient use of technology.

3.   Cabling and connections. Have these items been planned for? Although it is often not possible for cabling to be in conduit when technology is placed in an existing school library, there are few thing worse than seeing cable laid under duct tape. This is an area where you really can use the help and expertise of your technology coordinator or a knowledgeable parent—even an outside consultant.

4.   Bring Your Own Device (BYOD). This is an area of policy rather than environment. Are student devices such as personal notebook computers going to be allowed to be brought in? Think this issue through carefully, and reach consensus with your teachers on this policy. The school librarian can be a strong supporter of the use of all forms of social media and can be useful in helping teachers overcome their reluctance to allow this.

5.   Lighting. Many school libraries do not have sufficient lighting for the effective use of technology. In this regard, the local power company will probably come to your facility to survey the lighting in the school library and tell you how it can be upgraded. In some ways, lighting is as important as all of these other areas in considering the technology environment.

6.   Room and layout. If the technology is in boxes in your library waiting to be unpacked and you don't know how you are going to configure the room, you need to think quickly! How will the technology be supervised? Is the configuration efficient and conducive to good library usage? These are the types of things that are best settled before the technology arrives.

7.   Furniture. The key attribute for furniture is that it be flexible. Tables and chairs must be easily moved, because spaces in the library must be fluid. This means that purchasing something that must go into a particular place and remain there may cause problems in the immediate future.

8.   Ergonomics. This goes along with purchasing the correct furniture. Are the heights of the furniture correct for your students' use? Do the chairs provide a comfortable reach to the keyboard? Is the lighting correctly placed so that there is no glare and students can easily see the screens? Consider these and other ergonomic issues when building or changing the technology environment.

UPDATING AN EXISTING TECHNOLOGY PLAN

Not all efforts to work on a technology plan mean the creation of a technology plan from scratch. Some are in place and only need updating. In fact, after a technology plan has been created, the next time you consider the plan should be to update it, not to create a new technology plan. Some techniques you can use when it is time to update an existing technology plan include the following:

1.   Grade how effective the technology plan has been. This should not be just your opinion, but should include the opinions of teachers, administrators, students, and parents. The same people who were the stakeholders in the original plan should be the ones to grade it, but do consider the opinions of students, who are the ultimate stakeholders.

2. Get feedback from students who have gone on to high school and who can help you decide what is needed in your new update. Or you can ask college students. Many times graduates of a high school like to come back to visit, particularly recent graduates. Get them to review your old technology plan.

3. Form a new review committee. Get a new slant on the technology plan by bringing in fresh faces. Sometimes this is easier said than done, because there is a finite group of teachers in any building, and many may not be very helpful in evaluating technology; nevertheless, it is worth the effort to get new views.

4. Get ideas from attendance at library conferences, consumer technology shows, or even vendors who visit your school district. Sure, salespeople at conferences and vendors who call on the district are trying to sell you something, but this is an excellent way to gain ideas and knowledge about new and improved technologies.

5. Ask colleagues in a nearby district to review your plan. It is worth the visit to see what technologies they are using in their school libraries, and this can provide ideas for changes in yours. See what other people are doing with technology in their school libraries. Get out of your library and go on the road. Many things going on with technology in other school libraries; you just have to find it.

6. Readjust and maximize training. Has your training program been effective? If not, in the words of Madeline Hunter, "monitor and adjust." Do not continue ineffective training.

7. Do a technology inventory. What you are really looking for is technology that is stashed in closets or store rooms because it was found to be ineffective. Find out why it was ineffective and what could have been done to make it effective. The cloud may resurrect some computers.

8. Talk to those who question technology. This is very important. You get one picture from those who support technology but a far different view from those who question it. Take what they say seriously, because if you do, you may move them out of the questioning category.

9. Get ideas about using technology in the school library from preservice programs. If one is not available near your school, pay a virtual visit to see what is being taught in the program, then call the director or one of the faculty.

10. Incorporate technology into your curriculum plan. See whether there are technology items in your state standards and adapt them to your curriculum plan. If you don't have a curriculum plan, begin the process immediately.

STRUCTURE OF THE SCHOOL LIBRARY TECHNOLOGY PLAN

The following is based on Joseph R. Matthews' seminal work on technology planning in the library and lists the elements of a library technology plan as they might be adapted for a school library. These ten elements are not magic, but they provide a framework for successful technology planning in the school library. Following are the elements in a successful library technology plan:

1.   Executive summary. Although this is the first element listed, it actually is the last thing written. Though we would like everyone who reads the technology plan to read every word, some simply will not have the time or inclination to do so. The executive summary is for them. It will summarize all elements of the plan, but not in great detail. An effective executive summary is typically two to four pages.

2.   Description of the library. The description of the library should contain, at minimum, the following elements:

   a.   History. As a general rule, the history of the school library is the same as the history of the school. It may also include a description of any renovations that have taken place.

   b.   Physical description. Nothing is more effective than a diagram of the school library and, because this is a technology plan, some digital photographs.

   c.   The library's mission statement. If you don't have one, get one—yesterday! You cannot be effective without a mission statement.

   d.   Community served. This should go beyond just a statement of how many students you serve in what grades. Consult the latest report from your regional accrediting agency for a detailed community profile.

   e.   Staffing. Be sure to include nonprofessionals and vitas for all.

   f.   Budget. Budget information should be detailed and include historical budget trends.

   g.   Collection size and growth. You should be able to get this information from the reports section of your OPAC. The more detail you can provide, the better.

   h.   Services offered. This section should be a complete list of what is done in the school library, as well as why it is done and for what group of stakeholders.

   i.   Use of library. Does anyone use it after school? Do you have hours when the school library is open after school? It is difficult to justify increased technology levels if your library only serves the school staff and pupils during regular school hours.

j. Current technology. What do you have (include numbers) and how it is used? You must be specific in how it is used. Just saying that students use technology for research is not sufficient.

3. Challenges. Included in the challenges section of the school library technology plan should be the technology vision for the school library. There are several reasons why the technology vision is such an important part of the technology plan. First, it provides a continual purpose for the library. Second, the vision statement should both challenge the library and invigorate it. This is the opportunity for the school librarian to look ahead, to get out of the day-to-day routine and see what technology can do for the library. This process is invigorating and should be a bit of a catharsis for the school librarian. Third, a vision statement should be a critical part of change. If we think back to the difference between movement and change discussed earlier, we can see the importance of change and should be able to visualize how the vision statement is part of the process. Fourth, if properly constructed, the vision statement can positively affect the staff of the school library. The invigoration should carry over to the staff as they are able to see the positives of a move forward with technology. Finally, the vision statement is the standard against which progress with technology in the school library will be measured.

When assessing challenges, one of the methods is a SWOT analysis. This is a common technique often used in the strategic planning process, but it is effective when assessing technology in the school library. What does SWOT stand for? Strengths, Weaknesses, Opportunity, and Threats. These areas must be carefully analyzed in the process of the evaluation of technology. After the SWOT analysis has been completed, the school library will then want to complete an examination of external factors that will affect the school library:

a. Technology: A close look at the effects that different types of technology can have on the school library is called for here.

b. Economy: The state of the economy is a big factor when planning for technology in the school library. It is crucial you consider this and the effect the cost of technology will have on both the library's and the school district's budgets.

c. Markets: Do you know your audience for services? Does the technology positively affect them?

d. Politics: We hate to have this as an external factor, but the power of politics is inevitable. The school librarian must be very circumspect when approaching those in the political arena.

e. Law: Will any change of any local, state, or federal law effect the operation of the school library? What about the school code?

    f. Ethics: Ethical issues might include such things as copyright law or the use of filters for the Internet in the school library.

    g. Society: Are there societal forces that may come into play that will affect the procurement or use of different technologies in the school library?

4.   Emerging technologies. The section in the school library technology plan dealing with emerging technologies is at once both easy and difficult to construct. It is easy in that the section allows the school librarian to look into the future and try to figure what new technologies could be useful for the school library. The difficult part comes when the librarian attempts to predict what new technology will be useful. There is a big difference between could and will, and it is the job of the school librarian to attempt to discern the difference. Looking at emerging technologies is an area in which the technology coordinator and the IT staff can be of great assistance. They often have a better feeling for the new technologies.

5.   Current technology environment. Assessing the current technology environment in the school library gives the school librarian the opportunity to see what is good and what is bad with relation to technology in the library. When you are assessing the current technology, the following are some factors to consider:

    a. Physical environment. This was discussed in some detail earlier in this chapter, but it is an integral part of the technology plan itself.

    b. Network infrastructure. This would include the wiring and the server capacity. A schematic of the network topology would be helpful.

    c. Network: In this area, you will be discussing how reliable the network is and how fast it responds with different levels of network traffic.

    d. Computer hardware and software—servers. A table can be beneficial when describing the servers and server software serving the school library.

    e. Computer hardware and software—student and staff workstations. Remember that you are describing the technology environment at this point, not evaluating it.

    f. Library information system software. This should be a detailed description of your OPAC.

    g. Library-wide software applications. In a school library, this category might be very brief but should describe software used throughout the library to assist in the management of the library.

    h. Desktop software applications. This description should include the productivity software used, the Internet browser, and the antivirus software.

i. Technical support. This should be a detailed description about how the school library gets its technical support. Typically this will be your IT department, but there may be better ways of obtaining it.

j. Data—backups and virus protection. Both these things are key, and if you are not doing them or do not know how they are done, you should.

k. Staff skills: What is the level of your staff's technology skills? And what are yours?

6. Website evaluation. Had we been discussing school library technology plans fifteen years ago, there would have been no need to discuss the school library's website. Today it is a necessity. There are three stages that must be discussed when looking at the school library website. Every school library needs to have an online presence to deliver electronic resources to its users. The second stage is the creation of a digital library. This concept will be discussed in detail later in this book. The third stage is the ability of users to personalize the website for their own use. A school library website can have all three stages and still be ineffective if the creator did not pay close attention to some website design issues.

a. Why was the site created? This should be obvious to the user, but sometimes webpage creators are so concerned about the bells and whistles they forget the basics.

b. What is the library's goal for its website? Again, the obvious answer is to help people find information, but if the steps to do this are not clear, then some reevaluation may be in order.

c. Is it obvious to users what the library wants them to accomplish? This is closely related to the previous point.

d. What keeps the user at the site? Is it easy to do things and find information? Is there a lot of scrolling involved? Does it load quickly? All these are things to consider.

e. Why would a user want to return to the school library website? Again, the obvious answer is to find the things they need, but ease of navigation and a visually pleasing site are important.

When we are evaluating the school library's website, there are also a number of usability factors to take into consideration.

a. The graphics used should neither help nor hurt the site. Beware of large graphics, particularly if large numbers of your students still use dial-up connections.

b. You must have text links on the page. Remember that not all of your students will want to read a lot of text.

c. The navigation on the site and the content should be inseparable. Students (and teachers) are impatient. Make the navigation easy for them.

d. Remember searching and surfing are different. Make sure links to Internet search engines are prominent and near the top of the webpage for ease of use.

e. There should be locally developed information of your school library webpage. These factors will encourage users to return to the page.

f. Your webpage should be easy to find and well organized. Do not bury the link to the school library webpage deep on the school's webpage. It should be at the top of the page, highlighted.

g. It should descend from the most general type of information to the most specific.

h. Each webpage in the website should be able to stand on its own. The index page should be just that—a page directing users to more information.

i. Speed. Quick page loading is essential. Remember what we said about students' being impatient.

j. The webpage should be current. All links should be checked and updated frequently to avoid link rot, the process whereby links disappear from the Internet

k. Use the same standards or authority for information on the webpage as you do for the purchase of other library materials.

Multimedia is another consideration. If you have links to multimedia, you should have two things on the webpage. First, you should warn users that helper applications may be required; second, provide a link so users can easily download the helper applications.

7. Recommendations. This is the section that will bring the whole plan together. This is where you recommend what technology you want for the school library, a plan for getting and using it, and the cost of the technology. You may want to structure this part of the plan with the following continuum:

Action Step—Timeline—Responsible Person

Though there are no hard and fast rules for constructing the recommendations or for the breakdown of what should be recommended in the technology plan, one author suggested a breakdown as follows:

40% hardware
20% software
20% professional development
20% upgrades and future technology.

8. Plan review and update. The plan review and update is an integral part of the school library technology planning process. A technology plan should

be a dynamic, not a static, document. When the plan is adopted there should be a schedule for regular review and updating of it. Technology changes—so should the technology plan.

FUNDING TECHNOLOGY AND TECHNOLOGY PLANS

Funding for technology has always been iffy. Because technology has only become as important as it now is in the past ten years, many school librarians and school district administrators have had to adjust their budget categories to account for the procurement of technology; and technology can become very expensive very quickly.

In an ideal situation, the school district or the library will have a budget category for technology that is funded each year. It may be divided into several different subcategories, such as hardware, software, or networking, but regardless, there is a constant budget category for technology. The important thing to keep in mind is the technology budget category for the school library should be part of the library's discrete budget, not the technology department's budget or a curriculum budget.

At times, because of the high cost of technology, school districts have issued bonds to cover the cost of procuring technology. This can be effective, but the corollary is that after the bond money is gone, there is often no money left to sustain technology. If your district uses bonded indebtedness for the procurement of technology, be sure that they are also willing to include the budget item for technology as discussed above. The funding of the technology plan will be the biggest challenge you will face in the entire process. All the pie-in-the-sky technology plans will go for naught if there is no process in place to fund it. The funding issue is one that should be discussed and negotiated with the administration, in particular the business manager.

Nontraditional Funding Ideas

Williams discussed several nontraditional funding sources for technology. This is a somewhat new concept for many school librarians, but anyone who has conducted book fairs to raise funds for their library should be familiar with some of these nontraditional funding sources.

1.   Grants. We will discuss grants in some detail in the next section, including the elements that generally make up a successful grant proposal.

2.   Companies. Contact companies in your area that have even a tangential association with technology. They may be willing to either give funds or pieces of technology. Many of the larger concerns, such as Walmart and

Interesting idea (handwritten margin note)

Sony, have been particularly willing to do this. Don't forget to contact companies that employ your school district's graduates.

3. Publish and sell a book to raise funds for technology. This is really easier than it sounds. Many organizations self-publish items such as cook books as fundraisers. It may take a lot of legwork and coordination, but it can yield good returns.

4. Update your technology plan. You ask how this is a nontraditional funding source? By updating your technology plan, you can add new and updated technology to it and then go to your school board to ask for funding. Again, remember to tie it to the curriculum.

5. Beta test software. Many educational software companies are looking for sites to beta test their products. When you become one of them, the company will give you beta releases of the software to test, and often the final version when it is released.

Grants

Many school librarians forget about grants as a funding source for technology, because we think of ourselves as funded through taxation. Furthermore, many school librarians are not comfortable preparing grants, because they have no experience doing so. Forget these preconceived ideas. Forget that your school district does not have a grant writer. Go to your state department of education's website and see what grant opportunities are available. Talk to local foundations to see whether any of their grant categories could be used for school technology funding. It may surprise you, but many local charitable institutions may fit your needs and are generally willing to keep funds in the community. If you do have a grant writer in your district, all the better, but they are generally administrative positions and disappear when budgets become tight.

Getting grants can be a bit of a complicated process. It certainly is more than calling the charitable institution and just asking for money. There is often giving schedule and, with the larger institutions, a request for proposal (RFP) process. The proposal submission process can include the following elements:

1. A statement of the problem (or need) and a needs assessment. Remember the needs assessment you prepared for the technology plan? It can be reused here.

2. Methodology. The methodology should clearly state how the requested money will help fulfill your library's mission and objectives. Be clear here— no educational jargon. You are not necessarily dealing with educators, so they might not understand complicated "education speak."

3. Plan of operation. This would be where you would describe the design of the project—what you want and how it will be used. A hint here would be to address the community in some way. Charitable institutions like to see multiple users of their money. For example, if you are asking for funds for computers, include a plan for the community to use them.

4. Evaluation. This is a key to a grant proposal as it is to your technology plan. How will you measure success? Be sure to spell this out clearly and in measurable terms.

5. Key personnel. Who will make the grant work? Who will administer the money? Foundations will want names, not titles.

6. Adequacy of resources. Have you asked for enough budget to do what you say you want to do? If the agency likes your plan, they will want to give you the money you need. Do not treat the budget request as if the funds are coming out of your own pocket.

7. Impact. What will the effect of their funds be? Will it improve learning? How? Will it improve reading score? By how much? These are things foundations can relate to.

8. Organizational capability. Can your library support the resources? It is counterproductive to ask for forty computers when your library only has room for twenty or is not wired to network forty.

9. Budget. The more specific the budget is the more likely the project will be funded. Do your research, and keep the budget up to date.

ROLE OF THE SCHOOL DISTRICT TECHNOLOGY COORDINATOR

A question that I often ask in class is: "Who is your best friend in the school district with relation to technology?" If the school librarian's answer is anyone other than the district's technology coordinator, he or she may want to reconsider his or her relationship to technology. In fact, whether you call this person the IT director, the technology coordinator, or the network manager, this person should be your best friend. The school district technology coordinator is responsible for all facets of technology in the school district; if you are that person's best friend, someone they can depend on, your library will be at the top of the list for their services.

Conversely, if you are always whining and asking for help for things you could easily do yourself, your school library will slip to the bottom of their priority list. Be self-sufficient. Help your technology coordinator, making this person your best friend.

RESEARCH AND DISCUSSION QUESTION

Funding for technology in the school library is often difficult to obtain from local tax sources. Research the grants available for school library technology in your state, and prepare a presentation that could be used for your school board to describe these sources and how the funds would be used for technology. It is important for your school board to understand how the technology will help the students, not just the school library as a whole.

REFERENCES

American Association of School Librarians. "Standards for the 21st-century Learner." www.ala.org/aasl/standards.

Anderson, Larry S., and John F. Perry Jr. "Technology Planning: Recipe for Success." National Center for Technology Planning, 1994.

Burke, John J. *Neal-Schuman Library Technology Companion: A Basic Guide for Library Staff.* New York: Neal-Schuman, 2004.

Cohn, John M., Ann L. Kelsey, and Keith Michael Fields. *Planning for Integrated Systems and Technologies: A How-to-Do-It Manual for Librarians.* New York: Neal-Schuman, 2001.

"Determining Your Technology Needs." Forum Unified Education Technology Suite. http://nces.ed.gov/pubs2005/tech_suite/part_2.asp.

Doggett, Sandra L. *Beyond the Book: Technology Integration into the Secondary School Library Media Curriculum.* Englewood, CO: Libraries Unlimited, 2000.

E-rate Central. "Technology Plans and the E-Rate Program: A Primer for Schools and Libraries." www.e-ratecentral.com/applicationTips/techPlan.

Gordon, Rachel Singer. *The Accidental Systems Librarian.* Medford, NJ: Information Today, 2003.

Ingersoll, Patricia, and John Culshaw. *Managing Information Technology.* Westport, CT: Libraries Unlimited, 2004.

Jurkowski, Odin L. *Technology and the School Library: A Comprehensive Guide for Media Specialists and Other Educators.* Lanham, MD: Scarecrow, 2006.

Matthews, Joseph R. *Technology Planning: Preparing and Updating a Library Technology Plan.* Westport, CT: Libraries Unlimited, 2004.

Papa, Rosemary, ed. *Technology Leadership for School Improvement.* Los Angeles, CA: Sage, 2011.

Picciano, Anthony G. *Educational Leadership and Planning for Technology*, 5th ed. Boston, MA: Pearson, 2011.

"Planning Your Technology Initiatives." Forum Unified Education Technology Suite. http://nces.ed.gov/pubs2005/tech_suite/part_1.asp.

See, John. "Developing Effective Technology Plans. Minnesota Department of Education. www.nctp.com/john.see.html.

Sibley, Peter H.R., and Chip Kimball. "Technology Planning: The Good, the Bad, and the Ugly." EDmin Library. http://edmin.com/news/library/index.cfm?function=showLibraryDetail&library_id=16.

Wesley, Ted. "Perceived Educational Technology Needs Survey." NCTP. www.nctp.com.

Williams, Brad. *We're Getting Wired, We're Going Mobile, What's Next? Fresh Ideas for Educational Technology Planning*. Eugene, OR: ISTE, 2004.

"Writing a Library Technology Plan: Assistance for New Hampshire Libraries." New Hampshire State Library. www.nh.gov/nhsl/electronic/e_rate.html.

7

Copyright, Censorship, Filtering, and Security Systems

The four topics in this chapter, copyright, censorship, filtering, and security systems, may seem somewhat dissimilar to the casual reader, but they all relate to technology issues to a greater or lesser degree. They are also things that can cause headaches for the school librarian. Copyright affects the school librarian in such areas as photocopying and the fair use doctrine, copying software, and student use of electronic information in completing assignments. Internet filtering has been a controversial topic as long as the Internet has been used in schools. The experience with library security systems was, for many school librarians, a turning point in the concept of trust and ownership of materials. These are all key issues, and the influx of technology has only magnified them.

COPYRIGHT

No other concept in the field of school librarianship may be understood less than copyright. School law courses do not focus on it, and the copyright law itself is so complicated and has so many interpretations that it has become a specialty of its own. Many teachers believe that "Fair Use" applies to everything within the school and that copyright law does not really apply to them. In other cases, school librarians put a copyright warning on their photo copier and feel they have done their job with relation to copyright.

The term "copyright police" refers to the U.S. Marshals Service. It is unlikely that U.S. Marshals will visit your school district, but you do not want to be in violation of copyright law should they suddenly appear.

Copyright here is approached in two ways. First, common copyright issues will be presented and then some specific questions dealing with copyright discussed. Butter, in *Copyright for Teachers and Librarians*, posed some questions about materials to be copied:

1. Do you have permission from the copyright holder to copy? If the answer is yes, proceed: if it is no, you may not copy.
2. Is the material in the public domain? If yes, you may copy: if no, you may not.
3. Does the material fall under the fair use guidelines? If yes, you may copy: if not, you may not.

When in answering these three questions the answer is yes, you may copy. Perhaps this was simple enough in the days before wide technology proliferation in schools, but technology has created a whole Pandora's box of copyright issues. *Tech-Learning, the Resource for Education Technology Leaders* has prepared twenty scenarios that deal with copyright and teachers. This may not address all issues, but it should give you grounding in copyright as applied to technology.

1. A CD-ROM the librarian needs for a class is damaged or broken. May an archival copy be made? Yes, but it should be done in the library. If the same thing happens to a teacher, the archiving should be done in the library.

2. A single copy of a piece of software has been installed on a school server so students can access it throughout the school. Is this permissible? Yes, if it is only used by one student at a time.

3. The school has a site license for a piece of software. A newer version of the software is released, but the school elects to buy only five copies of the updated software, not a full site license. Students soon discover that work created on the new version of the software cannot be opened in the old version. Is it within copyright law to install the new version of the software on all computers to ensure backward-compatibility? The answer is no. The five new versions of the software can only be installed on five computers.

4. In states that mandate computer proficiency but supply no budget for software, schools can buy what they can afford and copy the rest. A gray area; some would say yes and some no. Contact the solicitor in your district for his interpretation and GET IT IN WRITING.

5. When you have more students and computers than software for a class, is it okay to make enough copies of the software for the entire class? No. You are restricted to the number of copies of the software that the school owns.

6. Students are creating webpages and have downloaded a large amount of material from the Internet. Are they free to put the materials on webpages

posted on the Internet? They may, but material protected by copyright must have the permission of the copyright holder.

7.   Websites containing copyrighted material may be posted to secure, password-protected websites. Yes, as long as the sites' security is monitored.

8.   Material, including films, that are downloaded and in use in schools fall under fair use guidelines. Generally true, but close attention should be paid to what file sharing sites are used.

9.   Audio clips can be downloaded from MP3.com and used in student projects. Yes, because MP3.com pays for its archives, as does United Streaming Video.

10.   Music and clip art downloaded from file sharing sites may be used by teachers and posted to the school website so others can use it. Material pulled from file sharing sites can be used but not shared.

11.   Students edit themselves into a video. Yes, this is allowable.

12.   Is it allowable for movies shown on commercial television to be digitized for computer use? It is allowable.

13.   Material that you have legally placed on your website is being used by another school. This is an example of fair use in action. If it is okay for you, it is okay for them.

14.   Teachers in the school's day care classes want to entertain the day care children using videos they have purchased. Not permitted. This is for entertainment and falls outside fair use.

15.   The creation of video compilations is considered to be fair use. No, the creation of video compilations is not permitted under fair use.

16.   The use of machines to overcome copy protection of media is not a violation of copyright. A moot point, as these machines are prohibited, but educators do have the right to use things that are blocked technologically.

17.   Digital images of streets and businesses may be posted online in web projects. Generally yes, but some sites, such as Disneyland, may be considered protected by copyright.

18.   Ethnic music from a commercial CD for a project is considered fair use. This depends on some length limitations.

19.   Production of a video yearbook using commercial music is okay under fair use. No. Yearbooks are not considered to be educational material.

20.   A multimedia CD was produced using material that was copied under fair use. May this CD be sold for profit this year? No, because this involves wider distribution of the material.

MYTHS ABOUT COPYRIGHT

Many, many myths about copyright exist, and they have almost become urban legends. The first of these is that educators can do almost anything they want with materials, because fair use trumps copyright law for educators. This myth is a very old one and usually cited by persons who want to use something that does not follow fair use guidelines, which will be discussed in the next section.

The second myth says all materials pass into the public domain after the same amount of time and are no longer protected by copyright. At one time this was perhaps so, but it is certainly not true today:

Date of Work	Protected From	Term
Created 1-1-78 or after	When published	Life of the author plus 70 years
Published before 1923	In the public domain	None
Published between 1923 and 1963	When published with notice	28 years plus 67 renewal years
Published between 1964 and 1977	When published with notice	Same as above
Created before 1-1-78 but not published	1-1-78	Life plus 70 years or 12-31-2002, whichever is greater
Created before 1-1-78 but published between then and 12-31-2002	1-1-78	Life plus 70 years or 12-31-2047, whichever is greater

No wonder it's so confusing

Brad Templeton has written widely about copyright and has posited several more important myths about copyright. The myths are widely held, and the description of why they are myths is thought-provoking:

1.   Works that do not have the copyright symbol (©) are not copyrighted. This has not been true, for the most part, since 1989. You have to assume that material is protected by copyright if it is published even if the copyright symbol is not present.

2.   If a copier does not charge for material, there is no copyright violation. Not true; it is a violation, and damages could be assessed.

3.   Usenet materials are always in the public domain. False. Nothing is in the public domain unless it meets the description above or the creator explicitly gives up copyright ownership.

4. Defending postings as fair use. It may be true, but fair use is relatively complicated and restrictive.

5. If you do not defend copyright, you lose it. False; you only lose copyright protection when you explicitly give it up.

6. Material you create based on another work belongs to you. False. These are what are called derivative works, and you must obtain the original author's permission. Of course this is not true if the original work is in the public domain. The many continuations of the Sherlock Homes stories would fall in this category.

7. Defendants' rights generally trump copyright law. Many people believed this right up to the time they were assessed damages for copyright violation in civil court.

8. Copyright violation is a civil matter, not a crime. Not true. As of the 1990s, commercial copyright violation was made a felony (you might lose your teaching certificate).

9. Copyright violation does not hurt anyone. This is absolutely false. Part of copyright law is the protection of the creative process. Using someone else's creation for your use is harmful!

10. I received the copy via email. No defense. Having a copy of something does not give you a copyright.

You see the myths. These are things many people believe about copyright but are not true. No wonder there are many lawyers whose specialty is copyright law.

FAIR USE

No concept of copyright law is more used but less understood than the fair use guidelines for teachers. As mentioned before, some educators use these guidelines as a carte blanche to do what they want, and copyright laws are ignored. These are the ones who say "but I didn't know" when they are sued for copyright law violation. Unfortunately, the fair use guidelines remind one of the Supreme Courts' discussions of pornography: "I can't define it, but I will know it when I see it."

It is beyond the purpose in this book to spell out the specifics of the fair use guidelines. Many good sources for this information are available, such as *Technology and Learning's* "Copyright and Fair Use Guidelines for Teachers," referenced at the end of this section. Before looking at factors that could be considered a fair use test, keep in mind copyright protection does not apply to the following list of items, and you are free to use them as you please:

1. Compilations such as phone books.
2. Materials in the public domain.
3. Freeware (but not shareware)
4. U.S. government works
5. Facts
6. Ideas, processes, methods, and systems described in copyrighted materials

The four-factor fair use test attempts to put some system to what is essentially educational anarchy. For each question, the uses on the left would generally be fair use, whereas those on the right would generally require permission. Remember, though, that this is not scientific certainty. Different people can interpret the same things differently.

Factor 1: What is the character of the use?		
Nonprofit	Criticism	Commercial
Educational	Commentary	
Personal	News Reporting	
	Parody	
Factor 2: What is the nature of the work to be used?		
Fact	Mixture of fact and imaginative	Imaginative
Published		Unpublished
Factor 3: How much of the work will you use?		
Small amount		More than a small amount
Factor 4: If this kind of use were widespread, what affect would it have on the market for the original or for permissions?		
Proposed use tipping toward fair use	Original out of print or unavailable	Competes with the original
	No ready market for permission	Avoids payment for permission in an established permissions market
	Copyright owner not identifiable	

Before leaving the morass of conflicting information about fair use, remember there are fair use quizzes available on the Internet. Try giving one to your faculty and see the red faces! A few statements that should help the school librarian and their faculty with regard to fair use in the library and education setting are the following:

1. Books and Periodicals
   a. Copying cannot be used to create or substitute for anthologies.
   b. Copying from "consumable" works such as workbooks or exercises is forbidden no matter what the salesman, your principal, or the third-grade teacher says.
   c. Copying is not a substitute for purchasing, nor can the same teacher copy the same thing term after term.
2. Television and Video
   a. Television programs may be taped for in-class use under the fair use guidelines.
   b. Only copy prerecorded tapes with the publisher's permission.
   c. Student–teacher-created tapes can be copied as time allows.
3. Internet
   a. Material may not be posted from another website without permission.
   b. Material from the Internet may not be compiled into a new work.
   c. Copyright material cannot be scanned for school use.
4. Music
   a. Music cannot be copied for performances.
   b. Music cannot be copied to avoid purchase.
   c. Copied music must include a copyright notice.

DEALING WITH COPYRIGHT ISSUES AND CREATING A COPYRIGHT POLICY

It is inevitable that the school librarian will have to deal with copyright issues, be it with print materials or with resources found in technology. As mentioned before, the school librarian must serve as the "copyright police" for resources found in and taken from the library; and it pays to have some plan in mind when dealing with these tough copyright issues.

Carrie Russell, in her article "Stolen Words," strongly recommends that school librarians know how to deal with copyright issues by doing the following:

1. Having a thorough knowledge of copyright law and not being hesitant to advise school staff members about it
2. Learning about changes to copyright law, in particular the DCMA
3. Being aware of the user's rights and taking all steps to find legal ways to allow access
4. Promoting and publicizing fair use guidelines
5. Considering the source of the information protected by copyright

One of the things a school librarian can do is create a copyright policy. This policy should be approved by your school administration as well as by your school board. This will not protect everyone in the district, but it can protect you and the district as a whole. A typical copyright policy might contain the following sections, which address both print and technology issues.

1. A statement or introduction indicating the school library's intention to comply with copyright law
2. A complete description, with examples of fair use in a school setting
3. The rights of publishers of websites on the Internet
4. Copyright law regarding website construction
5. How student work and digital archives will be handled
6. Link rights on webpages
7. Copyright netiquette
8. A statement of liability, in effect saying that those who violate the policy may be liable to prosecution
9. A user permission form

DIGITAL CONTENT

Veteran school librarians have long been dealing with print and audiovisual resources, and they have been learning how to deal with digital content. The newer graduate has learned of the challenge of copyright with all types of resources. Copyright issues with electronic resources and information on the Internet have increased the challenges. The piracy of software is of great concern both to the industry and to educators. Two factors have gone a long way toward easing this issue. The first is the level of security placed on computer software, making it much more difficult to make unauthorized copies. The second factor involves successful lawsuits by software manufacturers against school districts. Nothing makes a school district pay attention like having to pay damages in a civil case.

In spite of the level of security on some computer software, not all are so protected, and placing software on school networks without the requisite site license remains to plague the school librarian if the district administrators insist on doing this. Another issue that can be difficult to monitor is the use of copyright-protected material on school websites. While the old adage "why reinvent the wheel" may seem appropriate for teacher- and student-created websites, copying material from someone else's website is probably a violation of copyright law. When this is an obvious intentional violation of copyright and the teacher refuses to remove the item, it might require communication directly with the district superintendent. For those school librarians who are the webmaster for their schools, this can be a time-consuming assignment and even one that places the teacher and the librarian in a confrontational situation.

As stated, copyright law is somewhat vague with relation to the Internet, but two things are not vague. First, like ideas and facts, links on webpages are not protected by copyright. Second, after a website is saved to disk, it is protected by copyright. The entire issue of copyright online is far from settled—witness the controversy over Google's attempt to digitize large library collections.

PLAGIARISM AND RESOURCES ON THE INTERNET AND THE WORLD WIDE WEB

The issue of plagiarism has been the nemesis of both school librarians and teachers as long as the research paper has been assigned by teachers. Technology has changed the playing field for plagiarism, as you will see. Plagiarism is the using of someone else's words or ideas without attribution. In the days before the World Wide Web, plagiarism often involved copying passages of sources, passing off someone else's words or ideas as the writer's, or simply making up sources. Students at all levels through graduate school have ignored plagiarism as a crime, and in some cases, almost a game.

The proliferation of resources on the World Wide Web has changed the face of plagiarism entirely and, in some ways, made the job of the school librarian much more difficult. First, students often think anything they find on the Internet is free to use and claim it as their own in a paper. Second, the ease of copying material from a website allows the student to paste the passage into a word processing document. This is such a simple process that even the most technically inept student can use this technique. Copying and pasting makes it easy to plagiarize someone else's words or ideas.

The third thing that changed the face of plagiarism is the rise of term paper repository sites, such as schoolsucks.com. These sites have many disclaimers in which they deny their site encourages plagiarism, but the facts remain that the sites provide fully attributed papers, either for free or as custom papers for a fee.

These three factors make plagiarism one of the most troubling increases in academic dishonesty. Many students do not look at plagiarism as a crime or as unethical, but rather as a game, a matching of wits, they must play with teachers, especially when they really don't want to do the research and work needed to prepare a research paper.

HELPING STUDENTS AVOID PLAGIARISM

One of the most important lessons a school librarian can teach in the area of information literacy is the meaning of plagiarism and how to help students avoid this pitfall. You will most likely be the expert on the topic in your school. Teachers may be less likely to spot this unless they have students run a check system over their papers.

1. When you discover plagiarism, try not to be totally confrontational. While some students may be committed to plagiarizing, many others need to be reminded of what plagiarism is and how they are plagiarizing.
2. Teach about citing resources and have available examples of correctly cited sources and papers that acknowledge sources available for the students to look at and use.
3. Let the students know you are aware of the term paper sites, and you know about the ease of copying and pasting material from the Internet.
4. Encourage or foster discussions about plagiarism: the ethics and the legality of it.
5. Encourage English teachers to give specific writing assignments rather than general assignments. This makes it much more difficult to find papers at the term paper repository sites.
6. If a teacher comes to you with a paper that you suspect is plagiarized, do not hesitate to use a search engine or a subscription service such as turnitin.com to test it.
7. Encourage teachers to have their students use a search engine or subscription service such as turnitin.com to test their papers before submitting them.

These techniques are not foolproof, but they can make the process of recognizing plagiarism easier. They may not make students stop plagiarizing, but perhaps it will show them that they are likely to have their work recognized as coming from a source they have not cited or have copied.

FILTERING SOFTWARE

Early in the days of the Internet, users quickly discovered there was a great deal of material out there that school administrators, teachers, school librarians, and parents would not approve of. In many cases, the material was sexual in nature, but in other cases it included hate sites or sites that encouraged them to use their parent's credit cards. In these early days, it was believed if students accessed inappropriate material on the Internet, it would be enough to just take action against individual offenders rather than against all students. As the problem increased, many school districts took action either as individual districts or as a part of an educational consortium to filter Internet content in the schools.

As the Internet has continued to grow to its current size, with an estimated near trillion webpages, the pressure continues to try to control what school library users are able to view on the Internet. These efforts to control use became an issue for members of the American Library Association, who stated that filtering the Internet was a violation of users' First Amendment rights for access to information. This was upheld in 1997 by the United States Supreme Court.

Another effort was made to control access, and the Children's Internet Protection Act (CIPA) was passed. This act stated that schools or libraries receiving federal assistance either for Internet access or grants under LSTA must have Internet filters in place. In 2003 the Supreme Court upheld CIPA by holding that mandatory Internet filtering does not violate the First Amendment. Further rulings have mandated Internet filters for schools and libraries receiving E-Rate funds. With this in place, some school districts have tried to filter the Internet. Other school librarians have ignored the use of government funds for E-Rate and have provided an Internet use policy and asked parents and students to sign a "contract" for use of the Internet. This will be discussed in more detail below. First, the function of Internet filters is described, and what filters can and cannot do are listed.

Internet Filters and Their Function

If you are asked to support an Internet filter, there are four basic types. The first is client-side filters, which are installed as software on a computer and can be customized to meet the needs of the individual computer. It takes a password to disable the filter. This is the ideal filter for a small number of computers but becomes more unwieldy as the number of computers increases.

Content providers only allow their clients access to a portion of the Internet. The content they provide is monitored, and portions of the content may be added or deleted as the circumstances change. This type of filter is rarely used in library or school environments.

Server-side filters are very common in school districts. Everyone within the school district is subject to the filtering, though certain people within the district may be able to bypass the filtering. This is particularly effective in school districts because you can set different levels of filtering for different areas in the school district. The filtering can be provided by the school district's ISP or by the district's technology staff.

Search engine filters are rarely used by school districts but are sometimes used by home computer users. Search engine filters are offered by search engines such as Google to filter out inappropriate links from search results.

This discussion of filtering software really has not addressed how filters work. Internet filters function in one of two ways. They either block websites that have been reviewed or block sites based on keyword searches. The first is more reliable, because someone has actually seen the website, but the second is more common, because they are much cheaper to use. The difficulty with keyword filtering is that it does not differentiate among valid and invalid uses of particular keywords. Perhaps the most common example is the student who cannot access information about breast cancer because the word breast is on the proscribed list.

There are several things filtering software can do:

1. Restrict access to educationally valuable websites containing proscribed terms as mentioned above
2. Create issues for school librarians trying to teach responsible Internet use
3. Promote a political viewpoint

There are a surprising number of things Internet filtering software cannot do:

1. Block all objectionable materials
2. Block controversial materials
3. Evaluate information on the Internet
4. Take the place of the school librarian in student supervision
5. Evaluate the age-appropriateness of the websites
6. Keep truly advanced Internet users from bypassing the filter

Nearly fifteen years ago, *From Now On*, an online education technology journal, listed a dozen reasons why filtering is not effective in schools. Those "reasons" are as valid today as they were then:

1. They are not very effective. It is estimated that only about 70 percent of material considered objectionable is actually filtered.
2. They may work too well. This issue was discussed previously with the use of keyword filters.
3. Kids are kids. The challenge of beating the filtering software is irresistible to children.
4. The costs are often excessive.
5. They can create false security. As noted above, filters are only about 70 percent effective.
6. Liability may be increased. If students access objectionable material, parents may feel compelled to sue.

What about Social media Sites?

7. They may violate family values.
8. They may violate community values. Often filtering software is more conservative than most communities.
9. They may violate civil liberties. Court opinion currently rests with Internet filters, but that is always subject to change.
10. They may define obscenity too narrowly.
11. There are better ways to protect children than through the use of Internet filters.
12. Children are capable of thinking (filtering) for themselves.

Alternatives to Filtering Systems

Several alternatives to the use of Internet filtering systems are available. The first is having a viable acceptable use policy. This policy should define Internet and network use and should be signed by parents. Updating must be done on a regular basis. The second is to supervise students closely. The encouraging of student responsible use of the Internet can help alleviate the need for Internet content filtering and truly provide open access to information.

The school librarian who can go online and select appropriate sites for students who are going to be given research assignments is another way to control Internet use in a very positive way. Selecting appropriate, useful, accurate, and relevant websites for students is the kind of selection that school librarians have been doing since the beginning of the profession. Doing the "advance" work helps students focus on the paper and not find themselves inundated with too much information and the necessity of wading through the morass to find what they need.

LIBRARY SECURITY SYSTEMS

More than thirty-five years ago, when I began my school library career, other than the ever-present film and filmstrip projectors, the only technology the library had was a library security system. Several years before my arrival, the library was losing more than $4,000 per year in library materials, a significant amount at that time. This was in a high school of nearly 3,000 students with controlled access to the library. The year after a library security system was installed, losses were less than $100. This is in keeping with research that shows that school libraries lose 2 percent to 7 percent of a school library's collection annually.

As more and more school librarians purchase electronic resources rather than books, this may become less and less a factor. However, for the present, here is a discussion of types of security systems and how to manage them.

Types of Security Systems

Two types of library security systems are available from three major vendors who produce them. If your school library does not have a security system and you are losing substantial amounts of your collection, you might want to consider a security system. This is an area where doing research and visiting other school libraries can help you make your case to both your administration and to your school board. Also, your board may actually not object greatly to a one-time expenditure if it saves money over the long term. When you visit other schools, make sure you view ones that have both 3M security systems and Checkpoint systems. These are two of the three major vendors, and you can find reviews of both types of systems in *Library Technology Reports.*

The major types of library security systems are pass-around systems and desensitizing systems. Pass-around systems, also known as radio frequency or radio frequency ID systems, are less expensive than desensitizing systems. Inserts, called CPs, are placed in library materials, which must be passed around the security system. If materials are carried through the system rather than passed around, an alarm sounds and the gate locks. This occurs even if a piece of library material is checked out—hence the term *pass-around.*

Desensitizing systems are also known as full circulation or electromagnetic systems. With this type of system, a sort of electro-magnetic strip is place in library materials. When they are checked out, the material is desensitized and can then be carried through the security system without setting it off. These are more expensive but are considered more efficient.

Several items should be considered about security systems. First, for a security system to be effective, there has to be controlled access to the library. If students can come and go through multiple entrances and exits, the security system will never be effective.

When a security system is installed, you must begin with a deterrence phase. Explain to students what the security system is and why it is there. Be sure to explain it thoroughly to teachers who have always entered and left the library as they pleased and perhaps even borrowed things without checking them out. Put up signs asking for cooperation and reminding them about the security system. Also be very clear about the consequences for trying to defeat the security system, and emphasize enforcement.

The second step is to ensure that detection is fairly applied. If the alarm sounds, do not accept protests that the person does not have library materials. Make the person present everything they are carrying, and make them go through the system again. Although there are occasional false alarms, they are very rare. Never permit anyone, student or teacher, to circumvent the system when leaving the library.

The final step is your response to attempts to circumvent the security system. Violations must be met with firm, consistent consequences. Apply them without fail, or the presence of the library security system will be minimized.

This chapter has covered the challenges of copyright, censorship, filtering and security systems. The next chapter will introduce library information systems, such as circulation and the online public access system.

RESEARCH AND DISCUSSION QUESTION

You have noticed that both teachers and students in your school either are unaware of or ignore copyright law. After some discussion with the school administration, they have charged you to develop a copyright policy for your school. Your assignment is to prepare a copyright policy that can be adopted by your school board. Be sure to include information about fair use, and touch on digital copyright issues.

REFERENCES

Allison, L., and R Baxter. "Protecting Our Innocents." Monash University. www.csse.edu. au/publications/1995/tr-cs95-224/1995.224.html.

Bennison, Nancy, and Don Lee. "Library Security: Protecting Valuable School Resources." *Media & Methods* 37, no. 7 (August 2001): 13. *MasterFILE Premier*. EBSCO. April 22, 2009. http://search.ebscohost.com.

Bilal, Dania. *Automating Media Centers and Small Libraries: A Microcomputer-Based Approach*. Greenwood Village, CO: Libraries Unlimited, 2002.

Butler, R.P. *Copyright for Teachers and Librarians*. New York: Neal-Schuman, 2004.

Callister, T.A. Jr., and Nicholas C. Burbules. "Just Give it to me Straight: A Case against Filtering the Internet," *Phi Delta Kappan* 85, no. 9 (2004). www.pdkintl.org/kappan/k0405cal.htm.

"Copyright and Fair Use Guidelines for Teachers." www.halldavidson.net/copyrightchart .html.

"Copyright Condensed." Heartland Area Education Agency 11. www.somers.k12.ct.us/ ~dnorige/documents/copyright.pdf.

Craver, K. *Creating Cyber Libraries: An Instructional Guide for School Library Media Specialist*. Greenwood Village, CO: Libraries Unlimited, 2002.

Doggett, Sandra L. *Beyond the Book: Technology Integration into the Secondary School Library Media Curriculum*. Englewood, CO: Libraries Unlimited, 2000.

"A Dozen Reason Why Schools Should Avoid Filtering." *From Now On: The Educational Technology Journal* (March–April 1996). http://fno.org/mar96/whynot.html.

"Educators Guide to Copyright and Fair Use." Tech Learning. www.techlearning.com/ db_area/archives/TL/2002/10/copyright_answers.html.

Fair Use of Copyrighted Materials." University of Texas. www.utsystem.edu/OCG/ IntellectualProperty/copypol12.htm.

"Filtering." NetSafekids. www.nap.edu/netsafekids/pro_fm_filter.html.

Harris, Robert. "Anti-Plagiarism Strategies for Research Papers." www.virtualsalt.com/ antiplag.htm.

"Information Access and Delivery: Internet Access and Filtering Issues." The School Library Media Specialist. http://eduscapes.com/sms/access/filtering.html.

"Laws Relating to Filtering, Blocking and Usage Policies in Schools and Libraries." National Conference of State Legislatures. www.ncsl.org/programs/lis/cip/filter laws.htm.

Leland, Bruce H. "Plagiarism and the Web." www.wiu.edu/users/mfbhl/wiu/plagiarism.htm.

Lesk, Michael. *Understanding Digital Libraries*. Boston, MA: Elsevier, 2005.

Logan, Debra Kay. "Imitation on the Web: Flattery, Fair Use, or Felony?" in *The Whole School Library Handbook*, edited by Blanche Woolls and David V. Loertscher, 179–182. Chicago: ALA, 2005.

Miner, Barbara. "Internet Filtering: Beware the Cyber Censors." Rethinking Schools. www.rethinkingschools.org/archive/12_04/net.shtml.

Murray, Corey. "Study: Overzealous Filters Hinder Research." eSchoolNews. www.eschoolnews.com/news/top-news/index.cfm.

Peterson, Christine. "Filtering Software: Regular or Decaf?" www.txla.org/pubs/tlj-1q97/filters.html.

Renard, Lisa "Cut and Paste 101: Plagiarism and the Net." *Educational Leadership* (December 1999–January 2000): 38–42.

Russell, Carrie. "Stolen Words: Copyright in a Nutshell," in *The Whole School Library Handbook*, edited by Blanche Woolls and David V. Loertscher, 347–349. Chicago, IL: ALA, 2005.

Starkman, Neal. "Do the (Copy)right Thing," *THE Journal* (March 2008). http://thejournal.com/the/prinarticle?id=22173.

Templeton, Brad. "10 Big Myths about Copyright Explained." www.templetons.com/brad/copymyths.html.

"University Laboratory High School Library Copyright Guidelines." University Laboratory High School Library. www.uni.uiuc.edu/policies/copyright.php.

"Use of Entertainment Videos for Family Night." http://beckercopyright.com/id13.html.

"When Works Pass into the Public Domain." University of North Carolina. www.unc.edu/~unclng/public-d.thm.

Wiebe, Todd J., "College Students, Plagiarism, and the Internet: The Role of Academic Librarians in Delivering Education and Awareness." MLA Forum. www.mlaforum.org/volumeV/article1.html.

- Teachers can make a single copy of a ch. from a book or an article from a journal for their own use in preparing for their class
- 1 copy/per student of an article if ≤ 2500 words.
- 1 copy/student of _excerpt_ of work of prose ≤ 1,000 words or 10% of the work (whichever is less)
- 1 copy/student of ≤ 250 words of poem
- Ask for permission if there's time
- How long will it be used?
- Only 9x in one term & not repeated term to term (seek permission!)

8

Library Information Systems

Most school librarians, if asked about library information systems, would choose "circulation" or "Online Public Access Catalogs (OPACs)." However, circulation and OPACs cover only a part of what can be a library information system. Circulation and the OPAC are what was first provided to schools. For many school librarians, the installation of a circulation system in some technological format helped them with circulation of materials. These were expanded when the OPAC, once called an automated catalog in the early to mid-eighties, was offered to school librarians. College and university libraries and large public libraries had earlier installed automated circulation systems when they had access to mainframe or minicomputers for this use. However, a library information system is more than circulation and OPAC and technology had to move from larger computers to microcomputers for this to be affordable in all but very large school systems.

The development of the microcomputer and the accompanying software for a small local area network system made automation possible within school libraries. This happened school by school or within one district, where a coordinator of libraries helped at the beginning of the process. In the early stages, changing the card catalog into an online catalog was a slow, painstaking process.

DESCRIPTION OF A LIBRARY INFORMATION SYSTEM

A library information system may be described as a system of modules and functions within a combination of hardware and software. In their original incantation, library information systems were only quasi-networked. This means they were probably networked within the library, but for any of the modules to be used, a patron or librarian had to be using one of the computers within this very small local area network. One should keep in mind that much of this innovation was pre-Internet, so access from the teachers' or students' homes to the system was not yet on the radar screen.

The three original major modules of library information systems, circulation, catalog, and cataloging, have remained pretty much the same throughout their evolution. Others will be explained, but the "big three" remain.

PLANNING THE IMPLEMENTATION OR EXPANSION OF A LIBRARY INFORMATION SYSTEM

When planning for the implementation or expansion of a library information system some important issues must be considered including the circulation, catalog and cataloging modules among others. System issues fall into questions as shown below:

1.   What are the hardware requirements? Does the system require state-of-the-art hardware, or can older equipment be recycled for use? If all computers are used to access the system, then relatively powerful hardware will be required.

2.   Support agreements. School libraries using early versions of library information systems could live with support agreements that were not 24/7. With systems available from home, user support is required 24/7.

3.   Training. Nothing is less useful than technology put in place for any potential user without appropriate training. This is a sure recipe for the failure. See what training is provided and for how long (one day for everyone, over a week for smaller groups, or as needed over a period of time). Is there is an add-on fee for training from the beginning, or later when new personnel need training, or if follow-up training is needed as the product evolves? Explore the possibility of online training.

4.   Reports. The report function of a library information system is what information you will be provided so you can analyze data and produce information that your administration and school board would find both interesting and helpful to confirm the wisdom of your purchase. Your board spent a lot of money on a library information system. The reports you produce can help convince them that they made a good investment.

The Circulation Module

The circulation module requires attention to several factors including security, an internal calendar, importing patron records, error alerts, and checkout blocks. Security is the first consideration. Early in the progression of library information systems when they were, at best, small local networks, security was a major issue. It is still important but is now generally handled on a level above the library. If it is something someone else does, you will have an override password, and you know how to use the override password.

The module should have an internal calendar. Circulation periods need to be tied to specific dates and holidays and weekends so that they are automatically calculated into the system. Of course, you could bypass much of this if you allowed everyone—teachers, students, even parents—to check resources out for a semester with the understanding that an item must be returned immediately if it is requested by someone else.

The import of patron records and their removal must be easily accomplished. Every time a class or individual moves to a different school or a new one enters, you do not want to do the update manually. This may require some assistance from the vendor or your technology coordinator.

Error alerts such as incorrect barcode should have both audible error alerts and visible alerts. Both should not allow further work until cleared.

Checkout blocks are needed if for any reasons a patron should not check out further materials. This would be the case if a student has overdue materials or has failed to return a book that was checked out for a longer period of time but has been requested by another person. Be sure there is an override for this, though, because circumstances are seldom black or white.

The Catalog Module

The catalog module and data conversion are interwoven. The greatest challenge to building a library system was and is providing the records of what the library owns in a machine readable format. This is also known as retrospective conversion if you are moving from a card catalog to online access. In the past, the school librarian sent the shelf list off to a vendor who converted it. The costs for this procedure can be considerable, but if you are working in a library that has a card catalog, this is preferable to trying to input those records yourself or with the aid of willing volunteers.

Retrospective conversion projects do not produce a perfect catalog. Nor will the records sent to your OPAC from a vendor necessarily be what some catalogers would choose. However, you need to get those records into your catalog as quickly as possible, and the most efficient method is to buy the cataloging with the product.

After the catalog is in place, the catalog module should provide for ease in search. Users should be able to find author, title, subject, and/or key words. Key words should automatically be generated by the system.

Another function is truncation and wild card. Patrons should be able to use both truncation and wild cards so if they are not sure of a search term they can still get results.

It should be possible to provide "stop words" in the catalogs. This is not as major a problem as it once was, but it goes without saying that words such as "an" and "the" are treated as stop words.

Autocomplete spell-check is also necessary. The catalog module should automatically correct the spelling of common words as well as those in error because of such things as keyboard transposition.

Not used in Axis360!

Finally the catalog should be available through mouse or keyboard search. The system should search equally well either way.

The Cataloging Module

This module is different from the catalog module, because this module allows the librarian to import records. An efficient library information system should allow for the importing of records both from jobbers and from a large system such as OCLC or one or more statewide catalogs. Furthermore, users should be able to create complete, accurate records within the cataloging module if such records are not available elsewhere. If the library has local information to be included, this should be seamless.

The cataloging module should allow for the cataloging of websites. As the procurement of information from the web becomes more common, library information systems should have procedures for allowing information about websites to be added to the OPAC. It must also allow for merging records from the existing system when the system is upgraded or replaced.

These are the basic modules that should be part of any library management system. Other modules are available in some systems that can greatly enhance the utility of your system.

Other Modules

Among the other modules are serials module and acquisitions module. The first, the serials module, is used by school librarians who continue to purchase hard-copy periodicals or other serials. Most library information systems have this available.

The acquisitions module allows the school librarian to select and purchase materials for the library. Another helpful module for those school libraries in a consortium or even a state network is the interlibrary loan module, which allows teachers and students to borrow materials from other libraries in their area.

Moving to a single search, visually oriented library information systems have several other modules that are absolute requirements to provide the best search experience for students. They all relate to providing all available resources using a single search:

1. Electronic resource management systems. These are more for use by the staff than patrons, but they allow the management of magazine subscriptions with other electronic resources.
2. Metasearch. This is the single search school librarians and students have always wanted. It allows a single search for books, periodical indexes, electronic databases, and the Internet, and it can be done from school or home.
3. Digital library products. These modules allow librarians to manage the entire digital collection.

HOW SCHOOLS ARE USING LIBRARY INFORMATION SYSTEMS

School libraries are providing library information systems as described, but how are these actually being used? A survey conducted by Daniel Fuller, a faculty member at San Jose State University, in 2006, presented some facts that should be of concern to school librarians who are advocates of the best library service possible to their students.

First, most schools were using automation systems more than five years old. Although 75 percent of school libraries had automated by 2002, Fuller found that fewer than one in five were using the latest version of the library information system. This is a direct reflection on the decline in school library budgets. This situation was exacerbated by the economic downturn at the present time.

Second, Fuller showed that school librarians are very satisfied with the library information system they are using, even if it is not the latest and greatest. They find their systems stable and reliable and apparently have established a comfort level with their systems. In particular, they are satisfied with the different modules of their systems. The librarians are most satisfied with the circulation module, followed by the cataloging module, the OPAC module, and then vendor support. Though vendor support showed last here, 86 percent of the school librarians queried were either extremely likely or somewhat likely to use the same vendor and purchase the same system (Fuller).

Although school librarians appear to be very satisfied with their library information system, many are only scratching the surface of the system's capability. For example, a small (fewer than 50 percent) number of school librarians use their systems to print daily reports. Although this is somewhat understandable, with so many one-person school libraries, it is discouraging that the power of the library information system is ignored. Collecting such data helps confirm the value of the system as well as library usage statistics.

In considering the findings of the earlier study and present literature, some improvements would be helpful. These are discussed below.

ADVANTAGES AND DISADVANTAGES OF AND POSSIBLE IMPROVEMENTS FOR INFORMATION SYSTEMS

Nearly every school library management textbook published in the past fifteen years lists the advantages and disadvantages of library information systems. As time passes, the advantages become more numerous and the disadvantages far fewer. In the next three sections, one list of each is presented along with creating a list of some improvements that might be made to library information systems.

Advantages

The following lists the advantages of library information systems:

1. Library information systems provide more search options for patrons than traditional card catalogs. Any piece of data in the MARC record can be searched by most present-day library information systems.
2. Library information systems can encourage more school library use because of their ease of use.
3. Automated library information systems present the school library as being "up" on technology.
4. Library information systems allow remote access to the school library's resources.
5. Most library information systems allow single query searching allowing patrons to search not only the book collection, but also other electronic resources as part of the catalog.
6. A library information system simplifies the inventory procedure. School library resources now have barcodes, making checking whether a resource is there as easy as scanning a barcodes.
7. Routine tasks are made simpler, getting materials on the shelves quicker.
8. Library information systems reduce the cost of providing a catalog. Sustaining costs of maintaining are lower than such labor-intensive duties back when catalog cards had to be typed if no other method was available and all needed to be filed and the filing checked in the card catalog.

9. In addition to improved access to materials, library information systems also provide the checkout status of library materials. It is a very quick process to learn whether a resource is in the library or checked out by a teacher or student. This advantage alone makes the system purchase worthwhile. ˙

10. Library information systems encourage collection development and resource sharing. In contrast to the time when school libraries were self-contained, a library information system now makes it easy to see the holdings of other school and public libraries to encourage resource sharing. Furthermore, these days of reduced school library budgets make shared collection development a benefit to all, and a library information system can simplify the task.

11. Make importing and exporting catalog records much simpler. This simplification can substantially improve the quality of school library cataloging.

These are eleven good reasons for installing library information systems in a school library. In reality, all school libraries, regardless of size, should have one in place. The cost of the technology to implement such a system is so much less than in the past, as are the modules they offer in today's technology-rich atmosphere, that every school library must have a library information system. However, these systems are not without disadvantages.

Disadvantages

All of the reasons given in the last section for the necessity for a library information system are in place, but it does not hide the existence of some problems associated with library information systems. Most of these problems can be overcome if the school librarian plans carefully and is dedicated to the goal of providing students with the best educational experience possible.

1. Installation or update of a library information system can be time-consuming. The entire planning process, from idea to procurement, takes time, and school librarians rarely have extra time. This is particularly true in a school library with one librarian and no clerical help. Furthermore, after the system is installed, it must be maintained; this, again, requires time that may take the school librarian away from working with teachers and students.

2. Library information systems can be expensive. They have a multitude of costs associated with the successful implementation of a library information system, including such things as hardware, servers, furniture, and consumable supplies. If it is needed, the retrospective conversion alone can be extremely expensive.

3. Although library information systems can be labor-saving, they can create new tasks.

4. System downtime can be very frustrating. In an ideal world, no library information system would ever be down. The reality is systems do sometimes go down. It is not as common as it once was, but system downtime can be disastrous. Plan for it!

5. At times there are levels of knowledge that library information system users must possess to successfully use the system. These levels of knowledge do not build on each other but are discrete knowledge bits users must possess—and this means that someone must provide training. Again, this would logically fall to school librarian, and teachers may be reluctant to do the necessary professional development unless they are convinced of its usefulness.

    a. The first level of knowledge is a conceptual level of knowledge. This is knowledge of how to translate an information need into a search. At times it is a giant leap from searching for Shakespeare to searching for dramatizations of "The Taming of the Shrew."

    b. The second level of knowledge is a semantic level of knowledge. This takes the search to the formulation of a search query that returns only relevant results.

    c. The final level of knowledge is the technical skill necessary to actually operate the library information system. It does little good to have a state-of-the-art library information system if teachers or even students don't have the technical skills to conduct a search.

Improvements for Library Information Systems

No system will ever be perfect in spite of the claims of vendors. There are, however, a few easy steps, many of them simply common-sense, that can be taken to improve the school library information system:

1. Improve the database. This seems so simple as to be superfluous, but the reality is there is much poor cataloging in OPACSs. Cataloging, particularly original cataloging, is and should be a low priority for school librarians. Working with the database makes a huge difference in the quality when mistakes appear. These should be corrected immediately

2. Vendor improvements. Although improvements in library information systems sometimes seem to come very fast, school librarians should carefully look at these improvements. Some may be useful and may significantly improve the system, but others may not. It is important to take the time to test and make a considered decision.

3. New initiatives. Some of the same things discussed above also apply to new initiatives. Examine them carefully, and select the ones having the biggest positive effect on your library information system.

SELECTING A LIBRARY INFORMATION SYSTEM

When it is time to purchase, upgrade, or replace a library information system, care is essential in making the best decision. This can be approached in two ways. First, Rourke provided ten questions school librarians should ask about library information systems. Second, Doggett provided a more detailed checklist of items school librarians should consider when evaluating library information systems. Rourke's questions to ask include the following:

1. What is the size of the collection? Be sure the library information system is robust enough to handle the collection.
2. How many users can the system accommodate? This is an absolutely critical question. If the system you are examining cannot handle all your users, run—don't walk—away.
3. What modules are needed? Examine your needs closely and compare them to the modules available in the system. Although it is sometimes possible to add modules as time passes, it is often difficult to do so efficiently.
4. How many remote users—those who use the system outside the walls of the school—are anticipated? This can be a deal breaker even if at present you have no remote users. This is changing rapidly in schools, and if your library information system does not provide remote access, you may need an upgrade very quickly.
5. Do you still need to convert from catalog cards to electronic records? Think of vendors for retrospective conversion.
6. Should you weed before converting? Without a doubt. Be ruthless when you weed your collection. This may be the perfect time to get rid of those shelf fillers that need to go to make room for new items, particularly if you are reducing the size of your book collection.
7. How simple is the migration to the new system? Your vendor and its technical support team must be on site to ramrod the migration.
8. Can the interface be modified? Inevitably, you may not like some parts of the interface. Can you change it? How difficult is it to make interface changes?
9. Is the staff interface efficient and intuitive? If not, look at a different system.

10. What are the vendors' future plans? Is the vendor financially secure? The challenges of implementing a new system when the former vendor was purchased by another company can be difficult.

Doggett's Library Management System Vendor Checklist of questions is presented below. Your answers will be very helpful in decision making.

1. Cost
   a. Are there volume discounts for an entire school district?
   b. Can the system be phased in over a period of years to save money?
   c. Cost comparison with other vendors.
   d. Are the costs consistent with the services available?
   e. Is there a charge for updates?
   f. Is there an annual subscription cost?
2. Support Contracts
   a. What are the fees for phone and online support?
   b. How quickly does a vendor stop supporting a product when a new version is introduced?
   c. Is there both toll-free and help desk support?
3. Training
   a. Does the vendor provide training to the school library staff?
   b. Does the vendor assume responsibility for loading software?
4. Z39.50-compatible
   a. Is the system compatible with Z39.50 conventions?
5. Use
   a. Is there an integrated spell-checker?
   b. Is navigation intuitive?
   c. Does it permit Boolean searching?
   d. How long will it take to teach the system to students and teachers?
   e. Is there an efficient on-screen help system?
   f. Are closing routines simple?
6. Recommendations
   a. Have you surveyed other school libraries using the system to determine satisfaction?
   b. What weaknesses have others found in the system?
   c. Were some functions promised but not delivered?
7. Capacity
   a. Is the system compatible with your current computers and network?
   b. Can the system handle all required transactions?
   c. Can reports be run in background without system degradation?
   d. What are the systems patron and record capacity?

8. Flexibility
   a. Can the system grow?
   b. Can the database migrate easily to a new vendor's product?
   c. Can the system's interface be customized?
   d. Can custom reports be created?
   e. Are the systems compatible with those of all libraries in your district?
9. Vendor support
   a. How long has the vendor been in business?
   b. What enhancements to the system are planned?
   c. Does the vendor update when new hardware is purchased?
   d. Will the system function on both school and districtwide networks?

Considerations for the purchase, expansion, or replacement of a library information system are noted. Some recent trends in library information systems are now described.

RECENT TRENDS IN LIBRARY INFORMATION SYSTEMS

Breeding published an article in 2014 tying together many of the trends in library information systems. His findings point out that in some ways, little has changed.

The makeup of library information systems varies from school to school. Although the primary mission of a school library is to provide information resources to students, secondary missions can include such functions as providing professional materials for staff or even acting as an adjunct to the local public library. An example of this is in Westmoreland County, Pennsylvania, where the Robert Kerr Memorial Library in the Derry Area High School also functions as a branch of Adams Public Library, the local public library.

It is natural to assume that the library information system in a particular school is tailored for the population (grades) served by the school. This seems a no-brainer, but when schools can easily change their grade configuration, it sometimes becomes a complex problem.

School library information systems need to address the functions required at that level so they have specialized functionality. The main structure of associating student records with a grade, class, or homeroom distinguishes these systems from those designed for public libraries. Circulation policies and workflows must accommodate the school calendar, such as setting due dates corresponding to the end of each semester or term. Consistent with other kinds of libraries, ebooks and other electronic resources have become a growing component of school library collections.

In addition to the core automation system, K–12 school libraries may implement a variety of related applications. Management of media resources and equipment often falls within the role of the library. Schools also need automated tools to help manage textbooks. Tracking the overall inventory of textbooks, the assignment, and the return each term can be a major undertaking, especially in large school districts. Many of the developers of K–12 school library automation systems offer a specialized product for textbook management. Increasingly, the companies involved in school library automation aim to provide products and services that find use beyond the library, supporting other administrative and educational activities.

SCHOOL LIBRARY AUTOMATION COMPANIES

A limited number of vendors have systems available. They often have a specialization relative to developing products for a specific type of library. Though some overlap exists between public and academic sectors because of their much larger numbers of patrons, the school library arena has become very specialized. A number of companies provide automation products specifically for K–12 schools. Follett Corporation, a large privately held company with more than $2.7 billion in annual revenue, operates a variety of businesses that provide products and services to K–12 schools. Follett School Solutions represents a recent consolidation of four related businesses within Follett and includes among its offerings the Destiny family of automation products. Destiny Library Manager, available for individual schools or districts, is by far the most widely used automation system in the K–12 arena. Destiny has been installed in more than half of the K–12 schools in the United States. Follett also owns many of the legacy systems from the previous generation of school library automation, including Winnebago Spectrum, Athena, and Sagebrush Corporation, with its InfoCentre acquired in 2006. Follett also offers own Circulation Plus. These once popular legacy systems continue to wind down with most moving to Destiny

Follett does not target its development exclusively to the library but to the broader needs of a school district. It offers the Aspen school information system (SIS), a version of Destiny for textbook management. The company recently formed a partnership with Absolute.

THE FUTURE OF LIBRARY INFORMATION SYSTEMS

The future for library information systems is the ongoing move to visual systems with single search capability. With these systems, patrons will be able to enter a research question on one screen and the return will be books from the collection, items from fee-based databases, online periodical articles, and vetted websites. Furthermore, students will have had instructions in query formulation, so they will be able to create efficient searches. Another area for the future of library information system is that of digital libraries. Those concepts will be discussed in chapter 9.

RESEARCH AND DISCUSSION QUESTION

Your library is considering either upgrading or changing its library information system. Using a combination of the criteria presented in this chapter, visit three other schools using different systems and compare their capability. Using these data, prepare a recommendation to be presented to your administration and school board.

REFERENCES

Bazirjian, Rosann. "The Administration and Management of Integrated Library Systems." *LRTS* 1 (2001). www.ala.org.

Bilal, Dania. *Automating Media Centers and Small Libraries: A Microcomputer-Based Approach.* Greenwood Village, CO: Libraries Unlimited, 2002.

Breeding, Marshall. "Tech Trends and Challenges for K–12 School Libraries." *Computers in* Libraries. September 2013. http://search.proquest.com/docview/1440137000?ac countid=35812 (accessed October 18. 2014.

Brisco, Shonda. "Technology Connection: Visual OPACs," *Library Media Connection* (November/December 2008), 56–57.

Burke, John J. *Neal-Schuman Library Technology Companion: A Basic Guide for Library Staff.* New York: Neal-Schuman, 2004.

Cibbarelli, Pamela. "ILS Marketplace: School Libraries," *MultiMedia Schools* (September 2003). *MasterFILE Premier.* EBSCO. April 22, 2009 http://search.ebscohost .com.

Doggett, Sandra L. *Beyond the Book: Technology Integration into the Secondary School Library Media Curriculum.* Englewood, CO: Libraries Unlimited, 2000.

Everhart, Nancy. "How Relevant Are Standardized Subject Heading to School Curricula?" *Knowledge Quest* 33, no. 4 (2005). *MasterFILE Premier.* EBSCO. April 22, 2009. http://search.ebscohost.com.

Fiehn, Barbara. "Social Networking and Your Library OPAC," *MultiMedia Schools* (September 2008). *MasterFILE Premier.* EBSCO. April 22, 2009 http://search .ebscohost.com.

Fuller, Daniel. "School Library Journal and San Jose State University 2006 Automation Survey," *School Library Journal* (October 1, 2006). www.schoollibraryjournal.com.

Harris, Christopher. "Fishing for Information: The Next-Generation OPAC," *School Library Journal* (January 1, 2008). www.schoollibraryjournal.com.

Jurkowski, Odin L. *Technology and the School Library: A Comprehensive Guide for Media Specialists and Other Educators*. Lanham, MD: Scarecrow, 2006.

Kochtanek, Thomas R., and Joseph R. Matthews. *Library Information Systems: From Library Automation to Distributed Information Access Solutions*. Westport, CT: Libraries Unlimited, 2002.

Murphy, Catherine. "The Online Catalog on the Way to the Millennium," *MultiMedia Schools* 5, no. 3 (1998). *MasterFILE Premier*. EBSCO. April 22, 2009 http://search.ebscohost.com.

"Next-Generation Flavor in Integrated Online Catalogs," *Library Technology Reports* (July–August 2007). www.techsource.ala.org.

Woolls, Blanche. *The School Library Media Manager*. Englewood, CO: Libraries Unlimited, 1994.

9

School Library Websites

As school librarians move forward with technology, the question becomes whether your school library needs a website or an online presence. Administrators, teachers, and parents are well aware that student research is done on the Internet. If they are not taught different, their research consists of googling a search term and using the first three or four sites listed as the basis of their research regardless of the quality of the information returned by the search.

Student searching behavior is directly related to the school library when they have access to a library's website. Your students and teachers can use your website to find credible, reliable, and relevant current information. It is the library's portal to all things research-related. According to Warlick, your website allows you to help students become effective learners and to assist teachers in providing quality educational experiences (Warlick 2005). In developing your website the following questions will help in your planning for implementation:

1. What is the purpose of the website? Does it give only basic information about the library, hours, circulation policies, and other routine matters? Are you inviting teachers to post homework assignments? Are you providing web addresses for students to help them find information quickly for their assignments?
2. What do you want to accomplish with the website? Stages in the evolution of websites will be discussed later in this chapter.
3. What should website users be able to do? Can students and their parents find homework assignments? Will they find links to information such as sample bibliographic entries?
4. What will keep your users using your school library website? The answers to this question are found throughout the chapter.

CONTENT ON THE WEBSITE

Website planning begins with the answer to the question of why have one. It must offer basic information and describe the library rules and regulations, hours the library is physically open, and how to gain access electronically when a patron cannot physically come to the library. For resources housed within the library, how long materials may be used is explained, as well as what equipment is available to be checked out and for how long—also the requirements for use, such for Wi-Fi. Here also are directions to request interlibrary loan materials.

The second stage has all the information about the user-centered digital library. At this stage, students are able to do research and use the library page as the starting point for all research. Here are links to online databases and periodical articles. Here are the URLs to useful and relevant information to complete specific assignments. At a minimum, the library's website provides the following:

1. The ability to interact with the library's OPAC
2. The gateway to the library's electronic resources
3. Remote access to the library's databases
4. Library tutorials or how-tos
5. Virtual references
6. Access to library blogs and other Web 2.0 applications

CREATING THE SCHOOL LIBRARY WEBPAGE

The creation of webpages and websites is becoming almost as easy as using a word processing program. However, several caveats are associated with this type of webpage creation. Early webpage creation was a programming job done by computer programmers knowledgeable in HTML (HyperText Markup Language), and many computer professionals still consider this the best way to create webpages. Fortunately for most of us, there are other ways to create webpages.

If you are using Microsoft Office as your productively software, each of the applications—Word, Excel, PowerPoint, and Access—allow you to save your work as a webpage. However, there are two reasons why you may not want to use these as your web creation software. First, these programs do not allow the creation of fully integrated websites—and there is a difference between webpages and websites. A website is generally a group of related and linked webpages. Second, using these programs does not give you the close control over content that will best showcase your school library.

The second way to create pages and websites is by using web creation software. The two leaders in this field are Microsoft Expression

Web and Macromedia Dreamweaver. These are both relatively complex programs and are not particularly intuitive. They both have the capability of producing professional, functional websites after some level of training. Check with your district's technical coordinator, or perhaps a knowledgeable high school student, for help. You could also ask a local two- or four-year school what training might be available in your area. Both these programs will allow you to create individual webpages or integrated websites.

If you feel you just don't have the time to do a webpage justice, take a look at some of the webpage template services available, such as Schoolwires or WordPress. These types of programs do not have a great deal of flexibility, but you can turn out an attractive product.

These suggestions make it possible to build a website; the next issue is how to get your webpage or website actually on the Internet. Generally your Internet Service Provider (ISP) will host your website as part of the services your district pays for. If your district is its own ISP, then it follows that the district will host your website. In the highly unlikely event your ISP does not host webpages, it is likely your own personal ISP, such as Comcast, will provide a certain amount of server space to host webpages.

The next issue you have to deal with is how to get your school library website from your computer to your ISP's Internet server. This step gets very technical very quickly, so unless your technology coordinator is going to do it, you need a bit of technical expertise. The simplest way to upload websites to an Internet server is to use an FTP program such as Filezilla or CuteFTP. The file transfer program (FTP) allows you to post your website to your ISP relatively quickly and easily. If you are not sure about uploading your website, your technology coordinator should be your next stop.

WEB DESIGN

Many books written discuss effective and attractive web design and can improve your website. A very effective one is *Web Design for Libraries,* by Charles Rubenstein. It is a textbook but can be easily used by someone willing to apply himself or herself to the process. To get you started, the following are some very basic guidelines to make your website attractive and user-friendly.

Jennifer L. Wholleb (2006) provided guidelines to school administrators about considerations they should adhere to when designing a district website. Although this is at a higher level than most school library webpages, it gives a good insight into what administrators think is important in website design. The word "district" has been replaced with "library."

1. The website is the first place you can make an impression online when people want to find out about the school library. Be sure it is professional, attractive, and informative.

2. Make sure the most basic information people would want about the school library is easy to find. This includes telephone and fax numbers, street addresses, and e-mail addresses. It is nice to talk about great test scores "x," but make the basic information easy to find.

3. The school library's mission statement should not be the first thing you see on a webpage. Although the mission is important and should be readily available, if it is the first thing you see, you have to consider whether the mission of the page is to promote the mission or the school library.

4. Do not, under any circumstances, use generic, educational clip art! It is too cutesy. Also, avoid stock photographs of the school library.

5. Keep your website easy to read and use. Complicated photos and graphics, music, streaming video—these are all nice things to have, but keep in mind that some of your users may still be using dial-up connections.

6. Keep your website up to date. Always have the most recent update date on the page. Out-of-date information and invalid links are worse than no information at all. This is one of the main reasons why maintaining a website cannot be one of those things you do when you have the time. There is never time!

7. Use standard fonts. Specialty fonts look unprofessional and can be extremely hard to read.

8. Do not make your website too busy. Remember less is more and content can be buried in cuteness.

9. Do not use "under construction" pages on the website. Don't put a page on the site until there is content on it.

10. Updating the webpage. Fix broken links when updating the webpage. Either correct the link, or eliminate it. Your credibility is at stake.

11. Forget the artsy introduction page. Get to the point.

12. You can never test the website too much. Test it with different browsers and on a dial-up connection.

In addition to the items on the Wholleb list, what do you want your school library website to look like? A simple answer is it should be attractive and draw users back. At the same time, it should be informative and easy to use. You know what your patrons need on a webpage and what they will use. On the other hand, you also have to think like a web designer. That is difficult at first, because most school librarians were never web designers, and it is more complicated than putting up a bulletin board. Your web designer role must grow and use what you can find out to determine what can be done to fulfill what your patrons want.

Expanding Wholleb's second point, of prime importance in web design are issues of accessibility and usability. Having accessible web pages means all patrons, including people with disabilities, can use all parts of your webpage. Anything on a webpage that is an image or words (and that is almost everything) must be considered for accessibility.

When you are constructing your school library website, consider the following about images:

1. Images can take considerable time to download. This is especially true if your students are using dial-up connections.
2. Images can take an inordinate amount of time to create and can be difficult to change.
3. Text in an image cannot be changed to allow easier reading.
4. Text from an image cannot be copied and pasted.

When you are working with your webpage there are some rules with relation to images and accessibility you may want to consider:

1. Always include an .alt attribute with a description of the content when the image has information.
2. Always include a "long description" attribute when the image has a large amount of information associated with it.
3. Make images as small as practical to speed downloading.
4. Do not use image maps unless you have a compelling reason.
5. Don't rely on color to mark things on the webpage, because some users are colorblind.
6. Make sure your webpage does not do unexpected things like open in a new window unless there is some indication of what will happen.
7. Make your default font and font size readable.

Usability is how well your teachers, students, and others can use the website to do what they want it to do. A few basic rules to follow in order to assure your site is usable are given here:

1. Consider what your audience needs.
2. Make sure your website is well organized so users can easily find what they want.
3. Ensure the site is easy to navigate.
4. Be sure the content on all webpages is clear, well organized, and well written.

Others have written about design issues that must be considered by school librarians when they are working at creating their website. Roger Black has created what he calls ten rules of good design:

1. Every page must have content, and it must be easy to read.
2. Use white as the first color on any website; white is a great background color and can take almost any dark font.
3. Use black as the second color on any website.
4. Use red or . . . for the third color.
5. Never letter space lowercase fonts.
6. Never use all caps; it does not emphasize and is very hard to read.
7. Use a poster for the cover of a webpage.
8. Never use more than one or two typefaces on a website.
9. Make things as large as possible on a website.
10. Break up a website occasionally, even though consistency is good.

Kochtanek and Matthews described some webpage design guidelines that repeat some of the items previously mentioned and add others. The authors broke these into visual considerations and practical considerations.

Visual Considerations

1. Never use all caps for emphasis.

2. Ensure that links are in prose or definition lists.

3. Break up your content. Page after page of text is boring.

4. Again, use only one or two fonts per website.

5. Use white space effectively.

Practical Considerations

1. Never use more than three images per page. Think of the poor user who has a dial-up connection.

2. The background and text on a webpage should neither clash nor blend together.

3. Use light background colors. White is always good!

4. Use no more than four colors per screen.

These lists have given some very specific suggestions concerning website design. They can be distilled to the following.

1. The graphic design of a website will neither help nor hurt the website.
2. Text links are absolutely vital. Try your best to avoid using images as links.
3. The content and navigation of a website are inseparable.
4. It is essential that all websites have at least one search engine.
5. No matter what else is true, a website must be good to be used.

WEBSITE DESIGN ERRORS

This section is the list of items that can, if used, turn out very bad webpages. All anyone has to do is surf the web for a while to see what is bad, and there is plenty of it. It is a list of don'ts.

1. Don't use frames. Webpages using frames are nothing but trouble for users. They often display incorrectly and can be almost impossible to print. Fortunately, new web design programs, such as Microsoft Expression Web, have effectively eliminated the use of frames.
2. Don't use bleeding-edge technology. Many if not most of your students or teachers will have the technology—use it because it's cool.
3. Don't use scrolling marquees and animations. All they do is slow page loading and distract the user from the real mission of the website.
4. Don't use complex URLs. Though it is always desirable to go directly to the location of information, sometimes you want to back off a screen or two to simplify the URL.
5. Don't use orphan pages. Orphan pages do not contain any identifying information and do not provide navigation back to the previous page.
6. Don't use long scrolling pages. They are deadly! Most Internet users, adults and student, will stop scrolling after about two pages.
7. Don't leave out your navigation bar, site search, or site map. Your users should not have to guess where they are on your website.
8. Don't use nonstandard link colors. Your users with color blindness issues will be completely lost on the website.
9. Don't use old information. Of all the issues we discuss, dated information will cause your website to lose credibility quicker than anything else.
10. Don't use things with long download times. This may be a direct result of a large number of big images.
11. Don't use distracting splash pages. Of particular note are glitzy introduction pages. Skip it, and get right to the content.

12. Don't use unnecessary design items. As we mentioned previously, they distract from the ease of use of the website.
13. Don't use the same web design for the school's intranet. Doing this can create a lot of unnecessary confusion.
14. Don't put your navigation bar anywhere by at the top of the page. This is another case of leaving the user blind on the site.
15. Don't have an ineffective navigation scheme. A particularly egregious error is to ignore navigation links back and forth on webpages within a website.
16. Don't use Flash! Don't use Flash!
17. Don't test your page with a single browser. It is absolutely essential that websites be tested with all the popular browsers. You will be surprised at the differences.
18. Don't use too much content. Sometimes less is more.
19. Don't leave broken links unfixed. This is known as "link rot," and the more rot on your website, the less reliable it is.
20. Don't leave off links to sites outside your library. This leaves the impression with your students that only information within the library is useful when they know they have the world through Google.
21. Never forget to alphabetize or annotate lists. These are things we as librarians routinely do, but often do not on a website.
22. Don't forget to have a link to your library's website on the district's homepage—a real must if your website is to be useable.

WEB DESIGN AND COPYRIGHT

In chapter 5, copyright issues with relation to the Internet were discussed. Although not all of these apply equally to school library websites, the more you know, the less likely you are to get in trouble. Many who have worked with webpage design and construction have probably violated copyright law in some way, but you should try to avoid this.

Copyright issues and the Internet remain somewhat murky, with several key issues not yet adjudicated. When you look at what you might consider to be a good website and want to follow the old adage "why reinvent the wheel," you do not have the right to borrow content and graphics from the site. When you do, you may have receive a letter or e-mail asking that the content be removed from the website or at least give credit.

Many of these unresolved issues deal with links and images, and there are many corporate lawyers waiting to tell you to "cease and desist." Unfortunately, many educators feel if an image is used for educational purposes, it falls under fair use and is not subject to copyright law. Two examples should banish the notion:

1. Your webpage's theme is ideal for some Bugs Bunny images, so you find some on the Warner Bros. site and copy them for use on your webpage. Warner Bros. attorneys will send you a polite but firm letter to cease and desist very soon after the page is posted.
2. As a school librarian, you want to provide links for your teachers and students to purchase concert tickets without having to use Ticketmaster's site. Again, Ticketmaster lawyers will instruct you to remove the links or face legal action.

Three First Amendment issues can get you in some legal hot water. The first of these may seem less applicable to school libraries than other types of libraries, but the other two definitely pertain to school libraries:

1. Interactive discussion forums. These are just so full of legal issues that the best advice librarians can get is to not get involved with them.
2. Advertising. This is a large issue in most schools. There probably is a school district policy addressing this issue.
3. Accessibility. This was discussed at some length earlier in the chapter. School districts are bound by ADA guidelines for accessibility on websites, just as its facilities are bound by ADA.

Just to help distill this, the copyright holder has five rights granted by law:

1. The right to reproduce the copyrighted work
2. The right to prepare derivative works based on the work
3. The right to distribute copies of the work to the public
4. The right to perform the copyrighted work publicly
5. The right to display the work publicly

WHAT SHOULD BE ON A SCHOOL LIBRARY WEBPAGE

Nearly all the literature has provided lists of things that would be good on a school library webpage. Although some of these lists are discussed here, it is strongly recommended that you explore the web to see what is out there that is good and that you would consider bad.

A 2004 article from *Learning and Leading with Technology*, by Donna Baumbach, Sally Brewer, and Matt Renfroe, titled "What Should Be on a School Library Web Page?" is very useful to aspiring webmasters. In general, these three authors include the following as possible items on a school library webpage:

1. Online public access catalogs. Also include the OPACs your students might have occasion to use.

2. Reference resources. Include both fee based and free resources.
3. Reference assistance. You might want to include such things as hints on how to search your catalog or databases. This would be the perfect place to use a blog to assist students with their reference or research issues.
4. Curriculum connections. This category is so broad that you will have to limit this to the "best of."
5. Literacy materials.
6. General information. Hours, phone numbers, email addresses, etc.
7. Dynamic material. This might be the place you put such things as best-seller lists or student-produced reviews of new books.

Matthews, in his book on planning for technology, provides some more general items about the features on a school library webpage.

1. Include as much locally developed information on the page as is practical.
2. The page should be well formatted and edited. Sloppy just doesn't cut it.
3. The page or site should be easy to locate. Again, links on both the school district's page and the school's page are requirements.
4. Getting to information on the site should be clear and direct.
5. Consistency is a plus.
6. You must have at least one browser search engine on the homepage.
7. Information should be systematic and hierarchal.
8. Each page should be able to stand on its own.
9. Do everything you can to make the page load more rapidly.

Other issues to be addressed in what should be included in a school library are reported below:

1. A focus on teaching: Teaching is what you do, and your website should reflect it. Whether you do it through a library blog, a teaching/learning wiki, a collection of slideshows, or any number of other elements, your site should showcase that learning takes place in the library.

2. Examples of student work: One sure way to get parents to visit your site is to make it a gallery of student work. Posting student work on your site not only provides students with an opportunity for real-world publication, but it also emphasizes your role as an instructional partner within the school.

3. Opportunities for participation: If teaching students about digital citizenship and the ethical use of information is part of your mission, then your website should be an online laboratory where students get to put those skills to work. Many interactive Web 2.0 tools such as Wallwisher and ThingLink

provide students, teachers, and parents the chance to contribute to the library's web presence

4. Evolving resources for your evolving audience: If school libraries are to be thought of as the place to find the most up-to-date, most relevant, and most cutting-edge resources, our websites must contain resources of equally high quality. Out-of-date links will not make this happen. Resources shared on our websites need to be

- updated frequently to reflect student needs
- directly linked to student learning and to the school district and state's mission
- a part of our own practice in the library

5. Flavor: Your website should give visitors a taste of the library experience that you have created. If your library is a fun, busy, active place filled with opportunities for students to grow and learn, your website should reflect that (5 Things).

SCHOOL LIBRARY WEBSITE EVALUATION

Evaluation is an important part of creating and maintaining a website. You can follow all of the suggestions listed above and create a website that you think will be valuable for all of the stakeholders involved, but you need to evaluate your creation to make sure just how valuable it actually is. Website evaluation is multifaceted. You need to have all of the stakeholders in your school evaluate the website, including administrators, teachers, staff, students, and parents. Although some will just give the site a cursory look and say that it looks fine, you will also receive cogent, constructive criticism. It is likely that the best evaluation will come from students. Why? Students are the users who will be accessing the site most often. Whenever you evaluate your website and find the things that need to be changed, you revise or redesign your website as rapidly as possible.

REVISING OR REDESIGNING YOUR WEBSITE

Almost as soon as you have opened your website, you will see things you should change or things to be added. It is unlikely that you will be able to change or add things at a moment's notice; rather, keep a list of what must be changed. A few general guidelines to simplify the revision of a website are shown below. Some of them are repeated from the things to consider in developing a website: They are important enough to repeat here.

 Create a standard template for the entire website, containing the library name, logo, and a navigation bar.

2. Put what your users want on the website, as well as what you need to have there.
3. Verify and edit your text information.
4. Do not use generic education clip art or .alt tags.
5. Use dark text on a light background.
6. Have frequent dynamic information—nothing more than one month old.
7. Put things on your website that can't be found anywhere else.

INTRANETS

School librarians are often asked to participate in the creation of a school district intranet. An intranet is a website created by the school district and limited to employees of the district. It is typically only available inside the district's firewall. The construction and use of a school district intranet has several benefits:

1. Eliminate paperwork. This may be chimerical.
2. Create a "best practices" forum or blog.
3. Develop blogs or discussion groups to share problems and successes.
4. Provide a news outlet.
5. Feature effective search tools.

RESEARCH AND DISCUSSION QUESTION

Your principal has given you the responsibility of preparing a policy ensuring that the school website and all its consistent pages are accessible under ADA guidelines. Prepare a policy that could be followed by a school district, and also prepare a short presentation for parents explaining the policy.

REFERENCES

Baumbach, Donna, Sally Brewer, and Matt Renfroe. "What Should Be on a School Library Web Page?" *Learning and Leading with Technology* 32, no. 1 (2004): 46–55.

Bromann-Bender, Jennifer. "You Can't Fool Me: Web Site Evaluation." *Library Media Connection* (March/April 2013): 42-45.

Burke, John J. *Neal-Schuman Library Technology Companion: A Basic Guide for Library Staff*. New York: Neal-Schuman, 2004.

"Evaluating Websites." Multnomah County Library. www.multcolib.org/homework/webeval.html.

"5 Things Every School Library Web Site Should Have." www.librarygirl.net/2011/08/5-things-every-school-library-website.html.

easybib.com

Gordon, Rachel Singer. *The Accidental Systems Librarian*. Medford, NJ: Information Today, 2003.

Janowski, Adam "Instant Web: Just Add Content," *School Library Journal* (January 2005). www.schoollibraryjournal.com.

Jurkowski, Odin L. "School Library Website Components." *Tech Trends* 48 no. 6 (2004): 56–60.

Jurkowski, Odin L. *Technology and the School Library: A Comprehensive Guide for Media Specialists and Other Educators*. Lanham, MD: Scarecrow, 2006.

Kennedy, Shirley Duglin. "Web Design that Won't Get You into Trouble." *Information Today*. www.infotoday.com/cilmag/jun01/kennedy.htm.

Kochtanek, Thomas R., and Joseph R. Matthews. *Library Information Systems: From Library Automation to Distributed Information Access Solutions*. Westport, CT: Libraries Unlimited, 2002.

Matthews, Joseph R. *Technology Planning: Preparing and Updating a Library Technology Plan*. Westport, CT: Libraries Unlimited, 2004.

Minkel, Walter. "Remaking Your Website in Seven Easy Steps." In *The Whole School Library Handbook*, edited by Blanche Woolls and David V. Loertscher, 192–193. Chicago, IL: ALA, 2005.

Rubenstein, Charles *Web Design for Libraries*. Santa Barbara, CA: Libraries Unlimited, 2015.

"School Library Web Site Development Tutorial." Iowatown School Library. http://krueger .uni.iowapages.org/tutorial.html.

Valenza, Joyce. "A Webquest about School Library Websites." Wikispaces. http://school librarywebsites.wikispaces.com.

Walbert, David. "Best Practices in School Library Website Design." LEARN NC. www .learnnc.org/lp/pages/969?style=print.

Warlick, David. "Building Web Sites That Work for Your Media Center," *Knowledge Quest* 33, no. 3 (2005). *MasterFILE Premier*. EBSCO. April 22, 2009. http://search .ebscohost.com.

Wholleb, Jennifer. "Twelve Essentials of a School District Website." *The School Administrator*. (May 2006). www.aasa.org/publications.

*Reliable Sources

Links to:

AR Rules
AR Book Find
Tumble Books/Ebooks
Story line Online
Encyclopedia Online Subscr.
Interesting Author Pages
Public Library Link

Open Hours
Book Lists
Catalog Link
Databases
Big 6 Research Process
- Bib Maker
- Copyright

*Google Classroom
— Ed. Websites for kids

* Lending Policy   *Catalog   *Citing Sources

10

Digital Libraries and Digital Collections

This chapter discusses the relationship of the digital library to traditional libraries and the concept of the digital library, as well as its potential effect on the school and library information seekers. Attention is given to how it fits in the scheme of education in the 21st century. It then focuses on online materials for the school library's digital collection.

DIGITAL LIBRARIES AS SUPPLEMENTS TO TRADITIONAL LIBRARIES

The school library must be the center of learning in the school. Dedicated school librarians have worked hard to overcome issues that sometimes made the library unavailable. School buses took children home, teacher unions frowned on school librarians staying after the end of the school day, and sometimes the library was closed so its space could be used for testing. Certainly in elementary schools, when the library becomes the release time for teacher preparation, resources are held hostage. The digital library is a solution to making resources available to students 24/7.

Traditional libraries no longer offer hard-copy reference sources for students. These are available online. Even the traditional fiction section is morphing into eBooks that students can read on their cell phones. It may well be that the traditional library has become a supplement to the digital library. But what is a digital library?

THE DIGITAL LIBRARY

A starting point for the discussion of digital libraries is that the definition is not an easy one. Early in the first decade of the explosion of the digital library, Borgman (1999) divided them in two: the researcher who considered the digital library "content collected on behalf of user communities" and the practitioners who considered them "institutions or services" (227). Certainly school librarians today would consider them both content for their communities and a service for their patrons.

Kochtanik, in his 2002 book *Library Information Systems*, defined a digital library as a library providing services in a digital realm (239). Many students in library science education programs since that time have used Kochtanek as a textbook, but this definition is no longer as broad as it should be. Not only does the definition vary, but digital libraries are often called by different names.

Most school librarians are well aware the possibilities offered by a digital library, sometimes called a virtual or electronic library or even a library without walls. They have constructed them on library websites, allowing teachers, staff, students and even parents to access and use electronic library resources available inside and outside the school. As described in chapter 9, a simple webpage can offer access only with a link to the catalog or, more detailed, through the OPAC and all other available electronic resources within the school. Most likely, the website has links to resources beyond the school. One has only to visit the wide array of school library websites to see the variety of digital libraries currently available growing in number.

CHARACTERISTICS OF AND CONSIDERATIONS FOR DIGITAL LIBRARIES

Kochtanek enumerated three characteristics considered to be the base of digital libraries. First, a digital library is a collection of texts, images, or data that have been digitized. This is limiting, because a digital library is a place to go to other websites far beyond a repository for digitized collections. It should be a collection of links to other data sources. Second, a digital library should have a system to index and navigate or retrieve information. This is where the school librarians' expertise in organizing information is essential. Third, a digital library should have at least one specified community of users—in this case, the users of the school library.

Let's consider two examples of very large digital libraries. The first is that part of the Internet, the World Wide Web, considered the world's largest digital library, even though it lacks much organization and doesn't have a good system to index it.

Another early digital library, Project Gutenberg, was a digitized book collection begun in 1971 at the University of Pennsylvania. Project Gutenberg still exists as a collection of electronic record of print materials no longer protected by copyright and thus in the public domain. Other worthwhile items digitized by Project Gutenberg are a wide variety of local history materials.

A current and controversial digital library was started by Google Books. Google has contracted with many of the nation's largest libraries to digitize their collections and make them available in the public domain. This entire concept has been challenged in the courts.

Considerations

From a theoretical viewpoint, there are considerations that must be dealt with when a school librarian is constructing a digital library. This is not just the usual colors, fonts, and appearance issues, but rather issues cutting to the heart of visual libraries.

1. An enormous number of digitized items are available. Which ones will you use? How will you use them? Will you provide and constantly monitor links to where they currently reside online so your users will not find they have disappeared? Of the huge number of digitized books out there, which will your users want, need, and use?
2. Tools are being—or already been—developed to allow you and your patrons to retrieve this networked information. Which of these tools do you need? Is there a cost associated with acquiring them?
3. Copyright issues associated with digital content have been discussed in an earlier chapter. How do you prevent access to resources that are protected by copyright? How do you ensure fair use?
4. Interoperability standards are in place. You may need to get help from the technology coordinator to make sure they are met.
5. The design of the digital library should be user-centered. As stated in the chapter on web design, this is not the time to add flashy things if they make it more difficult for the user or you.
6. Creating and maintaining a digital library requires a tremendous administrative commitment even when you have the skills to do it. It is certainly time to consider ways to make this a part of an eager student's service assignment. It does take a great deal of trust to turn a website over to a student, but this would be a great place for a student who has the technology skills and who may not fit into other areas of service.
7. Must funds be available for a digital library project? In today's educational funding arena, this is key, but not being able to offer a digital library means students may continue to surf the web without finding appropriate, relevant resources

As mentioned before, the digital library should be the beginning point of research in the school library and thus should be able to be customized by users so they have the resources they need at their disposal. In a digital library environment, users need the following tools:

1. A productivity suite. Microsoft Office, including PowerPoint, is the standard.
2. A wide variety of graphics programs. Over time, students have become more and more proficient with graphics programs.
3. The web creation software you or your district has settled on.
4. Communication tools, including email, chat, and Web 2.0 applications.
5. Foreign-language translation software.
6. Assistive technology for students requiring it.
7. Distance education software.
8. Management tools appropriate for teachers and library staff.

Push/Pull Technology

Early in the days of technology in libraries, it was thought that push technology would be the panacea for many technology issues, but that never came about. Push resources useful in customized environments include automatic notification software and a messaging system. Many educators do not like being contacted by a parent regularly, but it is an integral part of push technology.

Pull technology is web search engines allowing users to pull information in from the World Wide Web. Many users, teachers, and students think the only search engine is Google. Google is good, but there are other good search engines. You should consider metasearch engines such as Dogpile and search engines expressly designed for elementary school–age children.

DIGITAL LIBRARIES AND ONLINE EDUCATION

Ten years ago, any discussion of library services for online education was one properly for postsecondary education. This is no longer true. Cyberschools and digital schools are surfacing all over the country, some very successful. Students do not have to travel long distances on a daily basis, and many parents who wished they could homeschool their children are using this to substitute for their lack of teaching knowledge.

Online education will be discussed in some more detail in another chapter, but public schools are going to provide some online education, too, and this will do much to increase the chasm between the "haves" and the "have-nots" if electronic access is unequal. When a school district provides distance education, there is a concurrent obligation to provide online library services. Assistive funds are within the purview of the school administration, but school librarians need to remind the administration that students who no longer have in-house access to information must have it provided.

The solution to this issue comes from David Loertscher, in his article "The Digital School Library: A Worldwide Development and a Fascinating Challenge." He proposed that every school library in the world construct and deploy a webpage that would be "the central hub of information essential to every student and teacher" (109). This webpage would become the starting point for all information searching. Such an information system would be available on the Internet and would be available from home 24/7. This has, in the past, been a challenge for those homes where there is no Internet access. This is rapidly becoming less an issue, as most students have cell phones and can access their libraries as well as other information sources.

The chapter will end with a discussion of the advantages and disadvantages of a digital library. These will help in approaching administrators about the need for a website and the creation of a digital library if you still do not have one.

ADVANTAGES OF A DIGITAL LIBRARY

The most obvious advantage of a school library digital library is simple: Materials are available twenty-four hours a day, seven days a week. No more is access to information prohibited because there is class in the library, it is after 3:30, or the library is closed for testing. The digital library is always available. Loertscher suggested several other advantages of digital libraries in his article "The Digital School Library: A World-wide Development and a Fascinating Challenge":

1. A digital library provides a starting point for all research. An example of this is the Hempfield Area High School Library in Greensburg, Pennsylvania. Borrowing from an idea at the Bank Library at Point Park University in Pittsburgh, each student in the library at Hempfield had an Internet-connected computer with a complete range of tools and a workspace. This was the beginning point for research for Hempfield students.

2. State and federal requirements are in place to offer adequate and appropriate educational opportunities for all students. This includes such student groups such as those students being homeschooled, those physically challenged, or those who are incarcerated. The digital library is a positive force in providing these required educational opportunities, particularly for students who are incarcerated and may not be allowed open access to the Internet. An intranet digital library will offer them needed resources.

3. The digital library is ideal in support of students' receiving their schooling using distance education facilities. They aren't attending a brick-and-mortar school, and they may be some distance from any library.

4. Digital libraries provide excellent opportunities for a broad range of patrons to find appropriate research materials all in one place.

5. The access to information is not dependent on the patron being in one location. The digital library is available anywhere at any time.

6. Digital libraries need not be dependent on each user having a particular type of computer or even a computer at all. Digital library content can be made available through any computing device, including tablets and cell phones.

7. Digital libraries can be customized so users can have access to what they want and need to use.

8. Because of the range of resources available through a digital library, school librarians can search for and bookmark more germane information for students. No more Google searches yielding 10,000,000-plus hits.

9. The school librarian is in full control of the selection of materials for the digital library.

DISADVANTAGES OF A DIGITAL LIBRARY

There are few real disadvantages to having a digital library. Issues with the time and technical expertise required to construct and maintain it are challenges, but providing library access on a 24/7 basis trumps other issues. Loertscher pointed out some issues that might arise with digital libraries:

1. Access is really an equity issue. The same issue of access is one that bedevils print libraries. Until recently, it seemed that a digital library required a computer for use. That is no longer true, as any personal computing device can gain access to digital libraries. At one time, the goal was to put a computer in the hands of every student. Now it appears that providing every student with a personal computing device may accomplish the same thing in a more cost-efficient way.

2. The whole idea of how many resources are enough and, as a corollary, how much is too much is a consideration. However, school librarians can choose appropriate materials for assignments in the same way they used to place appropriate materials on a book truck and wheel it into the classroom means that it is really difficult to have too much materials in a digital library.

3. Cutting and pasting is a challenge in relation to the web and plagiarism. This was discussed in the chapter dealing with copyright, but

the school librarian, in collaboration with teachers, can be helpful in making sure assignments are such that critical thinking occurs and the creation of new information becomes a part of the final product.

4. Moving students away from Google as a sole source will remain a challenge if assignments allow simple cutting and pasting or even getting a paper from the web.

5. The conflict between fair use guidelines and what is in a digital library remains a challenge.

6. Books as we know them continue to be used in schools today. As more and more children arrive in elementary school almost totally immersed in a digital environment, they may ignore hard-copy items. Only time will tell.

7. Budget drives all educational decisions. Digital libraries can cost more than traditional print libraries, but if you look at a 24/7 digital library, how do you compare those costs for access to information found in a traditional print library open approximately eight hours per day and never when school is out for holidays?

DIGITAL LIBRARIES TODAY AND HOW TO CREATE ONE

In a 2011 article, Tom Corbett discussed the changes in the role of the physical library:

[A]s the century unfolds, students will probably rely almost exclusively on electronic resources for their research and reading. In fact, the digitization of information (and entertainment) was already a defining characteristic of this "Information Age" and quite natural to the "digital natives" born into this era. It quickly became clear to our policymakers that the institution on campus already established to support research and reading would need to fully embrace this new reality. That institution is the library.

These goals can be accomplished by focusing on three important tasks:

1. Change the school library software platform by moving away from traditional Integrated Library System (ILS) functionality and toward a platform that is better integrated with newer Web services, including a best-in-class federated searching service;

2. Develop an improved acquisitions model that leverages the unique attributes of digital content; and

3. Transform the library's physical space into a collaborative work area that celebrates information gathering, analysis, and sharing. (Corbett 2011)

The technology-savvy school librarian takes big steps toward making the digital library a reality. In fact, the physical space becomes less important than the tools to access data in that space.

In 2013, Elisabeth Abarbanel, Sarah Davis, Dorcas Hand, and Matthew Wittmer published an article discussing the role of connecting digital resources and academic success. This could as well have been included in chapter 2, but the implications for digital libraries are evident. Of particular note is a table they constructed defining what is "hot" and what is not with relation to today's school library users.

This discussion of digital libraries is the first part of the opportunity to offer students wide access to materials outside their libraries. However, the school librarian still needs to make intelligent decisions about what to put into that digital library. This is covered in the next chapter.

RESEARCH AND DISCUSSION QUESTION

You are considering constructing a digital library for your school. Your two options are to prepare it as an Intranet or place it on the Internet. Prepare a paper evaluating the value of each option, along with a recommendation for presentation to your school administration.

REFERENCES

Abarbanel, Elisabeth, Sarah Davis, Dorcas Hand, and Matthew Wittmer. "The New School Library: The Human Connection to Digital Resources and Academic Success." *Independent School Magazine* (summer 2013). http://blog.schoollibrarymedia.com/index.php/2013/06/20/the-new-school-library-in-independent-school-magazine/comment-page-1/.

Borgman, Christine L. "What Are Digital Libraries? Competing Visions." *Information Processing and Management* (1999): 227–243.

Corbett, Tom. "The Changing Role of the School Library's Physical Space." *School Library Monthly* (April 2011).

Craver, K. *Creating Cyber Libraries: An Instructional Guide for School Library Media Specialist.* Greenwood Village, CO: Libraries Unlimited, 2002.

Kochtanik, T., and Matthews, J. *Library Information Systems: From Library Automation to Distributed Information Access Solutions.* Westport, CT: Libraries Unlimited, 2002.

Loertscher, D. "The Digital School Library: A Worldwide Development and a Fascinating Challenge." In Esther Rosenfeld and D. Loertscher, editors, *Toward a 21st Century School Library Media Program*, 108–117. Lanham, MD: Scarecrow Press.

11

Online Materials for the School Library

The previous chapter discussed the concept of the digital library. This chapter will address the information that should be available in your digital library, the content, and where you find that content. The digital library becomes the portal for your OPAC. Other content will include of subscription databases, and eJournals, the hidden web, and the use of Google Scholar and Google Earth. This chapter will not provide a recommended list of specific websites. By the time the book is published, many of those websites could have changed their URL or have disappeared altogether. You, like other school librarians, need to troll the Internet and find the online materials necessary for your teachers and students. It will provide some of the pros and cons of provided electronic access to your digital library.

The early 1990s saw the creation of digital libraries. Then there was some agreement about the general types of things that should be available on a school library's digital library. This chapter describes what should actually be available through your digital library. Briefly speaking, these include the following:

1. Resources supporting all of the educational needs of your patrons.
2. Resources to inform, motivate, or inspire your patrons.
3. Information literacy resources.
4. Resources to improve the value of the Internet for your patrons.
5. Links to other resources on the Internet.

This chapter describes what should actually be available through your digital library.

DIGITAL CONTENT: GENERAL CONSIDERATIONS

Loertscher provided a general starting point and some perspectives about the digital content required for an effective digital library. At the very center would be the core collection. This would closely resemble the core collection in a non-digital library and would provide the tools necessary for the majority of the information needs of school library patrons.

The second component of the digital library collection would be the materials related to the curriculum of the school. Of necessity, this would differ from school to school but might include curriculum-related e-books and databases, subject-specific reference materials, and any other digital materials supporting the curriculum of the school. It is in this phase that the contents of the digital library would begin to diverge.

The divergence becomes even more significant as you move into what Loertscher calls the "elastic collection." This is an innovative idea that would give the school librarian control over the contents of the digital library at any particular time. In this concept, school libraries could "rent" materials for the period of time when they are needed. The renting could range from expensive, extensive reference materials needed for only a few weeks for research to large numbers of copies of newly released popular fiction. The whole concept of the digital library could accommodate this "rental" idea; whether vendors would embrace the idea remains to be seen.

As mentioned before, the digital library should be the beginning point of research in the school library and thus should be able to be customized by users so that they have at their disposal the resources they need. The first category of resource users would need in a digital library would be tools:

1. A productivity suite. You are going to have to bite the bullet here and go with Microsoft Office (including PowerPoint). This is the standard.
2. A wide variety of graphics programs. Over time, students have become more and more proficient with graphics programs.
3. Whatever web creation software your district has settled on.
4. Communication tools, including email, chat, and Web 2.0 applications.
5. Foreign-language translation software.
6. Assistive technology for students who require it.
7. Distance education software.
8. For teachers, whatever management tools are appropriate.

The actual digital content is added from a variety of areas.

DIGITAL CONTENT: RESOURCES AND SPECIFIC AREAS

Digital library content may be organized in four categories. These are free websites, content developed by the school library, school library–developed interactive services, and fee-based electronic resources (Craver, 18). A digital library could have all four categories or have only one. This outline is expanded when appropriate.

1. Free websites. This category can be as extensive or as limited as the school librarian prefers. Early in the digital library creation process, the tendency was to include anything that looked even remotely good. As time passes, however, librarians became more selective and used only the best sites. Two things are crucial when you are including free websites in a digital library. First, make sure the links work! Check them often, and get rid of those that don't. Second, include a brief description of the website you have added. Users are less than eager to click on links with no description. Craver made some suggestions about the type of websites adding value to a digital library:

   a. Full-text sites
   b. Reference sites tailored to the age of your students
   c. Age-appropriate primary sources from the wide range of social studies primary source materials
   d. Interactive sites
   e. Instructional interactive sites for things such as bibliography creation or literacy tutorials
   f. Visual and auditory sites (19)

2. Internally developed content. This includes information specific to your library; however, much of the challenge in the creation of the digital library is making the library developed content attractive and accessible. Craver's article suggests including the following specific types of library developed content:

   a. General introductory information about the school library. This is an area that requires constant monitoring to ensure that information is timely and accurate.
   b. Policies and procedures developed by the library and approved by the governing body.
   c. Descriptions of special programs offered in the school library. This could include such things as reading competitions and special displays.
   d. Bibliographies and reading lists. These are lists you develop and those added by teachers, all supporting the curriculum.
   e. Web quests and library skill units. Using templates here can be beneficial.
   f. Forms for the patrons to use to request services. This is not as simple as it sounds, so you may need help with this.
   g. Reference services and term paper assistance.
   h. Your periodical holdings list (20).

3.   School library–developed interactive services. These types of services can be difficult to construct and even harder to maintain. They will yield great value but should be approached with caution:
   a.   Electronic reference assistance. This generally is most effective as an email service or as a blog.
   b.   Online request forms. As stated above, these are difficult to create and, in a situation with limited staff, difficult to fulfill. These may include library material requests or hold requests, and reservation forms for class or library instruction.
   c.   Interlibrary loan. This is best handled by a state or consortium program (21).

4.   Featured electronic services. This mostly features your OPAC and other electronic databases. They need to be a part of your digital library and if at all possible, they should available for home access.
   a.   Your OPAC. The OPAC is the single most important piece of online material in your digital library, because it has evolved into what some would call "one-stop shopping." Depending on the OPAC, when a student enters a search term, the OPAC can search the following:
      • The school's catalog
      • The catalogs for all schools in the school district
      • The public library's catalog
      • A statewide catalog
      • Links to colleges and universities around the world
      • The fee-based databases available, including periodical databases
      • Web sites vetted for credibility and reliability
   b.   Databases. These are defined as a collection of information on one or more related topics. The first electronic databases most school librarians worked with was one of the following: Orbit, Dialog, or BRS. These were not intuitive and often required a direct modem dial-up connection to access them. The searching costs were so high that often school librarians were the only people who could search economically.
        Today, commercial databases are available from a variety of vendors, such as Newsbank for newspapers and ABC-CLIO for curriculum-related subjects.
        The development of the periodical database began with computer-searchable versions of print products. Then links were developed between bibliographic citations and full-text articles. Now actual full-text magazine articles can be saved, printed, or even e-mailed depending on what the subscription allows. The three preeminent full-text periodical databases are Proquest, Gale, and EBSCO.

c. Trial subscriptions to databases. Vendors are often eager to provide trials to database. The caution here is to make sure your teachers and students know they are trials and may disappear, sometimes mid-project.

d. Online general references such as encyclopedias and dictionaries.

e. Subject specific database such as the American National Biography or SIRS.

f. Educational portals such as Bigchalk (23).

These are basic things to include in a digital library, but as you look at some of the digital libraries available, you will see a wide range of types of resources that provide a great deal of value to both your student and adult patrons. Another benefit of the digital library is the ability to provide resources in specific areas on the curriculum that may not be deemed as important as the major areas of history, literature, and social sciences:

- The arts. Because art materials are tremendously expensive and are often less widely used, an arts website can be a real money saver and even expand access to information about the art world.

- College information. Links to financial aid sources will be especially helpful in the high school. Students will also need access to the College Board site.

- Economics and business. Tremendous amounts of this type of information are available online. Much of the work of the classical economists is out of copyright and is available digitally, which is very helpful to high school teachers and students, as well as to parents.

- Education. This area is of great value to your principal and to other staff members, particularly those pursuing advanced degrees.

- Foreign language and cultures. This type of information has value for background and reference information for those studying geography, taking foreign languages, and wanting material in foreign languages.

- Geography. Although the study of geography seems to be in a decline, geographic concepts are very important in our society. World locations are very much a part of the daily news.

- Government and politics. Of particular note in this category are the digitized versions of almost any government publication.

- Health, medicine, and family. This is a bit of a catch-all category, but these resources have value in health and family and consumer science courses.

- History. The range of history primary sources is wide and varied.

- Homework helpers.
- Kids' links. Make sure they are age-appropriate for your students.
- Library links. This is a resource area that will probably be used only by you and your library staff.
- Literature. The World Wide Web has many good literature sites. Consider linking items in readings lists to author sites and criticism sites.
- Mathematics. The real test here is to include applicable sites for all levels of math taught in the school but not include things so complex that students are beyond their depth.
- Media. This is a great category for students and teachers! Be sure to include all local newspapers with a web presence, as well as other major media outlets, such as television and radio outlets.
- Writing. This is a great category for students writing papers. Include dictionaries, thesauri, and other author helps.
- Reference. This will undoubtedly be the largest area in your digital library site. Gone is the hard-copy reference collection. Everything is available somewhere online. Be careful here, though, because reference sites come and go with some regularity, and some are less accurate than others. Your teachers may refuse to let students use Wikipedia as a source.
- Religion and mythology. These resources, particularly those dealing with religion, can be controversial. Review the curriculum for appropriate topics, and review any sites you include in the digital library.
- Science. Many science education websites are available. Visit the science section of the Glenbrook North High School (Illinois) website to see what a creative school librarian can do with science.
- Sports and recreation. Some suggested resources here might be the websites of local professional and college teams, along with links to your school's teams. Recreation links should also provide local recreational opportunities or a link to the public library website that provides this information.
- Travel. This broad category includes travel sites of interest to students, parents, and school staff.
- Search engines. Links to search engines should be at a high level in the digital library. It seems difficult to recommend one over another, but as a minimum, Google should be there along with at least one metasearch engine. This is a category you can experiment with, adding new search engines as they appear and deleting those that are of less value (83).

ONLINE PERIODICAL DATABASES: ADVANTAGES AND DISADVANTAGES

Online periodical databases have many advantages and disadvantages, particularly when they are full-text online periodical databases. First the advantages:

1. Ease of search. This advantage is similar to one offered by OPACs as opposed to traditional card catalogs. In the past, in a print periodical index such as the *Readers Guide to Periodical Literature* there was searching only by author, title, and subject. With online periodical indexes, there are many more search options, with a major improvement being the ability to search by keyword.

2. Availability of full text in all holdings. With electronic databases, the full text is there. No more does the citation list a magazine not in the library's subscription list—or even if a copy should be available, point to a missing issue or one in which someone has removed the article from the magazine. Not all periodical databases provide full-text articles, but this would be the choice for most school library users who are seeking more than a bibliography.

3. Wider services. These include the ability to save an article, print an article, or email an article. They also provide a disadvantage that will be noted later—the ability to copy and paste a passage or an entire article.

4. Accessibility to multiple users 24/7. Students no longer have to wait to read an article another student was using. With the proper contract, online periodical databases are available for an unlimited number of users simultaneously. In addition, online periodical databases are available for outside-library use 24/7.

5. Space saving. School librarians no longer need to keep extensive periodical back files to satisfy research requests.

6. Cheaper and easier to update location information. With online periodical indexes, the update is part of the subscription, is seamless, and is often done daily.

Even with all of these positive statements about online periodical index, there are some downsides also:

1. Expensive initial costs. Some administrators and school board members can be put off by the high initial costs, but the school librarian can point out the broader coverage and lower cost per title.

2. Downtime. Even the best computer networks have downtime.

3. Searching is easy; browsing is hard. Today's students are used to instant results, and they will not see the value of browsing related topics. Browsing is very difficult with online periodical databases.

4. Loss of information sources over time. The coverage in online periodical databases can change as years pass. Some sources are added and some removed. You cannot control it, and a good technique to counter the negative effects is to keep a running list of titles added or deleted.

5. Ability to cut and paste. The ease of transfer of words, sentences, and paragraphs makes it a constant battle to keep teaching about copyright and the meaning of plagiarism.

Burke has provided additional issues that school librarians must consider in providing online databases:

1. Authentication. Typically no authentication other than IP recognition is required to access electronic periodical databases inside the school's firewall. Home access generally requires a user ID and password, because vendors do not want to give their content away. The license for the database will outline what this means, and students and parents need to be aware that the database is legally not available to a sibling home from college for the holiday or Aunt Mabel who would like to read about a health issue.

2. Technology requirements. Make sure all computers within the school meet the database's technology requirements. You should also provide the technology requirements to parents in the district.

3. Cost. As stated above, online databases are costly, and their purchase is unavoidable if you want to provide access to your students. One way to overcome this is to join a consortium for the purchase of databases. This can be as small as the district and the public library. Vendors may negotiate consortium discount prices for online databases. Second, some states provide these types of databases to all the libraries at no charge. It becomes a very economical service for the constituents in a government area, and the concerted efforts of librarians in all types of libraries should be turned to this as a project. Everyone benefits.

4. Canceling print services. Canceling the print version of magazines because they are in a full-text online database remains an issue all school librarians must consider. Doing this saves money from your print budget and can also save you storage room for back issues. Many school libraries now limit their print magazine subscriptions to what could be considered recreational reading and retain back issues for a limited amount of time. The challenge comes when titles are deleted from the database or, worst of all, the funds for the database disappear. This leads to a situation in which key titles are no longer available electronically or are no longer available in the school library.

5. Training to use the databases. Online database have much less value if users have trouble accessing the content. Training should be provided by the vendor, and school librarians pass this along to teachers and students. Students can also be trained to help teachers and other students conduct searches.

PLANNING TO PURCHASE DATABASE SUBSCRIPTIONS

Because of the cost of online database subscriptions, care must be taken in their selection. Peterson's plan is a decade old, but it puts a form to the process of selecting and purchasing databases:

1. Prepare a plan. The plan for the purchase of these products should be considered in your overall collection development plan.
2. Analyze the needs of both your students, teachers, and administrators. In particular, analyze whether the product fits the curriculum.
3. Analyze the product to determine potential management benefits to your school library. These benefits can range from financial benefits to space savings.
4. Attempt to link to a consortium for cost savings. As discussed above, many vendors will offer substantial savings for volume purchasing, and they sometimes offer discounts for extended term subscriptions of the school's budgeting process allows this.
5. Compare products to see how they will function in your library. A good way to do this is to ask for a trial period. Most reliable vendors will allow a trial period to test the need for, usefulness, and ease of use of the database with users. A table similar to the one developed by Peterson and shown below can help you in your comparison:

Vendor	Vendor1	Vendor2	Vendor3, etc...
Product			
Technical Support			
Admin Rights			
User Statistics			
Minimum Browser			
Requirements			
Home Access			
Print/Email/Download			
Training/Tutorials			

6. Evaluate the product. Make sure that as many who will be using the database have an opportunity to evaluate it. You promote the product and ask people to use it and evaluate it. Although a short period of time may not be enough to get thorough testing by teachers, unless the product fulfills many of your library needs, closely consider how your users evaluate it. If they don't like it or have issues with the product, perhaps you need to reevaluate whether it is a good purchase.
7. Negotiate a purchase price with the vendor. This is a true negotiation, because the vendor wants to sell the product, and you will have a limited budget to spend.
8. Promote the product to all stakeholders. After purchase, demonstrate the database to groups of teachers. If it is a database with wide potential use, share it at teachers' meetings, demonstrating the use of the product in the teaching process.

EJOURNALS

In the previous section, we dealt with full-text electronic periodical databases. In reality, this is the biggest piece of the eJournal pie. The vast majority of research publications that are available in a full text format are available in these databases. However, more sources are available for eJournals. Some of these are fee-based, others free. Often the publishers of journals will provide a website with links to both the current issue and, in many cases, to some or all of the journal's back issues. These websites can be of value but often do not have a search capability, so the searcher must have an issue date for an article, or it will be necessary to browse issues to find what is needed.

THE INVISIBLE WEB

The invisible web is also known as the deep web, the dark web, or the hidden web. What this all means is the greatest part of the web cannot be accessed using subject directories or standard search engines. In the early days of the web, certain pages were invisible to browsers and subject directories:

1. The pages were in non-HTML format.
2. The pages had scripts that contained a ? or other script coding.
3. Pages that were generated dynamically by other types of database software.

It has been estimated that there are more than 500 times as many websites in what is called the invisible web than there are in the "regular" searchable web. It is estimated that the web has more than 550 billion pages, with only about 1 billion accessible in the visible web.

As a general rule, invisible web resources can be shown to fall into one of the following categories:

1. Pages that contain dynamic content. These are pages returned in response to a query or accessed through a form.
2. Pages not linked to any other pages. This prevents web crawlers from getting to the content. These are typically single pages users have placed on the web.
3. Private websites that require a registration and a password.
4. Pages whose content varies by how they are accessed.
5. Websites that limit access to the pages by some technical means.
6. Pages only accessible through links created by JavaScript or another computer language.
7. Pages created in file formats not handled by search engines.

These categories seem to be invisible in themselves. Perhaps it would be better to say that a great deal of invisible web content is databases, but that might be overstating it a bit. Sherman and Price put together a list of the "Top 25" invisible web categories. If you were searching for the type of information contained in the categories listed below, you would be far better served searching the invisible web rather than the visible web because there are far more resources available.

1. Public company filings. These are documents the Securities and Exchange Commission requires to be filed on a periodic basis.
2. Telephone numbers. Currency is a major issue when using this type of database.
3. Customized maps and driving directions. This was once the exclusive preview of Mapbeast and Mapquest, but other sites, notably Google Earth and Google Maps, now provide this capability.
4. Clinical trials. Clinical trials for both for the researcher and the person who wants to participate in clinical trials are available here.
5. Patent information. This is an invaluable series of sites for anyone involved in the invention process.
6. Out-of-print Books. These sites give librarians and individuals the ability to search for and purchase out-of-print books.
7. Library Catalogs. Thousands of OPACs are available on the invisible web.
8. Authoritative dictionaries. The range from general dictionaries such as Merriam Webster's to very specialized, technical dictionaries.

9. Environmental information. Much more about the environment is available on the web than in print sources.

10. Historical stock quotes. These, according to some financial experts, have some predictive value.

11. Historical documents and images. These items are ideal for education. Many can be found at the Library of Congress American Memory Project (memory.loc.gov).

12. Company directories. This includes such formerly proprietary information as Hoover's and the Thomas Register.

13. Searchable subject bibliographies. These can have great pieces of information for the researcher.

14. Economic information. Because much of this information is in databases, it is part of the invisible web.

15. Award winners. These are lists from novel prizes to Emmy Awards.

16. Job postings. Although listed here, these are almost impossible to find on the visible web. Use Careerbuilder.com or Flipdog.

17. Grant information. In periods of economic belt-tightening, these resources can be "golden" for school librarians.

18. Translation tools. Sometimes they are almost too literal, but they continue to improve as time passes.

19. Postal codes. This includes not only ZIP Codes for the United States, but also postal codes from around the world.

20. Basic demographic information. This includes U.S. census information.

21. Interactive school finders. These sites try to match qualifications with schools.

22. Campaign financing information. The most comprehensive information comes from the Federal Elections Commission (www.fec.gov/finance_reports.html).

23. Weather data. Accuweather, which began as a government website, is a strong presence here.

24. Product catalogs. Some retailer websites are on the visible web, others on the invisible web.

25. Art gallery holdings.

We have listed and discussed categories of information that are generally part of the invisible web. That still begs the question of when and why one would use the invisible web. As a rule, you probably would use the invisible web when one of the following conditions is true:

1. You are familiar with the topic and think there is more information available than what you are seeing in the visible web.

2. You have a high level of expertise with search tools, such as searching using Boolean logic.
3. You don't want millions of hits; you want a precise answer.
4. You want all authoritative hits in an exhaustive search.
5. Timeliness is important.

Two issues remain with our examination of the web—first, what is not available in either the visible or invisible web and second, what tools will allow you to find information on the invisible web. First, we consider what is typically not available on either the visible or invisible web.

1. Proprietary databases and information sources. This is only available to paying subscribers.
2. Many government and public records. Individual privacy rights often trump the right to know.
3. Scholarly journals. High-priced scholarly journals are, for the most part, not available on the web.
4. Full text of all newspapers and magazines. This is changing somewhat, but authors' rights are unclear in this area.

The table below that provides some tools for searching the invisible web. This is adopted from Ian Smith, and the reader is cautioned that it may take a combination of these tools to actually find what you are looking for.

Tool	Description
Complete Planet	Tool is best used to search, not browse
Direct Search	Gets to the invisible web as regular search engines cannot.
Fossick.com	More than 3,500 specialty databases, mostly academic
Informine	Focuses exclusively on academic resources on the invisible web
Internet Oracle	Form and database search tool
Invisible Web.com	More than 11,000 specialized databases
Webdata.com	A database portal

GOOGLE SCHOLAR AND GOOGLE EARTH

The final section of this chapter will describe briefly two online tools to expand the use of your webpage or your digital library. Although these are not the only good online materials out there, they are two of the best. You should not be limited to them and should search for other online resources for use by your students and teachers.

Google Scholar

Google Scholar is an access point that allows your teachers and students to conduct broad searches of the scholarly literature. Google Scholar searches almost all academic disciplines and includes peer-reviewed papers, articles, theses, abstracts, and books. The material comes from academic publishers, preprint repositories, professional societies, and colleges and universities. Google Scholar allows the researcher to do the following:

1. Search many sources with one search.
2. Locate papers, abstracts, and citations.
3. Locate entire papers either on the web or in your library.
4. See what is being published in your academic areas of interest.

Google Earth

Google Earth is one of those online programs we have all seen, at the very least on news programs that use satellite representations to show locations of news events. Its powerful features make it an ideal online resource for students and teachers alike.

Google Earth is an interactive program allowing users to see a 3D version of geographical locations. It provides an aerial view of the location and increases or decreases magnification as desired. It also provides an alternative view available from Google Maps. Different layers can be added to the presentation to show different information. The program itself can be downloaded and used for free. A wide variety of helper applications are available for Google Earth to enhance its value in the library or classroom.

Russell Tarr, in his 2006 article in *History Review* titled "Using 'Google Earth' in the History Classroom," showed several applications:

1. Using Google Earth to enhance history
   a. Using terrains or overlays. These, obtained from the web, give students a geographic understanding of historical sites.
   b. Using 3D models. These are beginning to come into more common use as time passes.
   c. Tours using flyovers.
2. Obtaining existing resources

    a. Google Earth History Illustrated Community (bbs.keyhole.com)
    b. Google Earth Hacks: Historical Placemarks (www.googleearth hacks.com/dict40)
3. Aids for creating your own resources
    a. Sketchupp: 30 Model Creator (sketcup.google.com)
    b. Tagzania: Create collaborative tours as a classroom project (www .tagzania.com)
    c. Flickr Map: Geotag the photographs of your field trips (www.flick-rmap.com)

RESEARCH AND DISCUSSION QUESTION

Your director of library services has asked you to review different options for full-text online periodical databases. You are currently using EBSCOhost, and there is really no implication that EBSCO-host is not satisfactory—just a desire to see what else is available. The director wants you to prepare both a position paper and a PowerPoint presentation comparing the three major players in the market: EBSCO, Proquest, and Gale. Use the points developed in this chapter to compare these three products.

REFERENCES

"About Google Scholar." Google http://scholar.google.com/intl/en/scholar/about.html.

Botluk, Diana. "Features-Mining Deeper into the Invisible Web." *LLRX.* www.llrx.com/node/1054/print.

Brisco, Shonda. "Internet or Database?" *Library Media Connection* (February 2006): 44–45

Burke, John J. *Neal-Schuman Library Technology Companion: A Basic Guide for the Library Staff*, 2nd ed. New York: Neal-Schuman, 2006.

Craver, K. *Creating Cyber Libraries: An Instructional Guide for School Library Media Specialist.* Greenwood Village, CO: Libraries Unlimited. 2002.

"Invisible or Deep Web: What It Is, How to Find It, and Its Inherent Ambiguity." University of California. www.lib.berkeley/edu/TeachingLib/Guides/Internet/InvisibleWeb.html.

Jurkowski, Odin L. *Technology and the School Library: A Comprehensive Guide for Media Specialists and Other Educators.* Lanham, MD: Scarecrow, 2006.

Kochtanek, Thomas R., and Joseph R. Matthews. *Library Information Systems: From Library Automation to Distributed Information Access Solutions.* Westport, CT: Libraries Unlimited, 2002.

Lackie, Robert J. "Those Deep Hiding Places: The Invisible Web Revealed." www.robert-lackie.com/invisible/index.html.

Lamdgraf, Tedd, and Ronald Weaver. "At the Center: The Library in the Wired School." *Netconnect* (winter 2003): 12–14

Loertscher, David V. "The Digital School Library: A Worldwide Development and a Fascinating Challenge," in *Toward a 21st Century School Library Media Center*, edited by Esther Rosenfeld and David Loertscher, 108–117. Lanham, MD: Scarecrow Press, 2007.

Peterson, Janet Walker. "Stretch Your Budget! How to Select Web-Based Subscription Resources," *Computers in Libraries* (February 2003). *MasterFILE Premier*. EBSCO. April 22, 2009. http://search.ebscohost.com.

Rice, Marilyn, Daphne Johnson, and Michelle Pierczynski-Ward. "Google Earth." (n.d.): 12–15.

Smith Ian. "The Invisible Web: Where Search Engines Fear to Go." www.powerhomebiz .com/vol25/invisible.htm.

Tarr, Russel. "Using 'Google Earth' in the History Classroom." *History Review* (December 2006): 26–27.

Woolls, Blanche, and David V. Loertscher, eds. *The Whole School Library Handbook*. Chicago, IL: ALA, 2005.

12

Electronic Books (eBooks)

According to Church, an electronic book, or eBook is "a digital version of a traditional print book designed to be read on a personal computer or an eBook reader." What a simple definition for such a large and changing field! Many educators and librarians thought that the eBook would eliminate the need for each student to have a textbook and perhaps even mean the end of the book as we know it. We now know that both of these things have yet to happen. This chapter describes the book in a digital environment and explains how collections are chosen.

A very thorough introduction to eBooks in school libraries was developed and published in 2013 by the Minnesota Library Association, whose position statement on digital content and eBooks in school library collections is titled "eBooks and School Libraries." Many of the points made in this document are expanded below. All school librarians who aspire to move to the leading edge in technology and make their jobs essential in their schools should read and absorb these statements:

1. Ensure that the library's selection policy covers not just print material but also electronic resources;
2. Figure out the best mix for purchasing materials including electronic resources;
3. Know all parts of your school community;
4. Insure equity of access to library materials for all school stakeholders;
5. Purchase portable devices that serve the e-book needs of all stakeholders;
6. Review the physical capabilities of all students before buying electronic computing devices.

7. Carefully review the e-book packages offered by vendors to make sure they meet your library's needs.
8. Never forget! Not all books are available in e-book format-don't forget your print collection;
9. Have a method of replacing outmoded electronic devices lest they become expensive door stops;
10. Select e-book materials that account for all student abilities;
11. Allow BYOD;
12. Do not allow collection of student data without parental and/or school board approval;
13. Publicize the e-books you purchase. (E-Books)

On June 6, 2013, the American Association of School Librarians (AASL) adopted its "Position Statement on Digital Content and E-Books in School Library Collections" to help school librarians prepare to work in a digital environment. This paper provided fifteen ways to accomplish the mission to provide "anytime/anywhere access to reliable digital content" (Position Statement). It provided a more up-to-date definition, greatly expanded from Church's:

> Digital content is any content that is published in digital form. This includes online encyclopedias, digital textbooks, ad subscription databases that contain keyword-searchable articles and/or e-books. Digital content is accessed via the Internet and subscription databases; it may be leased or purchased directly from vendors. Such content may be downloaded. (Position Statement)

eBooks are read on an increasing number of digital devices including computer screens, proprietary e-readers, tablets or other mobile devices including cell phones, and they may offer hyperlinks to other resources. eBooks may be purchased, but some are limited to specific proprietary digital readers; others may be downloaded from public domains. Those in the public domain may be free. Others may be borrowed from resources purchased through the school library's subscription services.

The question is no longer whether to buy eBooks for the collection, but which ones to buy, what content to provide for them, and how the content will be delivered. If you and your students have access to any of the devices listed above from computer screens to cell phones, you may not need to buy any. In schools with a "Bring Your Own Device" (BYOD) policy, this does not matter. However, because many schools have some students who do not have their own devices, some consideration is given to the purchase of a device.

SELECTING DEVICES TO RECEIVE EBOOKS

The first consideration might be choosing the device providing the highest return on your investment. Proprietary bookstore e-readers such as the Kindle or Nook are very restrictive and allow users to download only content from the manufacturer's holding. Some proprietary tablets offer Internet access, which allows users to access other digital content through an Internet browser. The downside of the tablet—e.g., iOS, Android, Windows—over the bookstore e-reader is that tablet computers cost twice as much as bookstore e-readers, and they offer more than twice the functionality unless you are purchasing an upgrade Kindle or Nook. No matter the price tag, you must try to find the device that will best serve your patrons.

Although such devices are costly, prices are dropping. One of the most used eBook readers on the market is the Kindle, a reader sold by Amazon and using Amazon's own proprietary software. Amazon allows the downloading of books to the Kindle for about $5 a book. This is probably the closest to a standard that exists in the eBook field. The prices for the Kindle have dropped over the years since it was introduced, and the most expensive Kindle now sells for $199, with others priced at $79 and $119. The main competitor to the Kindle is the Nook, which is sold by Barnes and Noble. Pricing is competitive with the Kindle and, generally speaking, the same eBooks are available. Other personal computing devices such as the iPad have apps available for eBooks. In fact, there are apps for the iPad or iPhone that allow the downloading and use of both Amazon and Barnes and Noble content.

Deciding which device will serve the learning community best is contingent upon the school's user base and curriculum. The best way to find out the preferences of your user base is to ask them: students, teachers, administration, and, because many are providing devices for their children, parents. A very important question to ask parents is: "What devices do you have for your students to use in your home and the number?" One tablet for a family with three children might not be enough if that is the only access they have to read eBook content. If BYOD is voluntary, are these parents willing for their children to bring devices to school?

Other in-school decisions affect device selection. What computing devices are present on campus? To what extent do they support the access and download of digital content for all learners on campus? Does the campus provide an infrastructure robust enough to support the devices under consideration? Will students be able to download content without straining the current system? To what extent can the school/district rely on cloud computing for retrieving digital content? The issue of cloud computing was discussed in detail in chapter 5.

What existing policies will affect the use of devices under consideration? Is there a plan in place to modify network filters and firewalls to accommodate school-owned Wi-Fi? Is the use of student-owned devices in place or under consideration (BYOD)?

Are there platform preferences to consider? For example, what platform should a Windows-based, Google Apps school in an iOS-centric community choose for its mobile technology? How will this affect access to and downloading of digital content both on- and off-campus? School staff may decide against aligning their platform choice with the community preference, but it should factor community preference into the rollout process in terms of justification, marketing, professional development, and instruction.

[handwritten margin note: Platform Preferences can create problems]

Budgets are always a concern, and aligning a school district budget for mobile/digital learning can be a challenge. School district budgets must offer the flexibility to adapt to emerging software and hardware changes without losing access to digital content. The budget should include

- acquisition of e-content,
- maintenance of that access, and
- ongoing device access (i.e., apps, e-reader devices, or computers.)

How many or how much is always a consideration when it comes to the quantity of devices and digital content that a school library should purchase. When a program is in place, all students will require access to eBooks and digital content, meaning sufficient digital access available on campus to ensure that every student can successfully access digital content and produce work using digital tools. The school library must provide enough workstations and the corresponding mobile technology to meet individual, group, and class learning needs, especially if the campus does not have a BYOD program in place.

Grade level plays a role in digital content and device acquisitions. Some devices may be easier for very young children to hold and manipulate, whereas others offer features better suited to prepare learners for college and career. Elementary students are less likely to have their own device than older students.

Schools must align policy with practice where Wi-Fi access and data plans are involved. Student-owned technology is often used in the school library, making it advisable that school librarians(s) participate with administration in policy update discussions. Network access plays a role in filtering student-owned technology as long as the device uses the network. In some school districts (1:1: schools with 1:1 programs) each student is provided with mobile technology. In this model, the school district has more control over how devices are monitored and filtered.

In lower economic area school districts, administrators will need to know just how much they can rely on parents to provide BYOD support. Although students may not have a tablet, more and more children have cell phones to download content.

No technology should be considered if it doesn't support a curricular need or if its use is limited to only a part of the student body. Students with special needs, such as vision or hearing, must be accommodated.

SELECTING CONTENT IN EBOOKS

The selection process has some differences for eBooks and digital content from the hard-copy resources. A book has a table of contents and an index, and moving from one to the other means looking in the front or the back of the book. Some of the criteria can be applied to hard copy, such as the comparison of cost from one object to another and the reliability of the content, but some are very different, such as what devices support the content. Also, the preferences of the user must be taken into account.

- Is it easy to search for specific topics in the eBook?
- Does the content load quickly? We are living in an age that expects instant gratification.
- Is the content reliable? If the content can be revised, who is doing the revision?
- Which devices support the content?
- How does the cost of the resource compare with that of similar products?
- Are there other products that offer the same content?
- Is the content more accessible to students in digital form, or will print be just as good?
- Will students want the electronic version or the print version of that particular text?
- Is it available in electronic format for simultaneous uses for a similar price?
- Is the item for a class or for pleasure reading, and does the answer to that help you decide how to buy it?
- Are there advantages of disadvantages in digital content for students with visual, aural, or other learning challenges?
- Is the resource available in digital format, or must it be purchased in hard copy? Not everything has been published digitally, or the publisher

has chosen not to make certain items available to libraries. Some are not available because the school-selected device is proprietarily connected to a vendor that does not offer a specific title.

Some decisions with selecting content have to do with the format of that content.

Subscription Databases

Subscription databases often include informational e-book access. Some subscriptions contain all eBooks. You will have choices from the following:

Lease-only contracts and pay-per-view. Lease-only or pay-per-view vendors offer as much fiction as informational, but subscription terms vary dramatically.

Direct purchase for the life of the school library's need for the title. In all cases, titles purchased will stay in the school library collection until it is determined that they are no longer needed or used. However, the limit here is the proprietary restrictions. Many of these titles can be read only on computers, laptops, and some tablets with an installed mobile application (app); they are not often compatible with proprietary e-reading devices. Proprietary e-readers may limit downloadable content to resources that were purchased or borrowed from the manufacturer's bookstore or school library. What factors should affect the decision to buy digital content?

When considering how to best offer digital content to learners, it is not always necessary to acquire mobile reading devices. Most digital content can be accessed on a desktop computer.

- Licensing: How many simultaneous readers are allowed? Many e-books have embedded proprietary software restrictions (digital rights management) that limit the number of readers who can simultaneously access a title. When selecting a title to support classwide or gradewide use, it is important to account for licensing agreements and to formulate an acquisitions plan that supports enough single copies or adequate simultaneous access to one or more copies. Some vendors sell or lease titles for several readers, or even unlimited simultaneous readers. This option tends to be more costly (30–50% more, depending on the distributor) and is only sometimes available. Be really careful here. Not all publishers have determined what their business model for eBooks will be, and licensing terms can change at the whim of the publisher.
- Delivery: There is a distinction between downloaded and browser-viewed digital content. Most digital content, including public domain

and Creative Commons work, is accessible through a web browser. Some free mobile applications (apps) available for smartphones, MP3 players, PDAs, and pocket and tablet PCs facilitate digital content access and download, but many such apps permit access only to digital content acquired from the app developer/digital content distributor. Thus it is often necessary for users to download and navigate several applications to access a school library's entire digital collection

Free eBooks

The idea of free eBooks is much more exciting than the reality. Free books are available from the public domain or Creative Commons. Public domain titles include many classics like work by Charles Dickens and Mark Twain for which copyright restrictions have expired. Most are available in PDF format. These are available from the following:

Free eBooks may be read on computer screens/mobile devices, but not necessarily on other proprietary devices, unless those devices access the Internet. Regardless of the device, searching, accessing, and, when possible, downloading content first requires sufficient bandwidth and storage for offline reading. Another concern is the content formatting, which seldom includes easy-to-read fonts and page layouts.

Title: Project Gutenberg (www.gutenberg.org)

Contents: Over 15,000 eBooks. Generally older literature in the public domain.

Search Capability: Title, author, language

Title: Bartleby.com: Great Books Online (www.bartleby.com)

Contents: Reference, verse, fiction, and non-fiction in the public domain

Search: Title, author, subject

FOR THE YOUNGER CHILD:

Title: International Children's Digital Library (www.icd/books.org)

Contents: More than 600 children's books. Books are in their original language and not necessarily in the public domain.

Search: Title, author, illustrator, language, publication date.

TRAINING TEACHERS

You should try to find out whether your teachers and administrators are ready for a shift to the digital environment. Finding this out will help you decide what teacher training you might offer or find someone to help them prepare for the shift. Teachers will need to be convinced that these devices will help their students learn, and they should not be surprised to learn that their students are very enthusiastic about using digital tools and resources. In some situations, it may be possible to enlist the aid of students to help teachers as they begin to use these devices. A trained student can be someone to answer a quick question or offer a suggestion when a device is seemingly not working. The panic when a device won't turn on because the battery needs recharging is similar to an earlier age of technology when the teacher could not turn on the 16mm film projector because it wasn't plugged into the outlet.

Teachers must be aware of and using the collection. Your professional development efforts to teach your teachers how to use the resources should mean they will help publicize these resources to the students.

SELECTION POLICY ADAPTATIONS

Selection policies may have accommodated the selection of commercial databases, but the inclusion of eBooks and other digital content is a new concept. You should update your policies to reflect both digital review tools and print reviews of digital resources. Include discussion of vendor package evaluation relative to campus curricular needs.

School librarians must evaluate vendor packaging and policies. The decision may be whether the overall package is useful from one vendor or whether a different vendor package may be more useful. In some cases, a school will be best served by overlapping products. At all times, the policy will reflect how best to serve your community when deciding whether to buy the items in eBook format or print or in both.

For the future with the ongoing transition from all print to increasingly digital, students and their teachers will continue to need access to a combined collection that balances a breadth of opinion. Students will need to have resources that fit their learning styles. Adaptations to the selection policy will continue to reflect the need to support the curriculum of the school, the teachers, and the students.

USAGE OF EBOOKS

In 2013, the *School Library Journal* conducted a survey concerning eBook usage in school libraries. There really are no surprises here, except that perhaps the proliferation of eBooks in the school library is going more slowly than anticipated. The complete survey results can be found at www.the digitalshift.com/2014/01/k-12/slj-survey-ebook-usage-school-libraries -seen-rising-slowly/.

FURTHER CONSIDERATIONS

When we think about moving away from the traditional one textbook for one student to eBooks, two issues immediately arise. First, eBooks require a computer, a personal computing device, or an eBook reader to use them and not every student has, or can afford, one or both of these devices. Second, the downloading of the eBook requires an Internet connection and, preferably, a high-speed Internet connection. Again, some students cannot afford this; furthermore, some geographic areas do not have access to any Internet connection at all. Five years ago, this was true but the landscape has changed. Nearly every textbook company offers electronic versions of their textbooks at a substantial savings to students. There is one drawback to this, however. The textbooks are really only rented, not bought, and disappear after some time. This may not be a large issue in the long term as we think back to the college textbooks we kept with the idea we would refer back to them—and how few times we have actually done that.

The real change, though, has been in the willingness of schools to provide tablet computing devices to schools. Many schools, both secondary and postsecondary, are preloading textbooks that their students will use and then providing the devices to students.

In addition to equity of access issues, there is still no one widely accepted standard for eBook readers. Until then, the school librarian is rolling the dice on format. Think of the different video and music formats that have come and gone. Some of these issues mentioned in this paragraph have been overcome as schools have moved to BYOD (Bring Your Own Device) programs.

EBOOK VENDORS

The following vendors provide eBooks for a fee to school libraries. Note that you can purchase the eBooks you want—and because they come from standard vendors, school librarians can use purchase orders. These titles typically appear in your OPAC, and a link is there for users to go to the eBook.

When first building an eBook or a digital collection, that physical book or other resource isn't available to stand on the charge-out desk or place in a showcase. The challenge then becomes how to make students and teachers aware of these new digital materials when there is no physical object

Title: Gale Virtual Reference Library (www.gale.com/gvrl)

Contents: More than 500 reference titles in all curriculum areas. Home access to the works is provided.

Title: ABC-CLIO/Greenwood, eBooks (www.abc-clio.com/ABC -CLIOGreenwood.aspx)

Contents: More than 3,000 books, not all reference. About 10 percent of the works are specifically for grades 9–12. Greenwood now publishes all reference books in both print and eBook format.

Title: Follett Library Resources Company (www.flr.follett.com)

Contents: More than 12,000 eBooks available, ordered through Follett's Titlewave feature.

Title: Questia (www.questia.com)

Contents: More than 56,000 books (most protected by copyright) and more than 1 million journal articles.

There is also an index that attempts to provide links to all electronic books. The title is Digital Book Index, and the URL is www.digita bookindex.com.

to display. A first rule is to make it easy to find. All digital content must be in the catalog. Publicize the availability of the digital content materials as you did new books to your audience, and send lists to teachers to post on classroom bulletin boards. Make bookmarks to put in hard copy books that say, "Also available as an eBook." Get students to help you think of ways to "sell" your new collection.

The chapter ends with some additional challenges. Do digital vendors have access to identifying information? In the digital connection that allows a reader to access an eBook, the digital source of the content can track who the reader is. Many vendors promise that the connection is only identified by a number, but users of proprietary content, especially when a credit card may be included in the connection, have experienced some direct marketing along the way.

Cost will always be a consideration, and digital content can be expensive. Carefully research and compare the options. Negotiate with vendors, and be constantly on the lookout for cooperative purchasing options. Consortia offer potential ways to ease costs and share ownership. Take a leadership role and help your school district negotiate lower costs per student, even collaborating with other districts for greater discounts. Independent schools can often either join the consortium or work with vendors for similar rates. Watch for new trends in sharing; public libraries, colleges, and universities are starting to create models and innovate around interlibrary loans.

Because some digital resources do not work with traditional purchase order procedures, school librarians will need to explore new methods. Many eBook and other digital content providers require a credit card on file; school business practices will need to become more tolerant of this method. Business models will continue to evolve, and school librarians will need to persistently investigate changing purchase procedures.

RESEARCH AND DISCUSSION QUESTION

The superintendent is very interested in the concept of eBooks as a possible replacement for print textbooks and print reference materials for the school library. You are less sure the concept is feasible but have decided to compare two things: print textbooks versus eBooks and print library reference materials versus eBooks. Your comparison should present a frank appraisal of both and arrive at a clear, supportable conclusion.

REFERENCES

Bayliss, Sarah. "Libraries, Ebooks, and Beyond: Tablets in the Classroom." www.thedigital shift.com/2012/10/ebooks/tips-on-using-tablets-in-the-classroom/.

Church, Audrey P. "E-Book Resources for the School Library." *MultiMedia and Internet@ Schools*. www.mmischools.com/Articles.

"Ebooks and the School Library." www.mnlibraryassociation.org/?page=LegislativeCom mittee.

Harris, Christopher. "Ebooks and School Libraries" www.americanlibrariesmagazine.org/ article/ebooks-and-school-libraries.

Harris, Christopher "The Truth about EBooks," *School Library Journal* (June 1, 2009). www.schoollibraryjournal.com.

Lynch, Clifford A. "EBooks in 2013." www.americanlibrariesmagazine.org/article/ ebooks-2013.

Peterson, Karyn M. "SLJ Survey: Ebook Usage in School Libraries Expected to Rise Incrementally." *School Library Journal* (January 14, 2014).

"Position Statement on Digital Content and E-books in School Library Collections." www .ala.org/aasl/advocacy/resources/statements/digital-content.

Sanburn, Lura. "EBooks and Digital Collections for the High School Library. *School Library Monthly* (March 2014).

13

Integrating Technology into the Curriculum

The role of technology and its integration into the curriculum presents challenges not only to the school librarian, but also to the school community as a whole. School boards want it, administrators want it, and many parents want it. Teachers who see the potential want it, and students would be delighted to use it. With everybody wanting technology in the curriculum, one would think doing it would be easy. Unfortunately it is not easy, and challenges are numerous. Some people began implementation and then stopped; teachers who created a semester of PowerPoint presentations may think they integrated technology into their classes. Sometimes they then read the slides to their students in a darkened room. This technique is known as "death by PowerPoint."

Despite great amounts of evidence showing technology is most effective when it is integrated into the curriculum, many school districts opted instead to offer what they call "computer class" with "computer teachers." This is particularly prevalent in elementary school situations, in which classes go to a computer lab and learn how to "use the computer." In some cases, students are taught keyboarding; in others they use different educational software. The class is not taught as part of another class but is often, at least in collective bargaining states, an accommodation for the prep or free period for the classroom teacher. It resembles the principal who expects the school librarian to teach information literacy skills when there is no application.

In secondary schools, the computer class generally takes a different form, often closely resembling a college microcomputer application class. Although this may work relatively well in college, all too often the students cannot associate the learning with other situations and have little transfer learning into their classes.

Integrating technology skills into a class is effective at all levels from elementary through high school students. Elementary students do need to learn to keyboard and other word processing skills in coordination with preparing a report for science class. Furthermore, the concept of "just in time" or "as needed" instruction in technology addresses many issues. Is it important for students to know all parts of a software package, or do they just need to know enough to solve specific tasks? Research shows the latter is the case, but other issues frequently cloud the judgment of some administrators in school districts.

A chart from the *Digital Librarian* lists how technology can improve student achievement and how it can help develop 21st-century skills. The chart can be found at www.hscdsb.on.ca/pdf/publications/5/55/CEO%20Forum%20 2001%20Policy%20Paper.pdf.

TECHNOLOGY IN THE CURRICULUM: ADVANTAGES

Other than the obvious—that technology can provide students with an educational experience as a standalone—there are a number of reasons why integrating technology into the curriculum is a good idea. First, using technology in the educational process motivates students. Our students today are considered the digital native generation and will likely do better in class if motivated; they would be highly motivated if they are able to actually use technology in their classes. This table, also from the *Digital Librarian*, illustrates the learning preferences of the digital generation. It can be found at https://sites.google.com/site/thedigitallibrarian/the-ideal-tech-world.

Second, the integration of technology into the curriculum can provide unique instructional opportunities and unique learning opportunities through many unique applications for the use of technology matched to the unique pieces of technology. One example is the opportunity to add video clips to emphasize a point in a social studies class. The digital resources available from the Library of Congress and the Holocaust Museum give students an incomparable view of history as it happened.

The third reason why integrating technology into the curriculum is an advantage is that it supports new approaches in instruction. In the past, the teacher was "the sage on the stage," an individual who imparted information to the class spending most of the instructional time lecturing. Technology in the teaching process help teachers become the "guide on the side," a constructivist teacher, with the students taking a more active role in the construction of their education.

Finally, using technology to support teaching makes teachers more productive. The call today is for teachers to be more accountable in the learning process. Using technology properly keeps students more motivated and provides them better educational opportunities to become creative thinkers.

ATTRIBUTES OF INFORMATION-AGE SCHOOLS

As early as 2001, research done on the efficacy of using technology in the educational setting showed trends still true today. This research identified some attributes of schools in the information age.

1. Information-age schools provide interactivity in different venues. It might be email, instant messaging, or participating in video conferencing. These are all interactive experiences students and teachers can use in any number of different classes. Just think of the educational value added if students could actually interact with experts in the field they are studying.

2. In information-age schools, there is much self-initiated, student-centered learning, with the students often forming the question to be investigated. This returns us to the idea of the "guide on the side" in project-based learning or inquiry-based learning. In these cases, the students, with input or guidance from the teacher, formulate or frame the question to be investigated or solved.

3. The aforementioned role of the teacher as a guide or facilitator as opposed to the teacher as an information surveyor is definitely an attribute of an information age school. Rarely do you walk through the halls of an information-age school and hear teachers lecturing to students. Instead, you will find teachers who are facilitating instruction, using the technology as a tool in the learning process rather than an end in itself. The technology teacher is teaching students to program as a skill needed in the job market.

4. In information-age schools, the library is the center of learning, and the school librarian is a central participant in the learning process. Furthermore, the school librarian is not only the instructional leader, but also the technology leader of the school.

5. Continuous evaluation of instruction and learning is a characteristic of an information age school. When this research was done, in 2001, there was not yet the strong push for assessment in schools that there is now. Progressive schools even at that time were intimately involved with assessment throughout the unit rather than assessing at the end of a unit. Assessment was done on a continuing basis.

6. Information-age schools look different, and perhaps this is why some administrators fear it. These schools are not quiet, because learning is a noisy activity. Furthermore, most classrooms do not have a regimented

look; classes work in groups throughout, and even out of, the classroom. Students are coming and going from the classroom to the library and back. In sum, the school looks and sounds different from earlier schools.

APPROACHES TO INTEGRATION

In the first two sections of this chapter, the integration of technology into the curriculum is discussed, and the foregoing has presented some of the characteristics of information-age schools. In this section, some general techniques are given that you can use to help the teacher who wants to move toward integrating technology into the curriculum, presenting it as a tool rather than an end in itself. Technology is a tool to develop an effective unit of instruction rather than teach how to use presentation software. In reality, the only time when technology is an end in itself is, as stated above, is when the technology teacher is helping students learn how to program.

Information Literacy Skills

The school librarian may begin this process by modeling the use of technology in the way information literacy is offered to students. Instruction in information literacy provides great opportunities for students to work with technology tools as they learn the information literacy skills they will carry with them throughout their school years. The collaboration with teachers to determine the skills to be taught provides an opportunity to show the way technology is used to interest students in how to complete their assignments. You will be demonstrating the skill and how the skill can be applied.

As elementary school students begin doing basic research with electronic resources, they use other skills to prepare their reports, bibliographies, or presentations using the most appropriate computer software. At this level, school librarians demonstrate how to select and bookmark appropriate websites for the teacher so that students do not spend time on unproductive searches.

Throughout this book and in this chapter, instruction in the use of software has been emphasized as a key technology skill for students, is never taught in isolation. Information literacy research skills are not isolated. Gone is the research that was backbone of library and curriculum instruction, limited to the ubiquitous research paper as part of the English or social studies curriculum. In today's schools, research demands effective use of technology for a wide variety of resources well beyond finding information in books located using the school library's OPAC. Students are encouraged to use their research skills whenever they need to know something. In today's world, the cell phone may be the most useful tool for short answers. How many standing in a theater line use their cell phone to find out something about an actor in the movie?

As students are progressing through school, their searching skills are expanded and the sources available are widened. By the secondary level, research skills become more complex as do the computer applications. More types of technology are added to the equation, such as by streaming video and primary source documents. By the time students who have well-developed skills in information literacy leave for their postsecondary education or enter the job market, they will also have a level of technology skills that enables them to compete both in their postsecondary education and in their careers.

Teacher and School Librarian Collaborating

The best approach to integration of technology into the curriculum is, obviously, teachers and school librarian collaboration. For this to happen, teachers must be able to use the technology. School librarians who accept the leadership role in integrating technology into the curriculum are able to conduct staff development sessions to introduce technology. In these sessions, they can provide some examples of how a new piece of equipment may be used both as a teaching device and also as a way to get students interested in research and writing. This is usually a generic approach; the more specific applications come with later sessions discussing curriculum units.

Another approach to the integration of technology into the curriculum is to work with interactive programs. These types of programs are motivating and encourage students to learn more in an environment they like. The use of interactive programs in the curriculum is a challenge for teachers. It takes some level of training and much trial and error to use these effectively in the classroom.

Integrating technology into the curriculum works really well in cross-discipline units. The more participants, the more ideas are generated, and the more likely that problems can be identified before implementation. Even if the curriculum plans do not cross discipline units, if all the first-grade teachers will be teaching "weather," sharing ideas for ways to make things interesting through the use of technology will allow them to pick and choose what fits their teaching methods and the skills levels of their students.

Another approach to collaboration is between a single teachers and the school librarian. This is the classic collaboration and allows great opportunities for technology integration on a one-to-one basis. This gives the school librarian an opportunity to learn more about individual students and to learn more about a teacher's technology skills, as well as how the teacher approaches teaching any area of the curriculum. It is far easier for the teacher to express anxiety when others are not there to observe and very easy for the librarian to conduct the demonstration and then allow the teacher to put the demonstration into immediate practice.

Integration with Students

Integrating technology into the curriculum then becomes the application of technology in the curriculum with students. Here the school librarian is key to the process and assists in implementation from the beginning of each unit of instruction. One challenge is always flexibility in scheduling. A standard forty-five-minute class period is a definite challenge. Some schools have attempted to solve this issue with different forms of scheduling in high schools. In elementary, it is a little easier, because teachers usually have control over the class day. Whatever the format of the day, the school librarian helps the teacher plan ways to make this possible, breaking the unit into smaller pieces with suggestions for how information can be placed on the school library website for students to use when they are away from school so that not all activity needs to take place in the library or classroom.

An excellent opportunity for the integration of technology into the curriculum comes with collaborative learning, and this is sometimes not as easy for teachers to accept, because it is often difficult to judge the efforts of members of a group in the final presentations. Yet one of the skills most employers want their prospective employees to bring with them is the ability to solve problems using a collaborative approach. Because one of the important aspects of collaborative learning is the ability to use whatever tools are available to solve the problem, students must not only have the tools, but they must know how to use the tools effectively.

Other types of electronic resources can be integrated into the curriculum. For example, students can access electronic books; students can access streaming video, graphics, or sounds from the World Wide Web; students can participate in audio and video conferencing with other students or with experts in their field of research to broaden their research knowledge. The list of possibilities expands on a daily basis.

Students can also gain experience using both Flash and animation techniques as ways of integrating technology into the curriculum. There are more sophisticated programs and techniques that students can use to great advantage. Furthermore, they are technology skills that students will be able to carry with them into other venues.

PROS OF TECHNOLOGY INTEGRATION INTO THE CURRICULUM

Doggett, in *Beyond the Book: Technology Integration into the Secondary School Library Media Curriculum*, discussed, in some detail, the pros and cons of integrating technology into the school library curriculum. Although some of her points were covered earlier in the chapter, there is value in again considering these. Again even though the points deal specifically with the school library curriculum, they are equally applicable to the general school curriculum. Her pros are as follow:

1.   Integration of technology into the school curriculum facilitates school to career preparation. As discussed earlier, employers are looking for employees who can work in collaborative, team situations, and who are technologically able. This does not mean students must be able to work with every piece of software, but rather, they must show a capacity to learn to use the technology they will have to work with in their jobs. A comparison can be drawn to the 1960s and 1970s with education for several types of engineers. Employers looked at education in engineering as providing a base of learning and a capacity to be trained; the employer then provided the specific training required for the particular job.

2.   The second positive point for the integration of technology into the curriculum is a change of paradigm in the mode of instruction. Since the dawn of public schools, instruction has been nearly the same. A student from the 1850s who was placed in a public school one hundred years later would find nearly the same type of instruction, called by some "chalk and talk." The spread of technology has changed that. Teaching with technology requires a whole new skill set for teachers as most traditional teaching methods are not particularly effective in teaching with technology.

3.   Using technology as a tool in teaching opens new avenues for assessment. Many educators have been less than thrilled about "No Child Left Behind," but the movement caused administrators, school boards, and teachers to examine new methods of assessment. Schools are moving away from paper and pencil assessments—tests, quizzes, papers—and moving toward what is called "authentic assessment." When students are presented with real-life problems and scenarios, alternative types of assessment can be devised using technology that fairly evaluates student progress. Does authentic assessment easily lend itself to assigning better grades? Perhaps not, but it provides a more realistic evaluation of their performance.

4.   The use of technology in instruction can enhance students' critical thinking skills. The enhancement of students' critical thinking skills is a

much desired and seldom achieved goal of instruction. Part of the issue has always been that measuring critical thinking skills has been very difficult using traditional assessment methods. Using a technology-infused curriculum can provide some measure of critical thinking skills not available previously.

5. The use of technology in the curriculum also gives students wider access to information. Technology has significantly increased the amount of information available to students. Whether it is magazine articles, video snippets, or even pieces of music, information has become much more available to students. Take, for example, the use of general encyclopedias. In the past there were a finite number of volumes available, and if more than one student wanted to use the same volume, one could use it and the others had to wait. With access to electronic encyclopedias any number of students can use the same information at the same time. Also, the electronic resources are available both at home and at school, twenty-four hours a day, seven days a week.

6. Of all of the advantages of technology discussed so far, one of the most desirable is the currency. When instruction takes place in a more traditional setting, the instruction is typically textbook-based. With this type of instruction and the use of textbooks, the information is at least two years old because of the time cycle involved with writing textbooks. The use of electronic resources is current to the point full-text magazine articles are often available electronically before they are available in the print format.

7. The final advantage Doggett espouses for the integration of technology into the curriculum is one discussed before—motivation. Students today are part of the digital generation, motivated by the technology they can use. Technology appeals to students who are visual learners as well as those who are tactile learners. A major problem for educators is always motivating students. Introduce a lesson with a piece of streaming video or a part of a music video. These are the types of motivational devices technology can provide for 21st-century students and teachers.

Challenges for Integrating Technology into the Curriculum

Doggett presented these challenges to be overcome:

1. In the short term, it is more costly to integrate technology into the curriculum than not. In the long run, it is less costly, but most school districts have to pay in the short run, not wait for the long term. Furthermore, many parents, teachers, and students expect the latest and greatest technology, which sometimes is beyond the means of some school districts.

2. Closely related to the first item is the issue of rapid change. Change in technology is inevitable, and it is not cheap. When a new operating system is introduced, it means every PC must be updated if the school district is committed to currency.

3. Compatibility issues bedevil school districts all across the country, and those types of issues can wreak havoc with school district budgets. Sometimes one platform is a better choice for certain tasks than another platform. From an educational standpoint, having both platforms is sound, but from a business or budgetary standpoint, it is a problem that is very difficult to deal with.

4. The best plan for integrating technology into the curriculum can be completely hamstrung by a lack of training. Far too often, technology is thrown at teachers with the expectation that they will learn how to use it in their "spare" time. Some can do it, but it is not fair to expect people to learn new technology without training. This makes the opportunity for the school librarian to assume a leadership role and conduct staff development, something that will take time and planning that school librarians may have difficulty applying.

5. Equity, equity, equity. Does every student in your school have a computer? Does every student in your school have access to high-speed Internet? Do all your teachers have access to computers that can be taken home? Equity issues play havoc with assessing the effectiveness of the integration of technology into the curriculum.

Strategies for Integration of Technology into the Curriculum

Our approach to examining strategies for the integration of technology into the curriculum will be twofold. First, we will examine the strategies that facilitate this integration; second, we will look at different subject disciplines and see what techniques would work within each of the disciplines. This is not an inclusive list—jus things that they seem like good techniques and that either have been demonstrated as being successful or seem as if they would be successful. It is incumbent on you, the educator, to try things to see what works. Feel free to modify and adapt any of these ideas in the classroom. Keep in mind technology is such a dynamic field many of these strategies could be completely outmoded by the time you read this book.

PRODUCTIVITY SOFTWARE

Some of the most commonly used strategies facilitating the integration of technology into the curriculum are built around productively software. Productively software is a package such as Microsoft Office that includes different programs such as a word processor (Word), a spreadsheet (Excel), presentation software (PowerPoint), and a database package (Access). There may be other pieces in the productivity package, such as scheduling or email packages, but those are the major pieces. Productivity software gives the student the ability to use each piece of the software in conjunction with the other pieces or independently. In addition, there is file compatibility, which allows files created with one piece of the software to be imported into other pieces and then worked with interactively. For example, a student can create a spreadsheet and a chart from the data, then place it in a PowerPoint presentation. Any changes made to the data in the Excel spreadsheet are automatically updated in the chart, as well as in the PowerPoint presentation. What a powerful lesson this can be in "what if" analysis.

This short discussion here does not even touch on doing research online and then preparing a report using the word processing piece of the productivity software.

GAMES AND SIMULATION

Educational games and simulations have been around the education field for many years and represent some of the first educational software available for students. Gaming has become so popular with children that it has almost taken on a life of its own and eliminated the educational side of things. Even so, though, there are great educational games and simulations available in many disciplines and at many grade levels. Using these tools in the elementary grades can really motivate students and also provide much-needed reinforcement for skills building.

At the secondary level are also many games and simulations available for students. Who can forget, in the early days of Apple computers, working with the math and social studies concepts in Oregon Trail? I don't think anyone ever made it to the west coast alive! Oregon Trail still exists, albeit updated with all of the bells and whistles children today want.

Sim City, another game secondary students continue to enjoy, is both motivating and educational without being overpowering. Many textbook companies now offer online simulations with their books, such as MyITLab, MyMathLab, or MyWritingLab. Games and simulations still fill a need in the educational technology picture, for they are valuable reinforcers.

DRILL AND PRACTICE

Drill and practice technology goes back to the first days of the use of technology in schools. Drill and practice technology can be either linear or nonlinear and can give students valuable practice using such basic skills as reading and computation. The best drill and practice software provides reinforcement when a student responds incorrectly. Rather than indicating that the student is incorrect, the software provides the student with more practice in the concept. One question may arise with drill and practice software: Other than being a good motivator for some students because it is technology, can't the same thing can be accomplished with a paper and pencil at a much lower cost? If you are not careful here, you end up with technology for technology's sake.

TUTORIALS

In some ways tutorials are similar to drill and practice in their purpose. Modern tutorials not only can motivate the student, but also can break difficult concepts down into step-by-step interactive demonstrations. For example, one of the more difficult concepts for students when using Microsoft Excel is absolute and relative referencing. Tutorials demonstrating this concept typically have four distinct parts. First, the concept is demonstrated for the student. Second, the student is given the opportunity to demonstrate understanding of the concept. Third, if a student is still having difficulty with the concept, he or she is directed to a part of the tutorial to practice the concept and finally has the opportunity to show mastery of the concept. Tutorials have come miles since the early days of technology and provide students with the opportunity to master difficult concepts independently.

DISCUSSION

No matter what their form, chat, IM, and Web 2.0 discussion forums such as Facebook or Twitter are a true conundrum for educators. Many school districts have bans on interactive discussion for several reasons, generally because it is a nonproductive use of technology or because it allows students a chance to share things surreptitiously with other students.

Keeping all the negatives in mind, there are good, cogent, educationally sound reasons why students should have access to interactive real-time communication. For example, one of the key things in AP history courses are the discussion-based questions (DBQs). Teachers can conduct moderated chat on a regular basis to give students the opportunity to discuss their ideas. The key to discussion types of technology is for the teacher to control it, not just let it go without direction.

DISCOVERY, PROBLEM SOLVING, COOPERATIVE LEARNING

These concepts are called many different things but come around to the same process, generally done in a cooperative, or team environment:

1. A problem is posed. This can come from the teacher, or the students can frame it.
2. The students research the problem to discover what kind of information is available and to see whether tentative solutions already exist.
3. Students formulate a hypothesis in an effort to solve the problem or answer the question.
4. Students test their hypothesis.
5. Students present the results of their problem solving activity.

This is an integral part of constructivist instruction and can be designed to use technology in all aspects of the project. Many websites are available covering such diverse topics as project-based learning, problem-based learning, discovery learning, problem solving, or cooperative learning.

DISCIPLINE-BASED IDEAS FOR INTEGRATION OF TECHNOLOGY INTO THE CURRICULUM

This is really the fun part of this chapter for the author. In this last section there is a listing of things that work when you want to integrate technology into the curriculum. I have seen these things work, and you can adopt them to your needs or change them as you see fit.

Elementary

Many good elementary programs are available for educational use—far too many to try to list. An elementary librarian might be able to adapt some of the suggestions from the high school subject areas as well. This is the point at which teachers should begin to work with students using productivity software.

1. Preparation of short reports using online library resources and a word processing program.
2. Animated presentations using streaming video inserted in PowerPoint presentations.
3. Students' doing basic scientific research and prepare reports summarizing their findings.
4. Information literacy and library instruction. This can and should begin in kindergarten and continue through the elementary school years.

5. Math drill and practice using technology. Many programs are available—pick the ones providing the most motivation.
6. Reading software keyed to primary readers. The best of this software should be interactive.

Secondary

The following are listed by the subject area covered:

English

1. Video book reports including information about the author.
2. Student created tutorials showing research paper creation steps.
3. Senior projects.
4. As needed (just-in-time) technology tutorials.
5. Use of eBooks and eJournals to supplement subscription electronic databases.
6. Use of eBooks so multiple students can read the same book.

Mathematics

1. Use of manipulatives.
2. Use of many websites such as Dr. Math to assist students with difficult concepts.
3. Instruction in and use of graphing calculators.
4. Use of productivity software, especially Excel, to chart data.
5. Finding data online that then can be manipulated in Excel.

Science

1. Use of websites such as the Glenbrook South High School science website to explore more about scientific concepts.
2. Use special hardware, such as scientific probes, to perform actual scientific experiments.
3. Use of simulations to re-create scientific conditions that are too dangerous to re-create in schools.
4. Use productivity software to prepare lab reports.
5. Use proprietary software bundled with science textbooks to amplify scientific concepts.

Social Studies

1. Perform primary research using electronic collections such as the *Official Records of the Civil War.*

2. Use distance learning equipment to interview experts in fields such as economics and psychology.
3. Use interactive real-time conversation to gain insights in AP history classes.
4. Work with and digitize local history sources.
5. Prepare local history projects such as Planet Smethport.

Art

1. Prepare virtual art museum tours.
2. Using software to create buildings or design room arrangements

Foreign Language

1. Communicate with residents in foreign countries to polish language skills.
2. Use productivity software to present information about foreign cultures.

Music

1. Use electronic music sites to gain knowledge about music history.
2. Use proprietary software to design band routines.
3. Create a departmental website.

Tech Education

1. Use CAD and CAM software to complete problems and projects.

Since the advent of computer technology, one of the purported goals of school districts has been to provide every student with a computing device. These range from programs that provide laptops or tablets to every students to school with all class material preloaded on them. These are enviable outcomes to a goal that is difficult to achieve because of the high cost associated with providing every student with a computing device—but a goal that school librarians should be helping administrators figure out how to provide.

One solution to this is a movement called "BYOD," or Bring Your Own device. In these programs, students may bring their own computing device to school and is then able to connect to the school network. This is a controversial approach, as some or many of the students in the school do not come from homes where parents can provide a device for every student. They may have no computer at home and no connectivity or may have connectivity and one computer for the family. The student who brings a device to school may misplace it, or something may happen to destroy it. There are many other questions and possible pitfalls to the BYOD approach, and Mark Ray, in 2013, posed a number of questions concerning BYOD, then answered them:

1. What is a PCD? Shorthand for personally owned personal computing device.
2. Are teachers or students required to have a personal computing device in class? No
3. Are teachers required to implement the use of personal computing devices in their instruction? No, but many have elected to do just that in BYOD pilot programs.
4. Must there be district and board approval for BYOD programs? No, but existing policies have been changed to reflect the use of these devices.
5. Is technical support provided to BYOD participants? No, except for requiring Internet filtering. Personal computing device users are expected to know how to use their devices.
6. Are students at a disadvantage if they don't have a personal computing device for use at school? No, but in schools in which a high percentage of students with their own personal computing devices, this can be an issue.
7. Who decides when the students can use their personal computing devices? The teacher.
8. What network or software access do students have with their devices? They have access only to district-provided filtered Internet access.
9. Are any particular devices recommended for BYOD programs? No
10. Are students bound to comply with district technology policies? Yes, without exception.
11. What are the consequences if a personal computing device is lost, damaged, or stolen at school? The owner is of the device is responsible. The school or the owner's teacher has no responsibility.

As you can see, there are many issues with BYOD that have not yet been explored or researched. That said, as long as school district budgets continue to shrink, BYOD programs will continue to proliferate.

RESEARCH AND DISCUSSION QUESTIONS

1. Consider a unit of instruction in an elementary school, and integrate technology in at least seven days of instruction for that unit.

2. Select an academic discipline and design a unit plan using technology and integrating it into the instruction. The unit should encompass seven to ten instructional days and be complete to the point that it includes outcomes and educational objectives. Be sure the technology piece is not teaching technology skills in isolation.

REFERENCES

Burke, John J. *Neal-Schuman Library Technology Companion: A Basic Guide for the Library Staff*, 2nd ed. New York: Neal-Schuman, 2006.

Doggett, Sandra L. *Beyond the Book: Technology Integration into the Secondary School Library Media Curriculum*. Edgewood, CO: Libraries Unlimited, 2000.

Johnston, Michelle, and Nancy Cooley. *What We Know about Supporting New Models of Teaching and Learning through Technology*. Arlington, VA: ERS, 2001.

Lever-Daffy, Judy, and Jean B. McDonald. *Teaching and Learning with Technology*. Boston, MA: Pearson, 2008.

"Overcoming Barriers to Integrate Technology into the School Library Media Center." https://sites.google.com/site/thedigitallibrarian/introduction.

Ray, Mark. "BYO What?" *Library Media Connection* (January/February 2013). www.librarymediaconnection.com/pdf/lmc/reviews_and_articles/featured_articles/Ray_January_February2013.pdf.

Robbyer, M.D., Jack Edwards, and Mary Anne Havrilick. *Integrating Educational Technology into Teaching*. Upper Saddle River, NJ: Prentice Hall, 1997.

Rosenfeld, Esther, and David V. Loertscher, eds. *Toward a 21st Century School Library Media Program*. Lanham, MD: Scarecrow Press, 2007.

Smaldino, Sharon E., Deborah L. Larother, and James D. Russell. *Instructional Technology and Media for Learning*. Upper Saddle River, NJ: Pearson, 2008.

14

Web 2.0 and Related Technology

Most school librarians or students in library and information science programs have read or heard references made to Web 2.0. Some may wonder what the difference is between the World Wide Web and Web 2.0. Questions may arise about what can be done with Web 2.0 when we have yet to master the World Wide Web. However, most students do know about Web 2.0. So, if you don't know and need to, this chapter will give you at least a passing knowledge of what Web 2.0 is and how it can be used in school libraries. It is interesting to note that five years ago, all the material in this chapter would have been in the final chapter as we try to forecast the technology in the school library of the future.

In this chapter, several topics relating to Web 2.0 will be discussed, including a new concept called the Library 2.0, social networking, blogs, wikis, a brief introduction to videoconferencing, course management systems for distance education, and a brief discussion of virtual sites using avatars. Not all of these have been implemented in every school library. However, those school librarians who are on the cutting age should be mentoring their colleagues so that they can move swiftly into these. It is today, not the future.

Kroski, in her book *Web 2.0 for Librarians and Information Professionals*, defined Web 2.0 as a "participatory Web." This is evident from the listing above of the topics covered in the chapter. Each of those topics is participatory or even interactive to some degree. From an educator's viewpoint, rather than a student's, there are several reasons offered by Kroski as to why Web 2.0 is valuable.

1. It is valuable for the creation of content. In many cases, the creation of blogs and wikis can take the place of the creation of webpages. Although certainly not as sophisticated as the creation of websites and webpages, using blogs and wikis can be a "quick and dirty" way to create valuable content.

2. Web 2.0 applications generally have some level of interactivity. Our students are motivated by the use of interactive technology, and Web 2.0 supplies it.

3. Web 2.0 applications provide great opportunities for collaboration. What could do it better than a wiki, where students can create, add to, or change content? Can this be dangerous? Yes. Can it be beneficial? Yes again.

4. Web 2.0 gives students and educators the opportunity to participate in knowledge creating and communication.

Social software has emerged as the part of Web 2.0, and most people are familiar with this. Those parts will be discussed as well as one of the crucial components of the communication and interaction associated with Web 2.0. This crucial component is its openness, and it is this very openness that scares educators. The issue of interactive, real-time communication was discussed briefly in previous chapters, but it is an essential part of Web 2.0. If school librarians are to move forward with technology, they must embrace new concepts, not fear them.

In 2005 O'Reilly coined the term *Web 2.0* and described it as "the second generation of Web based tools and resources." At that time some of the characteristics of Web 2.0 and how it contrasted with the World Wide Web as we know it were presented as follow:

1. Web 2.0 moved from single-computer web access to connections with many computers. This is an essential point if collaboration is to be successful among teachers, teachers and librarians, teachers and students, librarians and students, and teachers, librarians, and students.

2. The move from single webpages and websites to dynamically created online resources in Web 2.0.

3. Some shift is happening from closed systems (Windows, MAC OS) to open systems and software (Linux). This is probably true but is an area of technology where school librarians may hesitate to venture unless they are true techies.

4. Web 2.0 takes the user from publishing things once to content continually added to and allows for user participation.

5. We move from single webpage authors and creators to a strong collaborative and consensus-building effort.

6. Web 2.0 is not about data storage, but rather about networking and socialization skills.

7. Rather than visitors coming to your website, you send the information to them.

8. Go from standards-based organizations (taxonomies) to user-based organizations (folksnomies). (O'Reilly)

LIBRARY 2.0 AND SCHOOL LIBRARY 2.0

Moving toward the interactivity of Web 2.0 in the general Internet arena, librarians have moved toward a new definition of technology called Library 2.0. This move to the Library 2.0 was initially defined by Casey in 2006. In effect, it outlines a framework for expanded web services in the library. Maness, in his 2006 article, defined Web 2.0 as "the application of Interactive, collaborative, and multi-media Web-based technologies to Web-based library services and collection." He further theorizes that the Library 2.0 has four elements:

1. Library 2.0 is user-centered. The user participates in the creation of dynamic content.
2. Essential parts of the Library 2.0 collection are video and audio in addition to text.
3. There are both synchronous and asynchronous communication opportunities available for Library 2.0 users.
4. Library 2.0 is always innovating and changing. (Maness)

Earlier in this discussion we said school librarians must be ready to move forward into this collaborative, interactive world of Web 2.0 and Library 2.0. Are librarians ready for this? Time will tell.

SOCIAL NETWORKING

Probably the best known part of Web 2.0 is the social networking parts. This would include Facebook, MySpace, and Twitter. Our students are in love with these applications; they are the chat of the 21st century. In many school districts, all these social networking applications are blocked from student use. An argument can be posed that blocking should be done for good, cogent educational reasons. However, when they are integrated into the curriculum and controlled, they can be educationally sound.

Lamb and Johnson, in their articles about social technologies, characterize social networking as a "computer-mediated communication environments that connect people for cooperation, collaboration, and information sharing." These social networking applications encourage interaction. This is the thing students really like. They are social people but seem to prefer the computer-mediated environment much as people who used the chat feature did. Second, they give students the opportunity to give and receive feedback. This is important in the assessment of the educational experience. Students and their parents seem to really like the connections they form through social networking. In their article, Lamb and Johnson point out several reasons for the popularity of social networking software:

1. Providing a sense of activism. Our 21st-century students have a very strong sense of activism, and social networking software plays to this strength.
2. A sense of belonging. Using social networking applications allows students to overcome social shortcomings. A caller can be blocked if someone is having a bad hair day. Speech problems are not heard, and communication happens from all corners of the world.
3. The students are able to contact one another as they see fit. Social contact is a 24/7 activity. One of the reasons school districts block this is that students text constantly in classrooms, often with other friends in the classroom.
4. Freedom. This is why many school districts bar the use of social networking applications. Some students do not deal with freedom as well as others.

A recent article by Doug Johnson, well-known maven in the field of technology for school libraries, pointed out some important issues for dealing with social media applications.

"SOCIAL NETWORKING TOOLS"

1. "Walls function like a discussion board but are meant for brief messages that can be easily seen, quickly read, and immediately replied to.

2. Friends and "friending" are terms that refer to the personally selected communities of people known to the user, built by invitation. Connections to friends can be social, interest group, work, or school related.

3. Notification of the activity of friends through news-feed like technology that relays what people are doing – uploading photos, playing games, making new friends. Their behavior, or experience, becomes "content" that others can learn from.

4. Messages or Notes are alternatives to email. Because users create their own universe of friends in social networking, private communication can be more selective than e-mail. Spam is less common in social networking communications." (Johnson, "Connections for Learning: Schools and the Educational Use of Social Networking")

WEB 2.0 FEARS

Web 2.0 makes it difficult to protect children from predators, because it is difficult to protect children from themselves when they make inappropriate or personal information public. It is also difficult to protect children from each other (cyberbullying).

Each of these are valid fears for parents, placing the onus on teachers and school librarians. They are important enough that a good portion of chapter 16 is devoted to cyberbullying.

ATTRIBUTES RELATED TO SOCIAL NETWORKING

However, our students are in the Net Generation, and they have a number of attributes related to social networking:

1. "Ability to read visual images. They are intuitive visual communicators and are less likely to be cognitive learners.
2. Visual–spatial skills. Their expertise with games allows them to integrate the virtual and physical.
3. Inductive discovery. They learn better through discovery than by being told. This dovetails perfectly with project or problem based learning.
4. Attentional deployment. They are able to shift their attention rapidly from one task another, and may choose not to pay attention to things that don't interest them.
5. Fast response time. They are able to respond quickly and expect rapid responses in return." (Johnson, "Connections for Learning: Schools and the Educational Use of Social Networking")

In 2010, *Library Media Connection* published an article that detailed what it called "Guidelines for Educators Using Social and Educational Networking Sites." They are discussed hereafter and are of great importance in understanding what can and what should be done with relation to social media by teachers and school librarians. They were written as guidelines for the use social networking sites by professional staff and may be used by school librarians for staff development if school districts do not include these along with discussion of appropriate ways to speak to or touch students:

1. Do not have students as friends. This is a common-sense dictate, because teachers are teachers rather than friends of students. It could be a sure was to lose your teaching credential or worse.
2. No friendships with students. See the foregoing.

3. Be concerned about security of data with those you have as friends.
4. Always be aware that whatever you post to a social networking site is out there for all to see. Use caution!
5. This is the same as email—there is no inherent right of privacy with social media, so be careful of anything that can be interpreted as criticism.
6. Again, be aware of privacy and security issues with those you may not know well.

Other guidelines for the use of educational networking sites by professional staff:

1. Do not say or do anything that you would not say or do in as a teacher in the classroom. (Remember that all online communications are stored and can be monitored.) See number 5 foregoing. There is an old saying about "fools names and fools faces."
2. Prepare an acceptable use policy for those using your network.
3. No pictures of students, EVER. Some school districts do not allow the use of student images even with parental permission.

Guidelines for *all* networking sites by professional staff:

1. Do not use commentary deemed to be defamatory, obscene, proprietary, or libelous. Exercise caution with regards to exaggeration, colorful language, guesswork, obscenity, copyrighted materials, legal conclusions, and derogatory remarks or characterizations. (Johnson, Guidelines, 2010)
2. If you think a posting will reflect badly on your role as a teacher don't post it. If in doubt, don't.
3. Due to security risks, be cautious when installing the external applications that work with the social networking site.
4. Always have updated malware protection on your computers in the school library.
5. Be careful not to fall for phishing scams that arrive via email or on your wall, providing a link for you to click, leading to a fake login page. Phishing schemes and scams are everywhere. If it sounds too good to be true it probably is—particularly if it comes from Nigeria.
6. If a staff member learns of information, on the social networking site that falls under the mandatory reporting guidelines, he or she must report it as required by law. (Johnson, Guidelines, 2010)

TWITTER

The social networking application currently most popular is Twitter. Twitter is a free messaging service that allows people to send and receive short messages, no more than 140 characters, called tweets. Tweets can be sent using a computer or any mobile computing device. If you want to see what others are saying, you "follow" them. Conversely, those who regularly follow your postings are called followers. Many tweets are pretty basic: "I watched the Pirates game tonight." An article, "Twitter for Librarians," suggested some good ways Twitter could be used in a library setting:

1. Twitter allows librarians to keep in touch with colleagues and friends.
2. It helps a school librarian to stay on top of the latest technology. This is really important in those ubiquitous one-person school libraries.
3. Because the major news sites, such as CNN, use Twitter, they will allow the librarian to stay on top of the news.
4. You can be made aware of conferences you may want to participate in. Some of the high-tech conferences use Twitter.
5. Twitter allows school librarians to participate in impromptu question and answer sessions.
6. You can always check Twitter to find out a little bit about your colleagues. Tweets can be very revealing. Although certainly not the primary purpose of Twitter, it can be used as a quick notepad.
7. Twitter can act as a low-level online reference service.
8. Use Twitter to announce new library services. Teenage and tech-savvy people will love this service.
9. Twitter is the ideal vehicle to post new materials lists.
10. Students who have Twitter accounts can elect to receive notifications about materials ready for them or about overdue library materials.

BLOGS

Blogs (web logs) store online postings and arrange them in reverse chronological order. The posting can be text, graphics, video, or audio, but the great preponderance of the entries are text. The use and creation of blogs is an example of one of the many types of communication that can have significant educational benefit as students collaborate to create and add to journals and gather reaction to postings. Although blogs originally were created and used on computers, they now can be used with any mobile computing device.

In McPherson's article "Literacy Links: School Library Blogging," the use of blogs in school libraries is discussed and several reasons advanced for the use of blogs in that environment. Generally speaking, in the school library blog, issues are raised and others respond using the blog reply. This is a bit of an oversimplification, but this is the idea.

School library blogs can be used to promote the skills of reading and writing. Not only are these key skills for our students, but encouraging them also helps show the school library's relevance to state and federally mandated testing. A way blogs can be used in the school library to encourage reading and writing is to encourage students to post book reviews to the blog. This would then allow students to reply to or comment on the review. The process of creating a book review encourages both reading and writing, as does the process of commenting on or adding to the review.

Using a book review and commenting scenario also encourages students' critical thinking skills. The opportunity begins in the actual creation of the review, but it is also strongly fostered in the responses to the review. This hasn't been tested, but anything that will improve critical thinking skills is a great benefit.

Using a school library blog should improve the students' information literacy skills. Often either the beginning posting to a blog or the responses to the posting call for some bit or amount of research. By doing this research, students should improve their information literacy skills.

WIKIS

The other powerful collaborative tool that gained importance as Web 2.0 increased in popularity is the wiki. A wiki, whose name is derived from the Hawaiian language, is a set of online tools allowing two or more people to work together to create something collaboratively in a virtual environment. McPherson held that wikis make the writing process a social process.

Joyce Valenza, formerly the school librarian at Springfield Township High School in Pennsylvania and now on the faculty at Rutgers, is a well-known school library technology expert. She believes that wikis allow users to "freely create, and, edit Web site content using their browser" (Valenza 2007). The wiki quickly becomes a tool for students to write, particularly collaboratively. Web 2.0 applications give students the opportunity to write and to receive comments and feedback in a nonthreatening environment. What a boon for those whose reading and writing skills may still not be fully developed!

Certainly the best known wiki is Wikipedia, an online encyclopedia with some information about nearly everything. As one reads the literature about wikis and Wikipedia in particular, two extremes appear: Those who feel Wikipedia is an excellent beginning reference source and those who doubt its reliability from beginning to end. The biggest issue with Wikipedia is that anyone, no matter their qualification, can post entries to Wikipedia or make changes to what is already there. This open atmosphere can cause trepidation among educators, and many colleges and universities will not accept references to Wikipedia in material submitted at those institutions.

The article "An Info-Skills Workout: Wikis and Collaborative Workout," by Annette Lamb and Larry Johnson, examined the characteristics of wikis and how they can profitably be used in education. With wikis, the emphasis is on authoring. Rather than just adding, wiki users are encouraged to submit things. Wikis typically use open editing tools, so there is little or no financial stake in them. Lamb and Johnson noted the following characteristics of wikis:

1. The content of the wiki is original and thus unique. Users are writing and posting original material to the wiki.
2. The wiki provides a space for collaboration that is both free and open. Collaboration is one of the keys with a wiki, as it is with many Web 2.0 applications.
3. A wiki allows for open editing. Students can check and recheck any postings to a wiki for accuracy, thereby increasing their research skills.
4. Using a wiki is simple. The tools used to create the posting are very similar to those found in most word processors. No problems with a high learning curve.
5. Wikis are constantly evolving.

Lamb and Johnson also enumerated several possible applications for the use of wikis in education. Although not a complete or all-inclusive list, it does provide reasons to have teachers willing to establish wikis:

1. Wikis can be used as an aid for collaborative problem solving. This is especially true if the collaboration does not need to be synchronous.
2. Collaborative research can benefit by the use of a wiki. Each member of the team can easily post research to the wiki.
3. Collaborative writing takes provides a vehicle for students to provide feedback to other students about their writing using the wiki.
4. A wiki is a great journal or notebook. Students can post to a teacher's wiki about what is being presented in class.
5. The wiki is a great vehicle for the creation of electronic portfolios. This is does have the challenge of someone else editing or changing a portfolio with an incorrect posting.

Wiki Uses for Classroom

6. A wiki can act as a portal, or a starting point for learning.
7. A wiki is more than a good device for collaborative research; it is a good place to aggregate research to be able to share it with others.
8. A wiki can be a very good study guide when it has enough contributions.
9. A wiki is a low-cost substitute for expensive video conferencing equipment.

Many good educational reasons show that it is important to use wikis in the school library. A few negatives about wikis have been mentioned and reinforced here. First is the open nature of a wiki that allows entries to be edited at will. This can be a dangerous thing with students unless it is closely monitored. Second, it can broadcast some students' difficulties reading and writing, and this is not good for their self-esteem. Finally, students who do not feel comfortable with the collaborative process are reluctant to participate. However, the value is there and teachers and their students should be encouraged to use this method of communication.

PODCASTING

Nearly every one of our students in the digital generation has an audio player of some description. The iPod is the perfect vehicle to provide content to students that is easy to access and inexpensive. By definition, a podcast is a "digital recording of a radio broadcast or similar program made available on the Internet for downloading to a personal audio player" (Eash). Most of our students don't look to mobile computing devices for much more than music, but there are some really good educational applications for podcasts.

Though MP3 files have been around for some time, the concepts of podcasting and RSS (Rich Site Summary) mean that users no longer have to go to the web to find the MP3 files or to download them.

The article "Podcasting in the School Library: Part 1: Integrated Podcasts and Vodcasts into Teaching and Learning" by Lamb and Johnson presented two discrete sections, the first presenting some criteria to consider when evaluating available podcasts.

1. The learner's needs. Does the podcast meet student needs exactly? It does little good to provide podcasts beyond what the students can understand.
2. Is the quality of the content high-quality? Is the person who did the podcast an expert in the field? Can his or her qualifications be verified?
3. What is the technical quality of the podcast? So many podcasts are out there of good quality that one can ignore those that are not.
4. If it is a vodcast is it well designed?

5. Does the podcast meet high standards of instructional quality? You would never want to make anything available to your students that is not of good instructional quality.

Lamb and Johnson ("InfoTech: Podcasting in the School Library, Part 1: Integrating Podcasts and Vodcasts into Teaching and Learning") then presented some possible uses of podcasts in the educational setting. Many of these applications refer to products available online, though it is certainly not beyond the ability of most educators to create simple podcasts.

1. Collaborative projects.
2. Discussion of current events. Many of these types of podcasts are available from news sources, such as CNN.
3. Government documents or government events.
4. Interviews. A wide variety of interviews are available for downloading.
5. Conflicting issues. Many of these are available from the news organizations.
6. Teacher lectures and notes. This is particularly valuable for students who are absent from class, and they are available 24/7.
7. Programs. Does your school do a band or choral concert? Broadcast it as a podcast that can be downloaded.
8. Reviews. Let's use the school's music program as an example and take this idea a step further. If your school is having its musical broadcast as a podcast, add reviews from satisfied viewers. What a great way to increase attendance!
9. Virtual tours. We have all been to museums that provide taped tours of their collections. Take it a step further and provide a podcast. (2007, 163–170).
10. Use podcasts to promote your school library. This is an especially good vehicle to promote reading and book promotion.
11. Use a podcast to show exemplary student products—perhaps papers, posters, or even a student-produced podcast.
12. Keep the public informed of what is happening in the school and school library through podcasts.
13. Provide professional development. The podcast is a great way to provide professional development programs in small snippets, and it can be available to teachers at any time.

School librarians can follow a few simple steps to create podcasts. These steps may vary in your library situation but are pretty universal:

1. Figure out what hardware and software you will need for the podcast.

2. Know what content will be on the podcast.
3. Practice the podcast until you are comfortable with it.
4. Record the podcast.
5. Test the podcast, and redo the parts you are not happy with.
6. Publish the podcast.
7. Make sure people know about the podcast by publicizing it.
8. Evaluate your podcast, and make the next one better!

COURSE MANAGEMENT SYSTEMS

Course management systems are an essential piece of the distance education process. Distance education or online education is the educational phenomena of the 21st century. It has proliferated to the point that the majority of college students have taken at least one online class. What can be better than instruction available twenty-four hours a day, seven days a week—not just at 10 a.m. Monday, Wednesday, and Friday? All the student needs is a computer.

Since the first days of distance education, there has been a K–12 presence. Initially the thrust was to provide education opportunities to students who would not have them otherwise. For example, in Indiana, Purdue University provided online instruction in calculus to students at schools too small to provide that level of mathematics instruction. In other areas, school districts formed consortia to provide instruction in subjects that did not have sufficient enrollment to support a teacher in each school.

The picture has changed significantly today. Digital schools are everywhere and provide high-quality education to such diverse groups as confined children, homeschooled students, and children unable to function in a traditional school environment. Two examples of statewide digital schools are the Florida Virtual High School and the Pennsylvania Cyber School. Because distance education is being decentralized to regional educational agencies and individual school districts, course management systems must be understood by an increasing number of teachers.

Course management systems are software systems that allow teachers to manage online instruction. In addition to full online courses, they are also used to manage both blended and face-to-face courses. Using a course management system ensures that all communication and learning tools are in one place, sharing a navigation system.

Choosing the right course management system can be a real challenge. The commercial systems are quite expensive but often provide a "finished look" that open or free systems lack. Another decision to make is whether you will host the system or will it be hosted on the vendor's servers. Here is just a brief discussion of some of the most popular course management systems:

1. Angel learning—a commercial K–12 system now owned by Blackboard.
2. Moodle—free and open course package. Widely used in K–12 environments.
3. Sakai Project—free and open-source, but high-end. Used by many large universities that produce their own systems.
4. Blackboard—commercial web-based. The most popular system at all levels. Blackboard now owns WebCT.

In 2005 Kathy D. Munoz, Bart Bos, and Joan Van Duzer conducted research at Humboldt State University comparing Blackboard and Moodle, contrasting a commercial system with an open course system. The results are interesting.

WHAT IS IT

Blackboard

- LMS partly owned by Microsoft
- Licensed worldwide
- Average license = $10,000/year

Moodle

- Open-source (free) LMS
- Customizable by local programmers
- Much flexibility
- Supported by programmers worldwide.

Advantages

- More polished
- Better gradebook
- Threaded discussion easier to use
- Announcements more prominently displayed.
- Easier to provide feedback.
- Easier to track student activity.

They reported that 35.7 percent of respondents favored Moodle, 21.4 percent Blackboard, and 42.9 percent neither.

RESEARCH AND DISCUSSION QUESTION

Construct both a blog and a wiki. You will need to research how to do each and then post meaningful content. Maintain each for one month (longer if you prefer), and then report back to the class with the results.

REFERENCES

"ABCs of Web 2.0: Avatars, Blogs, Collaborative Wikis: Avatars, Virtual Worlds, and Social Networks." Eduscapes. http://eduscapes.com/sessions/abc/abc2.htm.

"ABCs of Web 2.0: Avatars, Blogs, Collaborative Wikis: Blogs, Vlogs, Podcasts, and Web Feeds." Eduscapes. http://eduscapes.com/sessions/abc/abc3.htm.

"ABCs of Web 2.0: Avatars, Blogs, Collaborative Wikis: Collaborative Wikis, Documents, and Projects." Eduscapes. http://eduscapes.com/sessions/abc/abc4.htm.

"ABCs of Web 2.0: Avatars, Blogs, Collaborative Wikis: The World of Web 2.0." Eduscapes . http://eduscapes.com/sessions/abc/abc1.htm.

Achterman, Doug. "Beyond Wikipedia," in *Toward a 21st Century School Library Media Program*, edited by Esther Rosenfeld and David V. Loertscher, 148–153. Lanham, MD: Scarecrow, 2007.

Alexander, Bryan. "Web 2.0: A New Wave of Innovation for Teaching and Learning?" *EDUCAUSE Review* 41, no. 2 (March/April 2008), www.educause.edu/EDUCAUSE+Review/EDUCAUSEReviewMagazineVolume41/.

Berger, Pam "Student Inquiry and Web 2.0." *School Library Monthly* (January 2010). www.schoollibrarymonthly.com/articles/Berger2010-v26n5p14.html.

Bos, Bert, Kathy D. Munoz, and Joan Van Duzer. "Blackboard vs. Moodle: A Comparison of Satisfaction with Online Teaching and Learning Tools." Humboldt State University. www.humboldt.edu/~jdv1/moodle/all.htm.

Casey, Michael E., and Laura C. Savastinuk. "Library 2.0: Service for the Next-Generation Library," *Library Journal* (September 1, 2006). *MasterFILE Premier*. EBSCO. July 10, 2009. http://search.ebscohost.com.

Eash, Esther Kreider. "Podcasting 101 for K–12 Librarians." *Infotoday* 26, no. 4 (April 2006). www.infotoday.com/cilmag/apr06/Eash.shtml.

Hargardon, Steve "A Little Help from My Friends: Classroom 2.0 Educators Share Their Experiences," *School Library Journal* (October 1, 2009). www.schoollibrary journal.com/.

Harris, Christopher "School Library 2.0: Say Good-Bye to Your Mother's School Library," *School Library Journal* (May 1, 2006). www.schoollibraryjournal.com/.

Harris, Christopher. "SL2.0: Visioning the School Library 2.0." Infomancy. http://schoolofinfomancy/infomancy/?p=131.

Johnson, Doug. "Connections for Learning: Schools and the Educational Use of Social Networking." https://saywire.com/downloads/Saywire-White-Paper.pdf.

Johnson, Doug. "Guidelines for Educators Using Social and Educational Networking Sites," *Library Media Connection* (March/April 2010). www.doug-johnson.com/dougwri/guidelines-for-educators-using-social-and-educational-networ.html.

Kroskie, Ellyssa. *Web 2.0 for Libraries and Information Professionals*. New York: Neal-Schuman, 2008.

Lamb, Annette, and Larry Johnson. "InfoTech: An Info-Skills Workout: Wikis and Collaborative Writing," in *Toward a 21st Century School Library Media Program*, edited by Esther Rosenfeld and David V. Loertscher, 132–138. Lanham, MD: Scarecrow, 2007.

Lamb, Annette, and Larry Johnson. "InfoTech: Podcasting in the School Library, Part 1: Integrating Podcasts and Vodcasts into Teaching and Learning," in *Toward a 21st Century School Library Media Program*, edited by Esther Rosenfeld and David V. Loertscher, 162–170. Lanham, MD: Scarecrow, 2007.

Lamb, Annette, and Larry Johnson. "InfoTech: Want to Be My Friend? What You Need to Know about Social Technologies," in *Toward a 21st Century School Library Media Program*, edited by Esther Rosenfeld and David V. Loertscher, 178–183. Lanham, MD: Scarecrow, 2007.

Lamb, Brian. "Wide Open Spaces: Wikis, Ready or Not." *EDUCAUSE Review* 39, no. 5 (September/October 2004), www.educause.edu/EDUCAUSE+Review/EDUCAUSEReviewMagazineVolume39/.

"Learning Spaces: Course Management Systems." Eduscapes. http://eduscapes.com/hightech/spaces/course/index.htm.

McPherson, Keith. "Literacy Links: Wikis and Literacy Development," in *Toward a 21st Century School Library Media Program*, edited by Esther Rosenfeld and David V. Loertscher, 143–147. Lanham, MD: Scarecrow, 2007.

McPherson, Keith. "Literacy Links: School Library Blogging," in *Toward a 21st Century School Library Media Program*, edited by Esther Rosenfeld and David V. Loertscher, 154–157. Lanham, MD: Scarecrow, 2007.

McPherson, Keith. "Literacy Links: Wikis and Literacy Development," in *Toward a 21st Century School Library Media Program*, edited by Esther Rosenfeld and David V. Loertscher, 143–147. Lanham, MD: Scarecrow, 2007.

McPherson, Keith. "Literacy Links: Wikis and Student Writing," in *Toward a 21st Century School Library Media Program*, edited by Esther Rosenfeld and David V. Loertscher, 139–142. Lanham, MD: Scarecrow, 2007.

Maness, Jack M. "Library 2.0 Theory: Web 2.0 and Its Implications for Libraries." *Webology* 3, no 2 (June 2006), www.Webology.ir/2006/v3n2/a25.html.

Milstein, Sarah. "Twitter for Libraries (and Librarians)." *Infotoday* 29, no. 5 (May 2009), www.infotoday.com/cilmag/apr06/Eash.shtml.

O'Reilly, Tim. "What Is Web 2.0? Design Patterns and Business Models for the Next Generation of Software." O'Reilly. http://oreilly.com/Web2/archive/what-is-Web-20.html.

Rosenfeld, Esther, and David V. Loertscher, eds. *Towards a 21st Century School Library Media Program*. Lanham, MD: Scarecrow, 2008.

"Twitter for Librarians: The Ultimate Guide." College@Home. www.collegeathome.com/blog/2008/05/27/twitter-for-librarians-the-ultimate-guide/.

Valenza, Joyce. "Something Wiki Comes This Way . . . Are You Ready?" in *Toward a 21st Century School Library Media Program*, edited by Esther Rosenfeld and David V. Loertscher, 129–132. Lanham, MD: Scarecrow, 2007.

15

Common Core Standards and STEM

Few movements in education have been less understood or more politicized than the Common Core Standards. For those of us in education, this is a bit hard to understand: Standards have been a part of curriculum for many years. Perhaps the biggest difference is that the Common Core Standards were developed nationally rather than on a state-by-state basis, somehow impinging on people's idea of local autonomy of the educational system.

DEVELOPMENT OF THE COMMON CORE STANDARDS

The Common Core is a set of high-quality academic standards in mathematics and English language arts/literacy (ELA). These learning goals outline what a student should know and be able to do at the end of each grade. The standards were created to ensure that all students graduate from high school with the skills and knowledge necessary to succeed in college, career, and life, regardless of where they live. Forty-three states, the District of Columbia, four territories, and the Department of Defense Education Activity (DoDEA) have voluntarily adopted and are moving forward with the Common Core.

For years, the academic progress of our nation's students has been stagnant, and we have lost ground to our international peers. Particularly in subjects such as math, college remediation rates have been high. One root cause has been an uneven patchwork of academic standards that vary from state to state and do not agree on what students should know and be able to do at each grade level. ("Common Core and More")

For more information about Common Core Standards, go to http://www.corestandards.org/about-the-standards/.

BASICS OF THE COMMON CORE STANDARDS

As just noted, the Common Core Standards were developed to provide what many educators consider to be real world expectations across all states. The idea was not to impose a federal top-down curriculum such that every student across the country was on the same page at the same time, but rather to create a framework for teachers across the country. On the whole, students are required to delve into fewer topics but in greater depth. The Common Core's Career and College Ready Standards focus on more hands-on learning that correlates with what students will work with as they reach adulthood.

Of particular note is the fact that the Career and College Ready Standards emphasize student learning through technology and multimedia. Who among us cannot see that this is another opportunity for the school librarian to remain the epicenter of learning in the school?

This places the school librarian in the middle of two concepts. First is the need for professional development if the Common Core Standards are to assist students to learn through technology and multimedia. Research has shown that for training to be effective, it needs to be ongoing, not a one-shot deal. This is an area that makes technology tools and the role of the school librarian especially effective, as the use of technology to provide ongoing training for teachers should fall in the purview of the school librarian.

The second concept is what is known as personalized learning environments for students. This incorporates many of the concepts of the "flipped" classroom, in which students learn at their own pace and the teacher is more a facilitator than a purveyor of information. It is easy to see this education taking place in the school library. Digital content made available in an on demand digital library is the ideal vehicle to allow this concept to work. The use of technology in the school library should also allow the students to access experts from around the world without ever leaving the school through the use of collaborative distance learning technology (Common Core Standards).

Kristin Fontichiaro, a library educator in Michigan, along with the Iowa Association of School Librarians, formulated a short list of areas in which school librarians can be supportive in the implementation of Common Core Standards by helping their students accomplish the following:

1. Creating sound persuasive arguments with evidence
2. Reading comprehension strategies

3. Effectively using primary and secondary sources
4. Reading and analyzing complex texts
5. Reading and comprehending informational text in all content areas

The school librarian can be an integral part of the implementation process with Common Core Standards designed to prepare students for college and for careers. They were developed when business personnel said that students were not prepared to enter the workforce. Despite the political posturing, most would acknowledge that the Common Core Standards are clear, essential skills that need to be taught. Teachers are not being directed what to teach or how they should teach; teachers themselves are the best qualified to know how best to teach their students. The Common Core Standards give teachers targets. A little more troubling for teachers is that school administrators now have a vehicle to try to measure what successful teaching looks like.

For the school librarian, reading is at the very heart of the Common Core Standards. We are ideally situated to collaborate with teachers to identify literature and text in the content areas. Information literacy is at the heart of the Common Core Standards. We have an opportunity to step up and be an integral part of the Common Core Standards movement (Kramer).

One of the biggest consideration for Common Core Standards in school districts is how the school will deal with the assessments that are a vital part of the Common Core. Intel, in conjunction with Lenovo, developed a checklist that should be of assistance to the school librarian as they work with the district on Common Core assessments:

1. Define your vision:
   a. What are the end goals?
   b. What resources are needed?
   c. What plans and policies need to be implemented?
   d. What stakeholders need to be included?
   e. How will the changes be rolled out?
   f. What are the key milestones?
2. Conduct a gap analysis for the flowing areas:
   a. Devices
   b. Network
   c. Inventory
   d. Personnel
3. Provide regular progress reports to all stakeholders.
4. Address security issues:
   a. Physical security tools
   b. Virtual security tools

5. Prepare for students who will need special accommodations during testing.
6. Make sure students have the technology skills needed for online testing.
7. Practice to make sure there are no surprises during the actual testing.
8. Build a best-practices document so you can learn for others. (Common Core and More)

STEM: SCIENCE, TECHNOLOGY, ENGINEERING, AND MATHEMATICS

Science, technology, engineering, and mathematics (STEM) education is used to describe individual subjects, a standalone course, a sequence of courses, activities involving any of the four areas, a STEM-related course, or an interconnected or integrated program of study. A nationally agreed-upon definition for STEM education is currently lacking (Science, Technology, Engineering & Mathematics. Science, Technology, Engineering, & Mathematics (STEM) information. California Department of Education).

Paige Jaeger, in a 2013 article "STEM, eStem, and the Cybrarian: What Every Librarian Should Know," pointed out several items dealing with STEM that should be of interest to the school librarian. First, mathematics is the basis for almost all STEM. It is the essence of all computers. Technology, engineering, and mathematics are all based on numbers. Unfortunately, it seems many adults, including teachers, have an aversion to math. Jaeger notes that she is not sure which aversion is greater—reading or math. My experience has been that when my students work with Excel in Microsoft Office, as soon as formulas and functions are mentioned, their eyes glaze over and the whining begins. They are so poorly grounded in these math concepts that they just pull the curtain down and want to go no further.

One of the movements that is rapidly advancing in this country is the eSTEM movement. "When you see eSTEM, you are viewing a deliberate integrated educational paradigm shift where digital, technology focused STEM is the driver of the curriculum" (Jaeger).

Jaeger also notes that there are long lists of apps for portable computing devices for STEM applications. Although these apps offer explanations and experiments, they often do not offer high-quality, problem-based, inquiry-driven units. This is the opportunity for the school librarian to show his or her expertise. This is when the school librarian needs to be the academic coach, the guide on the side, to help those students who don't understand. What better role for the school librarian?

Also in 2013, Leanne Brown published an article titled "Developing Programs and Resources in the School Library to Support STEM Education."

This article cut right to the heart of the role of the school librarian with relation to STEM and could act as a roadmap for school librarians who need to move forward with STEM.

Based on earlier research, Brown found that school library collections are weaker in the sciences and stronger in language arts and social sciences, because past school librarians have had that type of background rather than a math or science background. It is a rare school library that has a librarian who has another certification in math or one of the sciences. Further research has shown some correlation between school library programs and improvement in social studies and language arts scores, but similar research has never even been attempted for the sciences or mathematics.

A 2008 Scholastic Research Foundation report found that school libraries have changed, with a wide variety of technology resources available to students, and that these resources help in integrating these resources in classrooms and throughout the curriculum. What was also noted, however, is that the school library needs to be better balanced in its collection and service.

President Obama noted that his goal with STEM was to think about new and creative ways to engage young people in science and engineering. Subramaniam, Ahn, Fleischman, and Druin noted that they feel that the school library and educational research will soon show the contribution of school library programs to mathematics learning. They further maintain that school libraries should be the hub of learning with all different types of media and should be places of discovery. The school librarian should be both a change agent and an innovator—the perfect job description for a school librarian.

Both Hiten and Brown have suggested some ways for school libraries to be active and supportive in STEM:

1. Create open exploration time for math and science, either before or after school hours. Make sure the lessons are fun but still educational.
2. Challenge students to create video games that include STEM skills in the design. This works well with elementary school–aged students.
3. Take full advantage of the subscription databases the library has to sharpen students' information-gathering skills.
4. Be the trainer. Create training for the STEM faculty to become more proficient with available technology.
5. Work with faculty to create podcasts related to STEM. Research has shown that these are especially valuable for special need students.
6. Integrate art into STEM, making it STEAM. This can be the ideal vehicle to interest female students in fields where they might feel intimidated.

7. Try to involve students' families in STEM education by creating make-it-and-take-it stations that allow students to take home supplies for simple experiments.
8. Use the National Science Digital Library (NSDL).

Brown also included some tips to make the school library a center for STEM education:

1. Remember that STEM programming can be as simple or as complex as you like.
2. Start small, collaborating with math and science teachers to create lessons and projects.
3. You need not have a STEM background to do STEM programming.
4. Make sure you use expert sites for your STEM activities.
5. Seek local funding for more complex STEM programs and activities.

RESEARCH AND DISCUSSION QUESTION

Your principal has tasked you to make your school library the center for STEM education in your school. Spend some time researching the Internet to gather research and program data, then design a collaborative unit that incorporates your skills as an information manager and the subject skills of the math and science teachers. Ideally, this should include a unit plan and the lesson plans that will make up the unit. Be sure to include any available technology.

REFERENCES

"Common Core and More." http://academics.nsuok.edu/Portals/39/pdfs/Checklist-Common-Core-10-Steps-to-Successful-Digital-Readiness-Assessment.pdf.

Common Core State Standards Initiative. "About the Standards." www.corestandards.org/about-the-standards/.

Fontichiaro, Kristin. "Common Core Standards." www.schoollibrarymonthly.com/curriculum/Fontichiaro2011-v28n1p49.html.

Hiten Samtani. "Meet the Makers." *School Library Journal* (June 19, 2013). www.slj.com/author/hsamtani/#.

Jaeger, Paige. "STEM, eSTEM, and the Cybrarian: What Every Librarian Should Know." *Library Media Connection* (May/June 2013). www.librarymediaconnection.com/pdf/lmc/reviews_and_articles/featured_articles/Jaeger_May_June2013.pdf.

Koester, Amy. "Full Steam Ahead: Injecting Art and Creativity into STEM." *School Library Journal* (October 1, 2013.). www.slj.com/2013/10/programs/full-steam-ahead-injecting-art-and-creativity-into-stem/.

Kramer, Pamela K. "Common Core and School Librarians: An Interview with Joyce Karon." *School Library Monthly* (September/October 2013). www.schoollibrary monthly.com/articles/Kramer2011-v28n1p8.html.

"President Obama, U.S. Secretary of Education Duncan Announce National Competition to Advance School Reform." U.S. Department of Education. July 24, 2009.

"Ready or Not: Creating a High School Diploma That Counts." Achieve, Inc. December 10, 2004.

Scholastic Research Foundation. "School Libraries Work." http://listbuilder.scholastic .com/content/stores/LibraryStore/pages/images/SLW3.pdf.

Science, Technology, Engineering & Mathematics. Science, Technology, Engineering, & Mathematics (STEM) information. California Department of Education. www.cde .ca.gov/pd/ca/sc/stemintrod.asp.

Subramaniam, Mega M., June Ahn, Kenneth R. Fleischmann, and Allison Druin. "Reimagining the Role of School Libraries in STEM Education: Creating Hybrid Spaces for Exploration." *Library Quarterly* (April 2012). http://ahnjune.com/wp -content/uploads/2012/03/libquarterly.pdf.

16

Educating Digital Natives and Countering Cyberbullying

In the five years since my earlier book on technology in school libraries, there has been a remarkable growth in what is called digital natives. These are our students, people who have grown up with all types of electronic devices and computing devices, such as cell phones, computers, and tablet computers. This is nothing less than a change that has enormous implications for the school librarian and education as a whole. Unfortunately, one of the outgrowths of the digital native is the explosion in the occurrence of cyberbullying, considered by many to be one of the gravest threats to our young people. It may begin with the confusion the older generation or digital immigrants have about the different new forms of communication available to the younger generation, those digital natives. This chapter presents educating digital natives and countering cyberbullying

UNDERSTANDING DIGITAL IMMIGRANTS AND DIGITAL NATIVES

This whole concept of digital immigrants and digital natives has somewhat murky beginnings. As early as 2001, the work of Marc Prensky showed an understanding of the difference between these two groups. In a seminal paper published in October 2001, Prensky stated that "the average college graduate spent less than 5,000 hours of their life reading but more than 10,000 hours playing video games and more than 20,000 hours watching television." In the fourteen years since then, the number of hours students spend with technology has only increased. Prensky is one who posits that these students think and process information in a completely different ways than digital immigrants do. He also bases his theories about brain structures on those of Dr. Bruce D. Perry of the Baylor College of Medicine.

Pransky calls what we, as digital immigrants do with technology as having an accent. We do such things as printing emails or printing documents to edit them rather than editing on the screen.

Prensky holds deeply to the idea that education must be changed unless we are willing to give up educating the digital natives until they reach adulthood and can teach themselves. He believes that educators need to change the way they teach, going faster, less step-by-step, and with much more random access.

Prensky feels that the content taught to digital natives should be both future and legacy. The first is a major change in methodology, and the second involves all the legacy content plus new content and thinking. These ideas should help even the most technologically literate school librarian recognize that change is inevitable. School librarians must help their teachers change teaching methods to meet the challenges of the digital native. Digital immigrants must understand digital natives and determine how to teach them.

METHODS OF EDUCATING DIGITAL NATIVES

A growing misunderstanding has arisen between digital immigrants and digital natives. Anyone with parents, children, clients, students, teachers, or employees knows there is a disparity—not only in technical skill but also in worldview—between the old and the young. Contrary to popular belief, this is not due to ineptitude or "techno-resistance" of baby boomers, but rather their entrance into the digital world at a later age. Digital natives are Generation X, younger people who grew up, in varying degrees, with technology. These natives understand technology in an intuitive manner that baby boomers rarely will.

Digital immigrants used the telephone to talk business or share personal happenings. They mailed letters to share news. For many, the public library was their introduction to the world of email, and they began to use this to maintain a relationship with their grandchildren. Their digital native grandchildren had many more gadgets to learn and use.

Digital natives have a great affinity and familiarity with the use of technology. They can use Twitter and Facebook. In fact, these two modes of communication, along with texting, have taken the place of email for many of these individuals. Many digital natives are no longer students but have completed their education and moved into the workforce. These individuals can download music and probably stream television and movies to their computing device—not necessarily a laptop but maybe a cell phone. They can do these things because they were on the ground floor when these tools were introduced.

The other issue here is what they are not able to do with technology. Let us just look at two areas, research and productivity. Many digital natives think that all research can be done with Google or another search engine and that all information on the Internet is free. This is not just digital natives; far too many digital immigrants also think this is true. The school librarian must work to change this thinking by teaching and reinforcing concepts of digital literacy, leading the teaching of efficient searching skills. School librarians introduce the use of acceptable data bases rather than depending upon a Google search. Digital natives need to learn that a Google search yielding 10 million results will be challenging when a student could use a subject specific databases that returns the desired results that will be accurate and relevant. No more "Shakespeare" that includes information about the fishing tackle company.

The second area the digital native falls short is in the use of productivity software. They may well be able to tweet and do the things mentioned above, but few can set headers and footers in a word processor document or apply the correct formulas and functions in a spreadsheet. My experience has been that when the word *formula* is mentioned, the eyes of many, many students glaze over. They just do not have the skills need to accomplish any kind of complex mathematical computation without a calculator. Keep in mind that I am not advocating the teaching of software packages in a computer class, but rather integrating the skills needed to complete an assignment into the overall instruction.

Dave Schechter, the Senior National Editor for the *New York Times*, discussed the education of our digital natives in an article titled "How Best to Educate our 'Digital Natives.'" He dealt in depth with an analysis of whether technology was actually improving the quality of education. Those that advocate the increased use of technology say that digital devices allow students to learn at their own pace, teach the skills needed in a modern economy, and can hold the attention of the digital natives.

Help parents take some responsibility for their children. This is where posting homework assignments on the school library's webpage is so helpful. For those students who have little help at home, suggesting that they go to the homework center at the local public library may help fill that gap.

CHARACTERISTICS OF DIGITAL NATIVES

School librarians and educators need to recognize, affirm, and make use of technology. It is here to stay. It is not an innovation that will go away. Rather, it will continue to change and change far more rapidly than we might want. However, the digital native will move along with each new opportunity, because technology is not foreign; it is and has been a part of their lives throughout their lives.

Although many digital immigrants are known to fly by the seat of their pants, digital natives are intuitive learners rather than linear ones. They seem to be flying by the seat of their pants when learning and seem to learn by doing, rather than by using manuals and taking a more systematic approach to learning. Because they learn by doing, they are more interested in project-based or problem-based learning. They are less willing to sit in a classroom and listen to a lecture. They may be sitting, and someone may be talking, but it is likely they are busily texting.

Another example would be the difference between the choice of using the *Encyclopædia Britannica* and Wikipedia. Wikipedia encourages users to contribute to and modify entries, whereas the *Britannica* is static. Their willingness to add new information to a project makes it very easy to assign group projects in which students add new knowledge to the group's previous work.

Digital learners have a great ability to multitask and can easily jump from one task to another. Some evidence has shown that this is caused by a real change in brain function, a change that digital immigrants have not undergone. Digital natives seem to view things in a less hierarchal way, and the digital native thinks of the Internet as the great leveler in society.

These students' brains are not wired to sit quietly and take notes while the teacher lectures. They want to be in an interactive environment in which they can talk, touch things, process information in different ways, and solve problems. Digital natives are demanding a sense of why they should learn something, as well as some control over what they are learning. This is a great challenge to teachers and school librarians. This generation of digital natives wants to know what they are doing and why they are doing it.

Digital natives' liking for games means that a game to teach a skill will be readily accepted and used to learn. Because they can multitask, they should be given opportunities to do so. It is unlikely that a digital native will want to sit quietly at a desk with hands folded until the next step is explained. He or she will want to be testing to find the best next step.

It is time to revamp the school library for all the new approaches to teaching. One way to do this has been discussed earlier—bringing much of those "special" teachers to the learning commons, where collaboration is natural. Providing opportunities for students to conduct their research virtually and also to work in small groups almost 24/7 to finish their projects moves them out of that school building into the world.

The Zur Institute published a report on how our digital divide affects everyone, from families through educational institution and into the workplace. Students must learn how to help digital immigrants accept and implement technology, and this begins with helping teachers. No school librarian can really be responsible for helping teachers who have technology challenges. Identifying those students who are not only capable but also understanding, with those who are less technology-oriented, are a school librarian's greatest asset. They become the "geek squad" for their schools, a great deal like students in the distant past who ran the 16mm projector and helped load film into it. Let's don't forget that not all students are expert digital natives, and students can help each other overcome any problems encountered with each new technology.

[handwritten margin note: Take advantage of your student "geek squads"]

Digital natives are constantly connected. They may not seem to be communicating, because they aren't doing so verbally. Cell phone conversations are not allowed in classrooms, but they are texting their friends, who may be just two rows over. They have friends both in real space and through virtual worlds all over the world.

Another big difference is between how digital natives and digital immigrants experience music. Digital immigrants listened to the radio and bought records of the most popular songs. Speaker systems occupied large parts of dens and bedrooms, and parents worried about how to cut down the noise levels. Today's digital natives download music to their computing device and expect the music to be digitally formatted, free, shareable, and portable. One cannot say that digital natives are more creative than previous generation, but they certainly manifest a creativity that is worlds away from the ways their parents expressed creativity. Digital natives can do things with technology that would not have been possible a few years ago (Prensky).

It was noted that one of the primary differences between digital immigrants and digital natives is in the language spoken. For digital immigrants, technology is a language that is not native to them any more than French might be. They have learned all types of technology, but it was a language learned incrementally. Digital natives, conversely, have used technology their entire lives and absorbed the language as easily as they would absorb French growing up in France.

CYBERBULLYING

In this section, we will discuss bullying as many of us understand the term and then move into a more detailed discussion of cyberbullying. This will include statistics on the occurrence of cyberbullying, what forms cyberbullying can take, and how teachers, parents, and teenage children can counter cyberbullying. Some high-profile cases that involve cyberbullying are reported, and resources are provided to help prevent cyberbullying.

Those who think bullying is a recent phenomenon may have forgotten their own childhoods. Bullying has existed both in the school environment and outside it for all of recorded time. The bullies who think their only mission in life was to make the lives of other children miserable have always been present. It was sometimes subtle, like name-calling, or overt, like taking money or even hitting. In those times, the reaction was often retaliation: Have an older brother or sister take care of the problem. At those times, persons being bullied by someone at school were usually safe within the walls of their homes.

Bullying today has a more insidious form, cyberbullying, "using technology, cell phones and the Internet to bully or harass another person" (Cyberbullying Statistics). Bullying is further defined as "intentional, repeated hurtful acts, words, or other behavior, such as name-calling, threatening, and/or shunning committed by one or more children against another. These negative acts are not intentionally provoked by the victims" (Cyberbullying Statistics).

The school librarian who is the leader of technology in schools should be the first line of defense against cyberbullying. The school librarian can be a strong advocate for those who are being bullied. To carry out these two things, it is essential that the school librarian have a firm understanding of what cyberbullying is; what parents, teachers, and the students themselves can do about it; what forms cyberbullying can take; and what resources are available to the school librarian relating to cyberbullying. Basic information on cyberbullying can be found at www.stopbullying.gov/at-risk/index.html. Some forms are listed below.

Forms of Cyberbullying

This list does not include all possible forms of cyberbullying, but it describes some of the more evident:

1. "Sending mean messages or threats to a person's email account or cell phone" (Cyberbullying Statistics). Certainly "mean" messages covers multitude of things, but threats are overt and, in most cases, criminal.

2. "Spreading rumors online or through texts" (Cyberbullying Statistics). This is one of the most insidious types of cyberbullying. Unfortunately, a single rumor can be devastating to one's reputation.

3. "Posting hurtful or threatening messages on social networking sites or web pages" (Cyberbullying Statistics). Hurtful may be in the eyes of the beholder, and threats, as already described, may be criminal.

4. "Stealing a person's information to break into their account and send damaging messages" (Cyberbullying Statistics). This type of behavior often leads to serious consequences for the bully and might be treated as criminal.

5. "Pretending to be someone else online to hurt another person" (Cyberbullying Statistics). One student may send messages to a girl or boy who is smitten with someone as if they are being sent by the person being adored, can cause unusually difficult situations, especially if the idol has no idea what is happening.

6. "Taking unflattering pictures of a person and spreading them through cell phones or the Internet" (Cyberbullying Statistics). It is suggested that this item depends on intent to a great degree, but it is malicious to take unflattering pictures with the purpose of making a joke.

7. "Sexting, or circulating sexually suggestive pictures or messages about a person" (Cyberbullying Statistics). The jury is still out on this. It is probably criminal, but it is such a recent serious phenomenon that there is little case law to follow up.

"Some cyber bullies think that bullying others online is a joke. Cyber bullies may not realize the consequences they face for cyberbullying" (Cyberbullying Statistics). At a very basic level, "the things teens post online now may reflect badly on them later when they apply for college or a job" (Cyberbullying Statistics). Nearly every college and employer now makes a close examination of cyber media to determine what their applicants have posted. A "joke" posted making fun of a classmate in the freshman year of high school may result in the bully's rejection to a desired college or university.

"Cyber bullies can lose their cell phone or online accounts for cyber bullying. Also, cyber bullies and their parents may face legal charges for cyber bullying, and if the cyber bullying was sexual in nature or involved sexting, the results can include being registered as a sex offender. Teens may think that if they use a fake name they won't get caught, but there are many ways to track someone who is cyber bullying" (Cyberbullying Statistics).

Cyberbullying Statistics

Some disturbing statistics have been reported concerning cyberbullying from both the i-Safe Foundation and the *Hartford County Examiner*. "Over half of adolescents and teens have been bullied online, and about the same number have engaged in cyber bullying" (Cyberbullying Statistics). Ten to twenty percent of teens experience cyberbullying regularly. It would be interesting to see what the overlap is here. Is there a trend wherein those who are cyberbullied also are cyberbullies themselves?

More than one in three young people have experienced cyberthreats online. More than 80 percent of teens use a cell phone regularly, making it the most popular form of technology and a common medium for cyberbullying. "Over 25 percent of adolescents and teens have been bullied repeatedly through their cell phones or the Internet. Well over half of young people do not tell their parents when cyber bullying occurs. Fewer than one in five cyberbullying incidents are reported to law enforcement" (Cyberbullying Statistics).

Girls seem to be "somewhat more likely than boys to be involved in cyberbullying. However, boys are more likely to be threatened by cyber bullies than girls. Boys are more likely to be threatened by cyber bullies than girls" (Cyberbullying Statistics).

Methods of Educating and Countering Cyberbullying

What Teachers and School Librarians Can Do

A first effort is to administer a student questionnaire to students (it is probably best to do this first using an anonymous document) to find out how much bullying, and what kind of bullying, is occurring. If students can respond anonymously, they may be more likely to give honest answers. The results may surprise administrators and teachers.

"Integrate curriculum-based anti-bullying programs into classrooms" (Cyberbullying Statistics). Some of these can be created by the students themselves. Good ideas for programs can be shared in more than one classroom, and schoolwide programs can be shared with other schools.

Teachers and the school librarian can work with their principal to change the school and perhaps the school board's bullying policy to include harassment perpetrated with mobile and Internet technology. The district and each school's policy should hold serious consequences for anyone who does.

What Parents Can Do

"Parents should learn about the Internet and what their children are doing online. Talk to them about the places their children should go online and the activities that students are involved in that relate to school assignments. Parents should aware of what their children are posting on websites including their own personal home pages" (Cyberbullying Statistics).

Under the worst possible circumstances, "any incident of online harassment and physical threats may be a criminal offense and should be reported to local police and the Internet service provider. If the child is bullied through a cellular phone, the problem should be reported to the child's phone service provider. If it's a persistent problem, the parent can change the phone number" (Cyberbullying Statistics).

"Talking to teens about cyber bullying means parents explain that it is wrong and can have serious consequences. Parents should have a rule that teens may not send mean or damaging messages, even if someone else started it" (Cyberbullying Statistics). Parents should refuse to let children keep their cell phones if they send suggestive pictures or messages. The difficulty here will be for parents to enforce the rules.

What Students Can Do

Parents may warn their students, but school librarian and teachers can fortify that warning. Students must guard their contact information. If someone gets any of these, school librarian or teacher should help get these changed if the school has control over the addresses. Parents should be told that the cell phone number needs to be changed.

Students should know that if they are being harassed or bullied online or by a cell phone, they need to immediately "tell a trusted adult: a teacher, parent, older sibling, or grandparent" (Cyberbullying Statistics). If this is physical harassment, they should" leave the area or stop the activity" (Cyberbullying Statistics). If it is online, they should stop chatting in "a chat room, with a news group, in an online gaming area, while instant messaging, or anything else" (Cyberbullying Statistics).

Students need to take a stand against cyberbullying among their peers. Students should speak out whenever they see someone "being mean" to another person online (Cyberbullying Statistics).

Students should keep cyberbullying messages as proof that cyberbullying is occurring. Parents may want to talk to the parents of the cyberbully, to the bully's Internet or cell phone provider, and/or to the police about the messages, especially if they are threatening or sexual in nature" (Cyberbullying Statistics). If there is no evidence of the cyberbullying, it becomes "he said/she said." As stated earlier, students should never divulge contact information.

Because of the ease of finding information on electronic devices, children "should not share anything through text or instant messaging on their cell phones or the Internet that they would not want to be made public. It may be that the person they think they are talking to in messages or online may not be who they think they are, and that things posted electronically may not be secure" (Cyberbullying Statistics).

LAWS ON PRIVACY AND INTERNET USE

The Family Educational Rights and Privacy Act (FERPA) is a federal law that protects the privacy of student education records. FERPA gives parents and students certain rights with respect to the student's education records. Generally, schools must have written permission from the parent or student to release any information from a student's education record. If a school fails to safeguard such records and a cyberbully publicizes the confidential information to classmates or on the Internet, the school may be in violation of FERPA. This is also the federal law that generally prevents college teachers from discussing with parents their children if they are older than 18.

The Children's Online Privacy Protection Act (COPPA) is a federal law that requires commercial online content providers who either have actual knowledge that they are dealing with a child 12 or younger or who aim their content at children to obtain verifiable parental consent before they can collect, archive, use, or resell any personal information pertaining to that child. It may be beneficial for schools to educate their staff and students' parents about the requirements of COPPA so that personal information concerning a child younger than 12 does not fall into the hands of online content providers or others. This is probably the least known of the three laws mentioned here.

The Children's Internet Protection Act (CIPA) is a federal law requiring that schools and libraries that receive specific federal funds (E-Rate in particular) to certify to the funding agency that they have in place an Internet safety policy. Such a policy should use technology that blocks access to obscenity, child pornography, or material harmful to minors. It may also include monitoring children while they are online (Cyberbullying Statistics).

ACCEPTABLE USE POLICIES

This also was discussed in some detail earlier in this book. The idea that schools could self-enforce acceptable conduct by students using the Internet was quickly overcome by government edict. In retrospect, based on the prevalence of cyberbullying this was probably a good idea.

"Schools should consider requiring students to sign a statement agreeing to comply with their school's rules on network or Internet use, and having parents or guardians sign a consent form and a release authorizing their child's use of the school network. In the release, the authorized student user and his or her parent or guardian, if the student is under age 18, agree to indemnify and hold the school system harmless from all claims that result from the student's activities while using the school's network and that cause direct or indirect damage to the user, the school system, or third parties" (Cyberbullying Statistics). Failure of either the student or parents to sign and agree to this policy should result in the student's not being able to use the school's network or use the Internet in the school. As with any releases, school officials should be advised by their solicitor.

"Ensure that your school district has a secure system to protect information, such as student education records, that don't fall under open records laws" (Cyberbullying Statistics). Most school districts try to do this, but with the hackers in today's world, it may take a consultant to make sure that data is as secure as possible.

School district policy should "prohibit students, staff, and others from using school computers to advertise or solicit for outside groups" (Cyberbullying Statistics). The use of school stationery to solicit without the approval of administration has always been a policy. The computer links are no different than a piece of school stationery.

Knowing the passwords allows access to a locked computer. Leaving an open computer or an easy-to-find password allows anyone access to the Internet for whatever use they wish.

"The district may have a technology coordinator to make sure that the school's network and Internet policies are followed. If no coordinator is available, then the school librarian becomes responsible for this and encourages teachers and students to help with the program" (Cyberbullying Statistics).

School Policies on Handheld Devices

Another method that school systems can use to discourage cyberbullying is to prohibit or limit the use of handheld devices such as cell phones, camera phones, and video cameras in school or in specified places such as locker rooms, bathrooms, or swimming pools. This is very, very controversial, but these prohibitions have been upheld in court.

Recently enacted or proposed legislation aimed at protecting privacy rights would provide support to school policies banning students' handheld devices. Many school systems and states in the late 1980s and early 1990s passed policies or laws prohibiting students from using cell phones or pagers in school because of the devices' association with drug dealers. The ringing and beeping from the phones and pagers, sometimes in class, also were disruptive. However, as cell phone usage has grown and their usefulness in emergencies, especially in letting children call their parents, has been demonstrated, some states and school systems have revised their policies and laws to allow school districts greater options. According to the website Education World, California, Maryland, and Virginia have lifted their previous bans on the carrying of cell phones in schools and allowed school districts to draft their own policies (Cyberbullying Statistics).

CASES INVOLVING CYBERBULLYING

The following are two examples of cyberbullying and their outcomes.

1. "In 2003, a Canadian high school student was humiliated when a videotape of him wielding a bladed light saber, mimicking a Star Wars character, was posted on the Internet and downloaded millions of times around the world. The videotape was stolen from a school filing cabinet. The teenager's parents filed a lawsuit against the parents of the

classmates who stole the videotape. The 15-year-old student has allegedly dropped out of school and is seeking psychiatric care.

2. A Tennessee middle school allowed security cameras to film students undressing in locker rooms and then allegedly stored the images on a computer accessible through the Internet. The students' parents alleged a violation of their children's rights, and sued the school for $4.2 million. Although this case did not involve transmission of the images by other students, the potential for access and misuse of such images by classmates is great.

Camera phones, cellular phones equipped with a camera that can be used to edit, copy, send, and post photographs on the Web, have been reportedly misused in schools and other places. In one reported case, junior high students snapped nude shots of a fellow student and threatened to post them on the Web." (Public School News)

Most educators are aware of the proliferation of cyberbullying. The school librarian is in an ideal position to be in the forefront in the fight against cyberbullying for two reasons. The first is that the school librarian should be the leader in technology in the school. The second is that it is often easier for the school librarian to establish a one-to-one relationship with students than it is for a classroom teacher who has a class of twenty or more students. Cyberbullying is insidious and harmful beyond what most can imagine. Any control of it will be beneficial to the students who are victims. If identifying and stopping cyberbullying permits one student to finish school rather than dropping out, keeps one student from committing suicide, or allows one student to go to school without fear, school librarians will have lead well.

RESEARCH AND REFERENCE QUESTION

Do more extensive research on the concept that the brains of digital natives are truly different from the brains of digital immigrants. Summarize at least three sources not mentioned in the text concerning this topic. Also prepare a presentation for parents of high school students that summarizes your findings.

REFERENCES

"Cyberbullying Statistics." www.bullyingstatistics.org/content/cyber-bullying-statistics.html.

Palfrey, John, and Urs Gasser *Born Digital: Understanding the First Generation of Digital Natives*. New York: Basic Books, 2010.

Prensky, Marc. "Digital Natives, Digital Immigrants." *On the Horizon* (October 2001). www.marcprensky.com/writing/Prensky%20-%20Digital%20Natives,%20 Digital%20Immigrants%20-%20Part1.pdf.

Public School News. "Cyberbullying: Protecting Children in the School Domain." www .tapsplf.org/images/pdf/safety/Cyber_bullying.pdf.

Scales, Pat. "Preventing Cyberbullying." *School Library Journal* (January 1, 2011). www .slj.com/2011/01/opinion/scales-on-censorship/preventing-cyberbullying-scales -on-censorship/#_.

Schechter, Dave. "How to Best Educate Our 'Digital Natives.'" http://newsroom.blogs.cnn .com/2011/10/20/how-best-to-educate-our-digital-natives/.

Zur Institute, "On Digital Immigrants and Digital Natives: How the Digital Divide Affects Families, Educational Institutions, and the Workplace." www.zurinstitute.com/ digital_divide.html.

17

Where Are We Going?
The School Librarian,
Technology, and the Future

For sixteen chapters, technology and technology skills have been described as essential if the school librarian is to continue to play an essential, central role in the school. Available technology and how it should be used in the school library have been described both from a theoretical and a practical viewpoint. The key skills and attitudes are suggested for the school librarian to become a leader in technology in their school. School librarians' failure to move forward with technology will certainly handicap their positions in helping students learn.

In this final chapter, our crystal balls will be polished to try to predict what the future might hold for technology that will appear and be adopted and used in the world of education or that will pass by. Technology is dynamic and ever-changing. Noted science fiction writer Arthur C. Clarke stated in 1962: "Any sufficiently advanced technology is indistinguishable from magic" (Levy 050). This reminds us of those first computer classes: Ask a question about how something works, and get what response? "It's magic." What the future might hold? What killer app is coming down the road? What will the next magic be?

TECHNOLOGY FOR THE TEACHERS

Change coming in instruction means changes for the way school librarians interact and collaborate with teachers. Some of these changes will include the following:

1. Interactive instruction. The move to interactive instruction has already begun as we become less the "sage on the stage," lecturing from the front of the room, and more the "guide on the side." Interactive instruction involves the integration of technology into all aspects of instruction.

2. Student ownership of education. Students are capable of and eager to take ownership of their own education. This is a difficult transition for many veteran teachers, because it is easier to change what you teach than how you teach. To allow students to break free and work collaboratively to find new ways to do things means giving them the trust that they will succeed.

3. Personal response systems. These types of systems are coming at all levels of instruction but seem right now most prevalent at the college level. Personal response systems can be as simple as handheld clickers or as complex as a computer-supported personal response systems allowing the instructor to monitor an entire classroom of computers and personal response systems. These systems have yet to have a significant effect at the K–12 level. However, with all types of technology the high costs of systems will come down, making their proliferation more likely.

4. Mobile assessment tools. Any device with a computing capability—PDA, cell phone, tablet, or laptop—can act as a mobile assessment tool. School librarians can make teachers comfortable with this technology.

TECHNOLOGY FOR INCLUSION

The concept of inclusion—having children of all abilities in the same classroom—is the current trend in education. To ensure equity for these students, technology must be available for these students—technology they can use easily and efficiently. Hardware and software has been available for students with learning disabilities, but improvements for students with other challenges need to be shared with teachers. The Library for the Blind and Physically Handicapped, a part of the Library of Congress, can provide assistance with students with sight problems. eBooks whose text can be magnified can help those who have partial sight. Computers that read text to students make it easy to "read" email messages from students in groups, as well as information on blogs or tweets.

Keeping technology available and up to date for students who face challenges will be an ongoing struggle. But the problems that technology is solving make it worth the effort.

TECHNOLOGY INNOVATIONS FOR THE 21ST CENTURY AND BEYOND

In 2008, Stephen Abram published an article titled "20 Things to Watch" in *Information Outlook*. In it, he noted twenty technology trends he felt would have a big effect on libraries and librarians over the ensuing five years, through 2013. When the article was originally published, some of the issues had already been dealt with. Where have we gone since then?

1.   Mobile devices. One just has to look at the prevalence of smartphones and PDAs to see how important mobile devices have become. They are everywhere! Each new cell phone is trying to replace the computer totally.

2.   GPS systems are already in most cars, but if your car is too old to have one, switch on your cell phone. Most mobile computing devices ask for Location Services to be used, although individuals concerned about privacy issues have difficulty with this.

3.   Open Handset Alliance (Android). This is an initiative advocated by Google to have all phones connect using the same standard. With the move to standards across all types of technology, it seems that almost any kind of content can be viewed on a handheld device. This is still "under construction."

4.   Tagging. This is one of the Web 2.0 applications having a great potential in determining social relevance in the rankings of search engines. Well under way, tagging is essential in Web 2.0 applications.

5.   Scrapbooking. Not paper and scissors scrapbooking, but the ability to find resources in online full-text databases and then capture them to your personal computer for later use. Again, well under way. Any viable full-text database has this capability.

6.   Software as a Service (Saas). This uses a server farm to store software. This can save school districts money and costs for security, back-ups, and malware are significantly reduced. Can we say cloud? Software as a Service is one of the major pieces of cloud computing.

7.   Microblogging. All social networking software now has microblogging features similar to Twitter's. The effect of Twitter and increased microblogging features could cause this to expand. Some evidence shows that Twitter may be becoming less important to our students, but it remains a prime information source for teachers.

8.   Social content. As we move forward with wikis and blogs, the ability to capture and share this content increases. Wikis and blogs have become integral parts of both online and face-to-face education.

9.   Social networking. The use of these applications just keeps increasing, and there has been no indication over the last five years that this trend will slow down. Millennial students generally use social networking as an alternative to email.

10. Social networking integration. This would connect school library webpages to social networking and tagging sites. This is here now.

11. eBooks. The opportunities for the integration of eBooks and other e-content are great for school libraries. The ability to have multiple copies of books and the ease of expanding a collection while reducing shelving in the library is awesome. The empty area of the library after the shelving is gone allows for makerspaces, different configurations for students to work in groups, and other uses of the library.

12. eBook devices. Amazon cannot keep the Kindle in stock in all its forms. Because there are other readers and ways to access eBooks, no one really knows the implications for education with the use of eBooks. Most tablet devices can use apps that deal with all types of eBooks.

13. Personal homepages. Library websites and virtual libraries are essential for the school library. These could be linked to personal webpages.

14. Cloud software. Cloud software is software that is not loaded on local computers but rather is hosted by another server such as Google. Furthermore, documents will not be saved locally, but rather on servers. The new version of Microsoft Office (Office 13) and Microsoft Office 365 encourage the use of the cloud for document storage and collaboration. The concept is good, but one must be aware of the security issues with cloud software.

15. RSS groups and readers. This is a very simple way to read blogs and Twitter feeds. For some, this has taken the place of reading the daily newspaper. These new RSS tools will allow the clustering of similar topics.

16. Podcasting and music. As podcasts continue to grow in popularity, companies, such as Wizzard Media, that gather them for distribution will gain importance.

17. Streaming media. This is what is replacing DVDs. Now that the "pipe" is large enough, this is the mode that will deliver video. In fact, DVDs are dying. Users connect their devices to their televisions and stream directly to them.

18. Custom search and microfederation. These are watch services that try to group blogs or databases by subject.

19. Open ID. The ultimate in single sign-on. This system would allow users to have one user ID and password for all things.

20. e-Learning. Teachers and librarians are now going to be developing curriculum and teaching in entirely new ways. This can be very exciting and also very challenging. It requires a great deal of collaboration, because it is a very good example of how many hands make for faster and better products.

Three recent articles have attempted to bring technology trends that school librarians should know up through 2014. The first, the *NMC Horizon Report: 2014 Higher Education Edition* was released in 2014. This is the eleventh time the New Media Consortium (NMC) has published this report, and it will be interesting to follow the trends as the years pass. 2014's trends are as follow:

1. **Social Media:** Educators, students, alumni, and the general public routinely use social media to share news about scientific and other developments. The impact of these changes in scholarly communication and on the credibility of information remains to be seen, but it is clear that social media has found significant traction in almost every education sector.
2. **Hybrid, Online, and Collaborative Learning:** An increasing number of universities are incorporating online environments into courses of all kinds, which is making the content more dynamic, flexible, and accessible to a larger number of students.
3. **Data-Driven Learning and Assessment:** As learners participate in online activities, they leave an increasingly clear trail of analytics data that can be mined for insights.
4. **Students Shifting from Consumers to Creators:** University departments in areas that have not traditionally had lab or hands-on components are shifting to incorporate hands-on learning experiences as an integral part of the curriculum.
5. **Agile Approaches to Change:** When educators are able to experiment with new technologies and approaches before implementing them in courses, they have the opportunity to evaluate them and make improvements to teaching models.
6. **The Evolution of Online Learning:** The value that online learning offers is now well understood, with flexibility, ease of access, and the integration of sophisticated multimedia and technologies chief among the list of appeals. (Lepi)

At the 2014 Florida Education Technology Conference (FETC), Julie Evans spoke to the group about the 2013 Speak Up Survey conducted by her organization, Project Tomorrow. Her remarks addressed what she considers to be the ten major technology trends on the horizon, based on more than 400,000 surveys from schools across the country:

1. Personal access to mobile devices
2. Internet connectivity
3. Use of video for classwork and homework
4. Mobile devices for schoolwork
5. Using different tools for different tasks

6. Paying attention to the digital footprint
7. Increased interest in online learning
8. Gaming is growing, and the gender gap is closed
9. Social media in schools
10. What devices belong in "The Ultimate School"? (Reidel).

See http://thejournal.com/articles/2014/02/03/10-major-technology-trends -in-education.aspx for the complete survey.

The final article is certainly more eclectic than the last two. In it Terry Heick has attempted to determine what tech trends are trending up for the 2015 school year, which are in the middle, and which are trending down. This seems like a long laundry list of items, but if the school librarian examines them closely, perhaps he or she will be able to see where to go to be relevant in today's schools.

Trending Up

1. Teacherpreneurs
2. Decentralizing academic standards
3. Rethinking data in the classroom
4. Adaptive learning algorithms
5. Digital citizenship
6. Focus on non-fiction, digital media
7. Depth of content
8. Experimentation with new learning models (including flipped classroom, sync learning, blended learning, etc.)
9. Teacher self-directed PD, webinars, streams, etc.
10. College as a choice
11. Collaborative learning
12. Digital literacy
13. Focus on learning spaces
14. Design thinking
15. Mindfulness, meditation, downtime
16. Teacher as guide-on-the-side
17. Gamification of content
18. Genius hour, maker hour, collaboration time
19. Workflows
20. Cloud-based word processing

In the Middle

1. Google, Microsoft, Apple, etc.
2. "Accountability"

3. Professional learning communities
4. Differentiation
5. Computer coding
6. Traditional reading lists of truly great literature
7. Pure creativity
8. Self-directed learning
9. Massive in-person education conferences
10. Colleges in general
11. Experiential learning
12. Cultural literacy
13. The physical design of most school buildings and universities
14. Memorization of prioritized content that leads to design thinking
15. Debate
16. Pressure on systems
17. Gamification-as-grading-system
18. Tutoring
19. To-do lists
20. Cloud-based learning

Trending Down
1. Mass education publishers
2. Common Core Standards, Race to the Top
3. Data teams
4. Scripted curricula
5. Draconian district filters
6. Humanities
7. Coverage of content
8. "21st century learning" as a phrase or single idea
9. The perceived quality of teacher certification & training programs
10. College as the standard
11. MOOCs
12. Agricultural literacy
13. The traditional classroom
14. "Low-level" recall of easily accessed data (facts) or skills (arithmetic)
15. Lessons that favor "verbally expressive" students
16. Pressure on teachers
17. Standards-based grading; pass/fail; student retention
18. Increased "instructional hours"
19. Whole class processes
20. Flash drives, hard drives, CDs, emailing files (Heick)

These lists are a sampling of ideas of where technology is going for school libraries. That said, these are nothing but guesses about the future. We may not have even guessed the next killer app.

RESEARCH AND REFERENCE QUESTION

Considering the various roles of a school librarian, try to predict ways that technology will enhance your responsibilities as a professional. Consider how you will interact with your peers, students, and parents, as well as the community in which you work. Prepare a report of your findings for your class.

REFERENCES

Abrams, Stephen. "20 Things to Watch." Information Outlook. www.sirsidynix.com/Resources/Pdfs/Company/Abram/IOColumn_67.pdf.

Heick, Terry. "30 Trends in Education Technology for the 2015 School Year." www.teachthought.com/Trends/30-trends-education-technology-2015.

Lepi, Katie. "The 6 Education Technology Trends You Should Know About." www.edudemic.com/education-trends-keep-tech-front-center/.

Levy, Steven. "Losing the Magic," Wired (May 2009): 050–051.

"NMC Horizon Report: 2014Higher Education Edition." http://cdn.nmc.org/media/2014-nmc-horizon-report-he-EN-SC.pdf.

Reidel, Chris. "10 Major Technology Trends in Education." http://thejournal.com/Articles/2014/02/03/10-Major-Technology-Trends-in-Education.aspx.

Smaldino, Sharon E., Deborah L. Lowther, and James D. Russell. *Instructional Technology for Media and Learning*, 9th ed. Upper Saddle River, NJ: Pearson, 2008.

Index

About the Author

WILLIAM O. SCHEEREN holds a BS in education from Indiana University of Pennsylvania and an MLS and PhD from the University of Pittsburgh. A former high school librarian, he currently teaches at St. Vincent College in Latrobe, Pennsylvania, and is president of the board and acting director of the Westmoreland County Federated Library Center.